Takin' Back My Name

Takin' Back My Name

The Confessions of Ike Turner

Ike Turner

with Nigel Cawthorne

Virgin

First published in Great Britain in 1999 by Virgin Books
an imprint of Virgin Publishing
Thames Wharf Studios
Rainville Road
London W6 9HT

A catalogue record for this book is available from the British Library.

ISBN 1 85227 850 1

Design by Roger Kohn Design

Typeset by TW Typesetting, Plymouth, Devon

Printed and bound by C.P.D. Wales

The real truth from the horse's mouth:

This book is dedicated to Tina Turner,
and to the memory of my loving mother,
Beatrice Cushenberry

Contents

	Acknowledgements	ix
	Introduction by Little Richard	xi
1	The Birth of Rock 'n' Roll	1
2	Delta Blues	6
3	Boogie-Woogie	17
4	Ain't Nobody Here But Us Chickens	28
5	The Kings of Rhythm	40
6	The Hunter	46
7	Sweet Black Angels	56
8	The House of Many Thrills	61
9	A Fool in Love	71
10	I Idolise You	80
11	Peaches and Cream	98
12	River Deep	110
13	Mountain High	128
14	It Starts to Snow	135
15	The Pleasure Dome	147
16	I've Been Loving You Too Long	165
17	Poor Fool	184
18	The Fifteen-Year Party	195
19	Tough Enough	218
20	On the Road Again	224
21	Battle of the Bands	235
	Epilogue	241
	Notes on the Ike Turner Discography	246
	The Personnel of the Kings Of Rhythm	247
	Discography	249

Acknowledgements

I want to extend my thanks to: Lil' Richard, Elena Davinci for using her house to write, Aunt Charlene Jack, Mel and Nancy Johnson, Vernon Minow, Lenny and Karen Marmor, Ann Thomas, Nigel Cawthorne, Michael Turner, Tawanna Melby, Ike Turner Jr., Ronnie Turner, Craig Turner, Beatrice Fakhrian, and to my fiancée Jeanette (Bazzell) Turner, and also to Tina Turner who made it possible for me to do this book.

Introduction
by Little Richard

Ike Turner has been famous to me all of his life. When I came to East St Louis, he was already famous. He was recording. Down where I come from – Macon, Georgia – you didn't hear of no black people recording. But Ike was recording with a lot of people.

Chess Records had a song out called 'Rocket 88'. When I was a little boy, that song fascinated me in a big way. I never heard a piano sound like that. I had never played the piano then. Soon I was trying. If you listen to 'Good Golly, Miss Molly', you hear the same introduction as the one to 'Rocket 88', the exact same, ain't nothing been changed. 'Rocket 88' was a very big record. It was huge. And I learned it was Ike's, so to me, Ike was big then. He had a whole lot of records coming out in my home town.

When people talk about rock 'n' roll, they talk about Chuck Berry, they talk about Little Richard, and they leave the main man out. Before all these people, Ike Turner was doing this thing. It ain't Little Richard, it ain't Chuck, it ain't Fats Domino – no, we came on later. This man was playing the blues, rhythm and blues. Rock 'n' roll came from rhythm and blues: rock 'n' roll ain't nothing but rhythm and blues up-tempo. Ike Turner was the innovator, for rhythm and blues and for rock 'n' roll. We just came and took it on home.

The first time I saw him, I was in East St Louis one night after we did a show. We were going out looking to have a good time that night, and went to hear Ike. He was at the Kiel Auditorium in St Louis, downtown. He tore the place down. His band were travelling. He was full of rhythm, his show was clockwork. There wasn't a bad moment. It would build; it made you want more. It is not that he is a hard driver – he is an entertainer, he loves what he is doing and he doesn't short-change people. They paid to see a show, and he gives them what they paid for – and a little more. They came for dinner, but they got two dinners. He just doubles it up. He gives his all, and he wants the band to do the same thing he does. That's what I saw when I saw him.

Then, about a year or two after that, he came to Los Angeles. He took me home. I was living on Virginia Road, and his kids used to stay in the house with my momma sometimes. I was getting ready to lose my house. I was crying and we prayed. Ike gave me a cheque for $3,500, a cashiers' cheque. He took me to the bank on Western Avenue. I never will forget that as long as I live.

When they first came to Los Angeles, I used to go over every day and Ike would be there with Tina and all of them. I remember when Tina couldn't sing like she can today. Ike came and asked me to teach her. He asked me, 'How would you sing this song?' And when I sang, he would tell Tina, 'Now, that's what I want you to do.' But when she talks today, she never mentions my name.

And I was looking like this first – the hair and all. Nobody ever mentioned that. You never get no credit for it. Not that I'm asking for any – I'm not asking for nothing, 'cos God has made me wealthy. I earned my money. But when I didn't have it, Ike helped me. And that's the reason I am writing this today, to let the world know the truth. I want the record to be put straight. The real story has never been told.

Tina got what she wanted, but she lost what she had. The bucket got a hole in it, can't buy no beer. I was with Tina at the music awards in New York recently and I didn't like the way she treated me. I thought it was very poor. That ain't the Tina I knew. I felt bad, I felt like crying. I was sitting at a table and I thought we were going to greet each other. I'm trying to catch her eye and I'm telling her, 'Tina, Tina I am so glad for your success. I am so proud of you.'

She said, 'How you doing?' Then she said, 'Are you doing w'll?'

I said, 'I'm not doing "w'll", I'm doing we-e-e-ell. I'm doing the same well that I been doing all the time.'

She can't even talk no more, with her English accent. I have nothing against her, but don't forget where you come from, 'cos you may have to go back there again. The planes fly high, but they come low, too. They have to land, don't they? They can't stay up there forever.

What I want the world to know about Ike – and he ain't going to say it about himself – is that he is a teacher. He's a disciplinarian. He knows how to discipline a person to get him or her to do it right. He don't take no gun to do it. What he asks you to do, he does himself, so he sets an example.

This guy can play every instrument. He don't play one instrument, he plays all of them. And he plays them well. He shows the people how they're supposed to do it, same as he did with Tina Turner. He showed Tina how to dress, he showed her how to act. Ike got her singing on a drive. She's attacking – she attacks them songs. He did the whole thing. It wasn't just the singing – it was from the top to the bottom, from the tip to the toe.

What the world doesn't know is that there are two sides to a coin, four sides to a room. A car has four tyres. You take away one tyre, and that car ain't going nowhere. This man taught this young lady. I've never seen another man do what he's done, and I don't think that any man ever has done it. He took this girl because he was so interested in her doing this thing right. He would put all his time into it.

It's the same thing with Michael Jackson. Michael Jackson's dad is not a bad man. He was a driver and he wanted his kids to be the best. He wasn't a tyrant, he wasn't severe: he was just a man who wanted his kids to be the top. Not middling, not the bottom, but the top. And that's what Ike does. He was interested in Tina's wellbeing.

Now Tina's band copy Ike's style. When I heard them doing 'Steamy windows', I said, that's Ike. She says she doesn't like the blues. That's nothing but the blues. She says she wants to sing something that is free and joyful and pleasant, like the rock 'n' roll groups. I say, you know where you learned that from? You didn't learn it from no Mick Jagger. You didn't learn that from David Bowie (he's a good friend of mine – I ain't putting nobody down). You learned that from Mr Ike Turner of Mississippi, by way of St Louis, Missouri. One chapter of this book should be called 'A Hole in the Wall' – I can see through what you talking about.

This man gave his all. Ike has been working all his life. How did he get this far? He didn't go to school to study all this. This man can play a piano better than any man I ever heard, and he can pick up a guitar and make it talk. Ain't nobody who plays like him. Which means that God endowed him. The man was gifted from on high. When he is onstage you can tell he is onstage, and when he goes off you can tell he's off. When he leaves the band, you can tell he ain't there with the band. It's a different sound, a different thing; a different thrust, a different energy. It's a different level that comes in when he is onstage. He projects. It rings, it flows, it builds, it comes up. Because it is a gift from God.

To me, Ike is one of the most underrated entertainers in the world. I have never met a person so underrated who has given so much. This man is one of the greatest producers I have ever seen in my life. And his own studio, Bolic, was one of the greatest studios I have ever seen. He had everything in this studio. He had his own booking agency, and he was showing people how to produce.

God gave Ike a gift and he shared it, he spread the joy. He got a country girl and showed her what God had given him. You might not have picked no cotton off the field, but you could pick up some off the floor that had fallen out of your mattress. And what Ike knew, he might not have known it technically or theoretically like somebody with a Bachelor of Arts degree, 'cos a degree ain't nothing but a piece of paper – if it ain't in your heart, it ain't nothing on the wall.

Long before Michael Jackson, Ike had all he's got. He had his own buses and packed stadiums all over the world. 'River Deep' was so big. When we came through Europe it was everywhere you turned. He is electrifying.

I think that Ike influenced the whole music industry, not just the one section. He is a person who hasn't been given his proper due. The whole field has been energised and inspired by him: I was inspired by him, and I think if I was, everybody else was. If people don't want to give him the respect he deserves, it's because they are jealous and envious. They just coons.

Ike is so underrated because a lot of lies have been told on him – a whole lot of lies. People in key places didn't like him because they couldn't use him. Because they couldn't use him, they lied on him. If I can't take you in the palm of my hand and direct you like I want to, then I say you're a bad person. You a bad boy, 'cos I can't knock you and put you over here. They can't do that to him, and that's what they don't like. He knows what he is doing.

But Ike ain't through. He's going to carry on. You can't beat what God gave him. He is so interested in things being real. You can't stop truth: you see, truth don't die. You can beat it, you can whoop it, you can throw it down, but it comes back. 'Cos you can't kill it. It's immortal. It's eternal. It's everlasting. It's the first and the last. It's the beginning and the ending.

Ike has a cult following. People come who want to hear him, people who admire and respect truth. It makes black history. He stood behind his craft but he's never got the recognition. I got some of mine; he ain't got none. And this man is not what people say he is. I know him. I ain't known him for three weeks, I've been knowing him for years. I have known him before a lot of the people who're talking were born. He is a good man. Ain't none of us no angels – you ain't got no wings either, do you? We ain't fixing to fly nowhere. We all walking, we all talking, we have all made mistakes.

I believe if Ike and Tina got back together again – and I ain't talking about no marriage: people are supposed to have sense enough to do business and ain't got to be married – just for a business venture; if they did a tour together, ain't nothing in the world that could touch them. It could be the biggest tour there's ever been. Can you imagine that? Michael Jackson, nothing – ain't nothing been as big as that would be. That would be a venture, boy, like there has never been.

We've got to learn to do business together as black people. It is a matter of sense and intelligence, of being realistic. I'm not taking anything away from Tina. She is one of the greatest entertainers I have ever seen on the stage. I take off my hat – I'll even take off my hair – to her. She is fantastic.

But I knew her before she got where she is; I knew then that she had talent and I knew the man who polished it. And not only did he polish it, he made the polish. I don't think you should talk about how awful and how dog-eared a person is. I think we need to give the proper respect and thanks. Where would I have been if I hadn't met this person? Talk about 'Nutbush City Limits' – I'd have been outside the city.

Tina, here is the man who gave you not only respect, but also his heart. 'Cos he had to love you to stay with you. He ain't stupid, he ain't crazy – he's intelligent. He had to be intelligent to get you where you are. If Tina hadn't been where he put her, she wouldn't have been as famous as she is today. They would have had to have reached down a long ways for her. It would have been a big haul. But she was already on a springboard.

And even with all that has been said that is not true, Ike still loves her. She is still a friend in his heart – he doesn't hate her, he wishes her the greatest success. He takes off everything to her and hopes that she continues to move. But don't stop the ship from sailing; don't speak against the water that brought you across.

Not only that, he's hip to that ship. He's been on that trip. He's hip to the kitchen and he knows what she's cooking. If people were to sit down and tell the truth, it is nobody trying to destroy nobody. We're just trying to show what God has done for all of us. We want to live and let live, we don't want to take nothing that we can't give.

Ike is a country boy, born to a life of poverty – he wasn't born rich. But this man has been on the mountaintop. This man knows what it is like to be wealthy. He knows what it is like to have money, what it feels like to be on the top, what it feels like to come back down to the bottom. And he knows what it feels like to come back again. He's been there, he's been up and he's been down – but he's back.

I pray to the Lord that somebody be blessed out of this, because Ike has stood the test. He's been in a mess but, God, he's also been refreshed. He's going all the way back. And he is going to be bigger than he's ever been.

1 The Birth of Rock 'n' Roll

The story of rock 'n' roll began one night in March 1951. Ike Turner and his high-school band, the Kings of Rhythm, had been playing a gig.

WE WERE PLAYING DOWN AT CLEVELAND, Mississippi, on Friday night and in Greenville on Saturday. Coming home from Cleveland on Friday we passed by Mound Bayou. Down by the highway we could see all these cars parked. On the Saturday night, the cars were lining up down there, and there were even more people. So we said, let's stop and see what shit is going on here. We pulled off the highway. We saw the sign that said B.B. King, but we didn't know who B.B. King was – I only knew him as Riley King.

I don't remember why or how, but Riley – B.B. – turned up in Clarksdale, Mississippi, where I'm from, one day, and I took him to our house. I was the kind of kid who was always bringing someone home with him. Mom accepted it. He had a three-string guitar – there weren't but three strings on it. He stayed a day or two. I remember Momma giving him some shoes to go and get half-soled, because they were worn through. He never came back.

So here was Riley – B.B. – playing this club, the Harlem Club in Chambers, Mississippi. We asked him to let us play a song. And we got up there and played, and we tore that place up, boy.

B.B. was playing blues, but we were playing what was on the jukebox – that was all we knew. The shit he was cutting was OK, but the jukebox was the thing that was hot. We played everything.

Afterwards the guy who owned the club, Hezekiah Patton, wanted us to play there because everyone was crazy about us. He hired us to work on Fridays, Saturdays and Sundays. And boy, did we pack that place, back to back.

B.B. told us, 'Man, guys as good as you are should be recording.' I said we didn't know nothing about record companies. He said he'd set it up for us. We had no idea how to get on record; it was the furthest thing from my head at that time. B.B. said he would have the guy at the recording company, who turned out to be Sam Phillips, call on Monday. He did call, and then that Wednesday we came up to record.

B.B. King had recently signed with Modern Records and had been recording at the Memphis Recording Service, whose studios were in a converted radiator shop at 706 Union Avenue, Memphis, Tennessee. The owner, radio engineer Sam Phillips, also founded Sun Records.

Phillips had dreamed of finding a white man who could sing and move like a black. Three years later, in July 1954, at the same Sun Studios, Phillips discovered a young truck-driver named Elvis Presley.

But on that rainy Wednesday in March 1951, a far more significant contribution to the history of rock 'n' roll was about to be made as Ike Turner and the Kings of Rhythm pulled out of strictly segregated Clarksdale to make the sixty-three-mile journey north along Highway 61, across the flat cottonfields, to Memphis.

We were in Johnny Dougan's car, a Chrysler. There were seven or eight of us and all the instruments too. Someone said that he thought we might need some original material if we were going to record. All we knew were jukebox covers – we didn't have any original songs, man, not one. So on the way up there we tried to write some songs. We just had to do it real quick so that we had something when we got there. That was how 'Rocket 88', about a new model Oldsmobile, was written. Jackie Brenston, our sax-player, came up with the idea. He was crazy about stupid shit like that.

Ike wrote the first verse and the band pitched in with the rest of the lyrics. They had a little more time to write the song than they expected: a tyre blew out and a bass amp fell off the top of the car. Then a highway patrolman stopped them, harassed them, and took them on a massive detour, across to Highway 51 to see a judge. Even so, when they eventually arrived at Sun, 'Rocket 88' was still not completed. But when Ike and the Kings of Rhythm were finally ready to record, Sam Phillips realised immediately that 'Rocket 88' was one hell of a song.

When we got there we had part of it written, and we finished writing it at the studio. Man, as we were going from the sound studio into the control room up in the front, we just had stacks of paper.

I did all the music, there wasn't no writing that – I just did it in the studio. Anyway, it turned out good.

When Sam cut it, he called Leonard Chess of Chess Records in Chicago and overnighted him one. He got real excited about it, thought it would be a big old hit – which it was.

At the time, there was a white radio station in Memphis called WHBQ. They had a guy, Dewey Phillips, who had a show named *Red, Hot and Blue*. Dewey was a friend of Sam Phillips, so Sam got him to play it on the show. That was how 'Rocket 88' took off.

On 12 May 1951, 'Rocket 88' entered the *Billboard* chart at number 4. On 12 June it reached number 1 – and it stayed in the chart until 8 September. The record sold over half a million copies at a time when Chess considered anything over 50,000 a hit.

It also inspired Little Richard – who stole Ike's thumping piano intro for 'Good Golly, Miss Molly' – and a hundred other artists across the South. Country-and-western singer Bill Haley covered the song when he chose to take a new direction in his career.

Sam Phillips claimed that 'Rocket 88', with its honking saxophone and steam-train rhythm, was the first rock 'n' roll record ever. Ike Turner is credited as its creator and

he is honoured as the founder of rock 'n' roll by the Rock
'n' Roll Hall of Fame in Cleveland, Ohio.

Although he is flattered by all the adulation 'Rocket 88'
has attracted, Ike himself contends that there is nothing
special about the record. He was just playing what he had
been playing all along. But at the age of nineteen, he
already had an encyclopaedic knowledge of musical styles,
from big band through jazz, bluegrass, doo-wop, blues,
rhythm and blues and country and western. And he could
dissect and reproduce any jukebox hit by ear and play all
the parts.

They put me in the Hall of Fame for cutting the first rock 'n'
roll record. OK. But I was playing rhythm and blues. That's all
I was playing. When I'm listening to Jerry Lee Lewis, it's
nothing but boogie-woogie, but they call it rock 'n' roll.

When I was doing 'Rocket 88', I wasn't really playing a
boogie, but that was the reason for what I was doing; the
reason I was playing it that way. But to me, if that's rock 'n'
roll – well, then I play rock 'n' roll. But I play anything. My
favourite music is country, anyway.

Ike concedes one innovation in 'Rocket 88', however: the
bass line is played on the bass strings of a guitar rather
than on a double bass. 'The upright bass, you couldn't
hear,' he says. 'We didn't know what notes we were
playing on it.'

There were others though: the spare studio sound, the
simple tape echo used to project the singer and of course,
the breathtaking tempo. Still, Ike maintains that if 'Rocket
88' was released today, it would be called rhythm and
blues rather than rock 'n' roll – because he is considered
an R&B act, and not because of his music.

It's funny about that. They say I'm the first somebody to do
rock 'n' roll. But why do they call what I play rhythm and
blues? I don't understand that. They took the name and they
put R&B on me because of my race, not because of my music.
'Cos I'm playing the same thing: if you play 'Rocket 88', or

anything I do right now, it's the same fucking thing. How did I cut the first rock 'n' roll record if everything I cut is R&B? It is the most racist statement I ever heard in my goddamn life.

And growing up in Mississippi in the 1930s and 1940s, Ike Turner knew all about racism. Very soon, he knew all about the rock 'n' roll business too. From their national chart-topping single, Ike and his band made just $20 each.

2 Delta Blues

Ike Turner was born in Clarksdale, Mississippi, on 5 November 1931. Clarksdale is found at the heart of the delta, the D-shaped lowlands that lie between the Mississippi and Yazoo rivers. It was a rail head for the surrounding cottonfields and cotton from the outlying gins was brought to the huge compresses there, where the bales were compressed and stored before being shipped out to the mills of America's north-east and Lancashire, England.

The town was, of course, strictly segregated. The blacks were confined to the east side of the railroad tracks that divided the town. Even today, few, if any, blacks live in the prosperous Oakhurst section of town. When Ike Turner was a boy, black kids had to walk on the other side of the street when the whites went swimming.

In the 1930s and 1940s, the jukejoints, clubs and cafés of the bustling area around Fourth Street and Issaquena were a magnet to the old Delta blues men, including the great pioneers such as Robert Johnson, Charley Patton and Son House. Now that cotton-picking has been mechanised, the sharecroppers have long since fled north. The town is run down, decaying, a shadow of its former self. Black folks say of these parts, 'The bloodhound run me away and the Greyhound never take me back.'

Ike's first memory is of riding down to Baton Rouge in the rumble seat of his father's car, on the way to see his grandpappy Heuri.

My momma was trying to give me a titty, but I didn't like that one. It had been burned when an oil lamp had fallen against it. I was crying 'cos I wanted the other one. I never will forget that.

> Ike's parents were Creole. His father, Izear Luster Turner, was a minister at the Centennial Baptist Church at Yazoo and Fifth in Clarksdale. The name I.L. Turner is still preserved on a stone tablet in the front wall. Ike thought that he was called Izear Luster Turner Junior after his father until he first applied for a passport. In the records in Jackson, Mississippi, he found that he was registered as Ike Wister Turner. By then both his parents were dead, so he was never able to discover the origin of his name.

My father was killed when I was about five years old. I was told when I got older that there was a woman my father was fooling around with on the side. This same woman was going with another man too, a white guy everybody called Bird Doggin. He was well known around Clarksdale for being a real redneck peckerwood. Well, something happened between this woman and my father – a fight, or he stopped messing with her. Anyway, she told Bird Doggin, and he became real angry with my father because of it. One day this man got together with a group of other white men, and they all decided to come and get my daddy.

I can remember that as they pulled up in the front of our house in pick-up trucks, my mother grabbed me up and slammed the front door shut. Those men just kicked in the door and rushed into the house. As the door flew open, my mother held me in her arms. We both fell to the floor. For me, because I was so small at that time, it seemed like we both fell a real long ways before we finally hit the floor.

They came into the house and grabbed my daddy. Then they put a blindfold on him, took him outside to one of the pick-up trucks and drove away with him. They were dressed in khaki. Hours later, they brought him back and tossed him into the yard in front of the house. My daddy was all bruised and bloody. He had been beaten up real bad. He had holes in his stomach where he had been kicked.

I remember Momma going out there and washing him up. Daddy couldn't remember where he had been, 'cept that he remembered the sweet smell of rotting vegetation like he had been out in a swamp or something. Mom took him to the white hospital but they wouldn't accept him because he was a black man. They didn't have a black hospital back then. I'm talking about the old days, not today, now. In Clarksdale, you was black and got sick, if you got hit by a car, you just died.

My mother sought help from the local health department. The health department people sent someone over and they put up a little house, 12ft by 12ft, something like a tent house made out of tarpaulin, in the yard outside. My father was to stay in this tent while he recovered from his wounds. I guess he was trying to get his strength back.

There used to be a little confectionery store up around the corner of Washington and Magnolia streets where I would go sometimes to buy a double soda and peanuts. We lived at 304 Washington in Clarksdale, the second house from the corner, and when the wind was blowing a certain way you could smell the odour that came from the wounds in my daddy's intestines as soon as you turned the corner coming back.

I can just remember trying to help my daddy. I remember the windows in his little house were flaps that you raised with a rope. I used to ask Daddy to let me pull the string. And he had a little metal cup that you put a paper cup in for him to spit in. I would go in the tent and get a paper cup from the dispenser for him.

The tent didn't have a bathroom and our outhouse was out on the back porch. When he could get up, he used to hold upside the house to get down the side to the back porch, holding on all the way. Then he would come up on the porch and go to the bathroom. My mother was working days, so I had to help him.

I remember Daddy used to sit on the back porch when he came out of the bathroom. He'd sit there with me and teach me to read. He had a little book with a picture of a bug in it, and he'd say, 'This is a bug.'

He'd turn the next page and there'd be a chicken, and he'd say, 'This is a chicken.'

There was a large cat that used to climb over the fence to get into our backyard so he could eat the chickens. My daddy had a .410-gauge shotgun that he kept right inside the kitchen door. One day when the cat came sneaking over the fence while Daddy was teaching me from this book he just picked up his gun and – bam! – he blew the cat away. I guess he wanted to make sure he killed the right one.

I was real close to my daddy. He stayed sick for two or three years, and finally he died around 1936–37. He was buried some way out of Clarksdale, near Jonestown, where cemetery plots were cheaper. Momma joined him there twenty-two years later.

My mother's name was Beatrice Cushenberry. But my older sister, Lee Ethel Knight, and I called her Momma B. I didn't have but one sister. She was some ten years older than me. I have a niece, Ethel Mae Knight, that we called Baby Sister. She felt more like my sister than my real sister. She is in Chicago. She and I are close – we're but two years apart.

We lived on the last street in town. Across the gravel road was a cottonfield. There was no electricity when I was a kid and we'd only just got a radio when we tuned in to hear President Truman announce that the atomic bomb had been dropped on Hiroshima.

Our wooden house was of the old 'shotgun' construction with the sitting room, bedroom, kitchen and back porch all leading into each other in one straight line from front door to back. But later, Momma built me an extra bedroom off the side of the house.

My mother was a big lady. One time there was a storm in Mississippi. I never will forget the wind shaking our house. A lady called Miss Porter lived behind our house on the next street. We could go there through the back and across the alley. Momma grabbed me in one arm and my niece, Baby Sister, in the other, and she bent way over down to her own waist with us in her arms – that's how strong the wind was – and carried us over to Miss Porter's house where we would be safe. I never will forget that. Mother was one helluva woman. I don't know that much about my father, and I don't give a shit about my stepdaddy. But I just know, man, my Momma was a *woman*.

Another time our house caught fire and Momma thought we

were in there. She took her hand and knocked the windows out – she didn't think about no brick to do it, she just took her hand and knocked them fucking windows out.

That's what I am still searching for in life today, at my age, that sort of security.

Momma was a seamstress. She covered couches, made drapes, bedspreads and stuff like that, and I used to have to earn my money by helping her sew. There was very few seamstresses in Mississippi. In those days, the top paying job was $25–$35, something like that. My mother used to make $200–$300 a week sometimes. She made real good money covering couches and stuff. She did some work at home and sometimes she'd go over to some people's houses over in Oakhurst and various places in Mississippi.

After Daddy's death, it seemed like just me and my mother. For a few years she really did spoil me. But if I wanted a bicycle, say, she wouldn't just give me the whole amount of money for it. She'd ask me how much it cost. If I said it was $15, she would say, 'OK, Sonny' – my nickname was Sonny – 'here's my $7.50, now you go get your $7.50 and you can get your bicycle any time you are ready.' She would put that money in the sewing-machine drawer.

I earned the rest helping Momma. She taught me how to make the thick cord she needed to put around the edges of the couch covers. She would give me a couple of dollars for making the cord. Then she would give me all the scraps left over and I would make throw rugs out of them. I'd help her sew to earn the other $5. That's what I'd do to get my bicycle.

Then I got a job working for Mr Brown, a blind man who delivered newspapers along a regular route. I would lead him around while he delivered the papers and he paid me 25c a week. I also had a wheelbarrow that I used to go out and hustle scrap pieces of iron, soda and milk bottles and other stuff that I could then sell to make money. I'd save up the $27 you needed to buy a hundred baby chickens. I would carefully raise those chicks until they became pullets, then I'd go through the neighbourhood and sell them. With the money I'd go back and double up, buying 200 more baby chicks. It taught me how to hustle, man.

I also used to go down to the Greyhound Bus Station on

weekends and play deaf and dumb to get a little change. I had a hundred ways of making money.

By now I was in the second grade at school. I was starting to develop a rebellious attitude against my mother because I was spoiled. Whenever she wouldn't let me have my own way, I would cry and cry until no more water would come from my eyes. When the water ran out, I would put some spit on my face to make it look like there were still tears coming down. Sometimes my mother would give in to me, and sometimes she wouldn't.

I was a little rascal then. There was a little boy named Percy Parker I used to play with. One time when we shooting marbles together he took all my marbles even though I'd won the game.

Percy was a kind of a bully then, and I was the cowardly type. But when he took my marbles I jumped on him. That's when I had my first real fight. Percy was a good boxer, but shit at wrestling. At that time I was a pretty good wrestler, so I threw him down on the ground and got on top of him.

I was punching him and things were going pretty much in my favour until he managed to get one of my fingers in his mouth. He bit down on it. My finger still in his mouth, he told me to get up off of him and lie down. After I did that, he sat straddling me and, my finger still clamped firmly between his teeth, he beat the cowshit out of me.

In those days, unlike today, if an older person in the neighbourhood saw a kid doing something he wasn't supposed to be doing, he would whip you good and send you home. So when Reverend Holmes saw me and Percy fighting that day, he gave us both a real good whipping with a switch from a weeping-willow tree. Then he carried us both home and told my mother what I had done. She gave me another good whipping.

My niece, Ethel Mae, and I were very close. Like I said, because we were only two years apart, I felt like she was my sister. My Momma would give us each a small sack lunch to take to school and 5c to buy extra. At school, during the 10 am recess, I would find Ethel Mae and pretend that someone had taken my lunch so I could get her 5c.

At home, Ethel Mae would do her chores and mine too, while I shot marbles with the kids outside. She did all the washing and ironing and scrubbed the floors. Each day before school we had to make our beds. They were the feather-tick kind, which meant that they had to be fluffed up and smoothed out by hand. I had to cut the wood myself, though – there was no way around it, because Momma was at home in the mornings. She didn't go out until after we had left for school.

One day it was raining really hard, with lots of lightning and loud thunder. Everybody stayed at home that day because of the storm. Baby Sis was in the kitchen cooking potato pies for me to sell out at the compress – another thing I did to earn extra money.

Our kitchen led directly into the bedroom, and that's where I was resting, having just finished polishing the furniture. Baby Sis was scared of lightning, so when some suddenly struck very close by, she ran to me full of fear and I hugged her for comfort.

While we stood there hugging each other, we could see Momma laying across her bed, sound asleep. She was wearing one of those country-type dresses, which was kind of flimsy. That was when I got the idea to use the hot comb to press the curly hairs on Momma's cat.

It was pure devilment on my part, because I don't know what I could have been thinking. 'Let's do it!' I said to Baby Sis.

· We put the iron hot comb on the wood-burning stove to heat. I went and raised Momma's dress up around her waist while she slept. When the hot comb was ready, Baby Sis and I took some hunko-lard and put it on Momma's hair down there. We were doing it the way we had seen Momma do it herself when she straightened the hair on her head.

Baby Sis brought me the hot comb off the stove. But Momma must have felt the heat, because as soon as we attempted to touch her pubic hairs with it, she jumped up and grabbed a stick, and she laid it on me good, shouting, 'I bet you'll never look under my dress again as long as you're black!'

My mother married again, but I never really got on with my stepdaddy, Philip Reese. I never really liked him, it's a shame to say. He's dead now, God bless him.

He was a painter, but he drank, man. He was an alcoholic,

I would say. He'd get drunk and if my mother was sewing he would come in and snatch the material from under the machine. He'd be cussing and snatching at the machine and at me. My mother would jump up and grab a hot skillet of grease and pop him on the side of the head with it.

Sometimes he'd say, 'I ain't got a chicken or child and when I eat a hamburger my family's full.' I can remember that like it was yesterday. It's just stayed in my mind.

The antagonism between Ike and his stepfather came to a head one day when Ike and Baby Sister had made a playhouse in the yard. Ike had installed a small stove with a little chimney in it. When his stepfather came home, he saw the smoke and gave Ike a whipping. But Ike was not going to take this lying down. He went into the house and caught his stepfather bending over. He crept up behind him and hit him over the head with a length of timber, knocking him out.

Terrified that he had killed his stepfather, Ike jumped on his bicycle and cycled out of town. On Highway 61, he grabbed on to the back of a truck which towed him at up to 75mph along the fast, straight road to Memphis. Just short of the state line, the flat delta of Mississippi gives way to the rolling hills of Tennessee and the road narrows as it passes through a cut. Unaware of the presence of his uninvited passenger, the lorry-driver did not slow down. In the nick of time, Ike realised that he risked being crushed between the side of the truck and the wall of the cut. He let go and had to pedal the rest of the way into Memphis.

I was sitting on the sidewalk outside the Peabody Hotel, resting, when a policeman came by on a horse and told me to put my feet back on the kerb, which I did. I was right across the street from the Hotel Clary, opposite the Peabody Hotel. I was so fucking hungry it was unbelievable. I went around behind the Hotel Clary. At first, I wasn't thinking about no job or nothing, I was just looking at the garbage cans to get me something to eat.

I lived in this alley for several days. I made me a bed to sleep on by taking all the bottles out of four or five Coca-Cola cases and turning the crates upside-down. Next day, I would get up and put all the bottles back in the crates so they couldn't tell I'd slept there. And then I would eat out of the garbage cans. Finally, a guy caught me there. He worked in the hotel and was fixing to go eat. I said, 'Hey man, can I go and get something to eat?'

'Yeah,' he said, 'they don't know you don't work here. Just go in, take your tray and get something.'

So I went in there with him, boy, and I was so hungry. I asked the guy, 'Can I get a job here so that I can eat like you all eat?' He told me to go talk to the hall porter or whatever he was. He gave me a job as a hall boy. I had to polish the mahogany doors – I remember it like yesterday.

I stayed there from Monday to Thursday – not even long enough to get my first wages. By then I'd started getting worried about home. And when I got off work I had nowhere to go – they'd started locking that back alley where I was sleeping.

I think I left my bicycle in Memphis, but some kinda way I got back to Clarksdale. On the corner of Fourth Street and Sunflower there was a service station. I knew that when my little niece came home from school, she would have to walk right by the graveyard and the service station, so I took my little ball of clothes and set them up by the gas pump. I sat way back from it, waiting on my niece to come, knowing she would see it.

When Baby Sister came by and saw the clothes, she said, 'Momma is worried to death about you.' Then she said something about my stepdaddy, so I knew he wasn't dead. 'You coming on home?' she asked me.

I said I wasn't. 'I'm taking your clothes home, then,' she said, which was what I really wanted.

I waited real good until I knew my Momma was home before I went back to get my clothes. She would not let me leave.

Ike was more than happy to be back with his loving Momma B. But he had a chance to see the big city – and to see that life could be different. In Clarksdale, the Klan was in control. Ike tells the sardonic joke:

'Where do the black folks hang out?

Well, two that was here are hanging on that tree over there.'

Memphians looked down on country people, thinking they had something to hide. Often they had.

The black folks in Memphis were serious. They were the hip ones, they got the right clothes. And in those days in Memphis, there was not a whole lot of racial shit. It wasn't 'separate but equal' – that was a load of shit. But white folks knew where white folks went, and black folks knew where black folks went in Memphis. The blacks weren't interested in the whites and the whites weren't interested in the blacks. There was more respect for each side. It wasn't equal, but the white folks didn't fuck with the blacks. You could go downtown where they were.

When a black somebody killed a white somebody in Mississippi, they'd put him on a train and ship his ass away in a coffin. They made a hole in the coffin so he could breathe. You kill a white man, and they get you to the Masons, the Masonic Temple, and they put you in a coffin and ship you like a body to Chicago.

But Ike had seen another way out of Clarksdale – Highway 61, the road he would take again ten years later.

Eventually he was to escape the bitter memories of his murdered father and the racial brutality of the deep South for good. And when his mother died he took his stepfather with him. He also forgave his stepfather for the fights he had had with his mother, though his sister never did.

After my Momma died in 1959 or '60, I moved my stepdaddy from Clarksdale to St Louis into a home of mine and I took care of him till he died in 1961. He was OK, but you know with kids, man, they brand you as mean and it sticks with them.

My stepdaddy had been with my mother since 1942 or

something. They had been together twenty years. So whether they fought or whatever they did, I felt he was entitled to half of whatever gains there were.

After my father died, the beneficiaries were my mother, my sister and I, and Momma left it at that. My sister didn't want to give my stepdaddy his share, so I said I was not going to sign for her to sell the house. She wanted to split it between me and her. I said, 'Lee, I don't want any money out of it. You split it between you, Baby Sister and stepdaddy, and I'll sign the papers.'

She said OK, and so I signed the papers. About a year later, I was on a tour and I went by my house in East St Louis, where I'd moved my stepdaddy. I'd told him he could stay there so they could sell the house down in Clarksdale.

It was snowing, but he came running outdoors to see me and he didn't have no coat on. I said, 'Where is your coat?'

He said, 'Son, I don't have one.'

And I said, 'You drinking up all your money?' He was getting money from the state or the city or whatever.

'No, Sonny,' he told me.

I said, 'What you do with the money off the house?'

He said, 'I never got no money.'

And, boy, that really got to me, that my sister hadn't kept her word.

3 Boogie-Woogie

TODAY THEY CALL STUFF CHILD-MOLESTING. Well, man, there was no such thing back then. When I was a small boy, about six years old, there was a woman named Miss Boozie Owens who lived with her husband in the same neighbourhood. Mr Owens worked as an auto-dealer at the Buick dealership at Clarksdale. Miss Boozie stayed at home raising chickens to sell in the neighbourhood. She was about forty-five, fifty years old.

I had just started school – not even first grade, what we called back then primer. I would leave my house at 7.30 am so I could walk to school by 8. The route I took went right past the Owens' house.

One day, just as I was about to pass by her house on my way to school, Miss Boozie, who always addressed me by my childhood nickname, Sonny, called me to come into her house. She was at home alone because Mr Owens left for work daily at 6 am. She asked me if I would like a job and I said, 'Yes, ma'am.'

She explained that she wanted me to feed her chickens every morning before I went to school, and that she would pay me a nickel a week for doing it. After accepting the job, I continued on to school. When I got home I told my mother about the new job. The fact that I was able to find work on my own initiative made her really proud of her son.

So I stopped by every morning to feed the chickens and empty out the bottom trays under the wire-mesh screen that the chickens stood on inside the coops. I would always replace the old newspapers with fresh ones that I had to trim with a putty knife to make them fit the trays. It was messy work and

17

when I finished I always had to go inside the house to wash my hands. Sometimes I would have spots on my pants as well. Miss Boozie would help me to clean myself up, because I had to be neat and clean when I continued on to school.

I guess because it was so early in the morning, Miss Boozie always had on her nightgown, which was made of that real thin see-through material that some window drapes are made of. After these chores became routine. Miss Boozie and I became very close. She was always very friendly.

One morning she came out and helped me with my job and I finished early. She said, 'Come on, Sonny, let me clean you up so you can go to school.' When we both went back into the house, she removed her robe and washed up first. She still had on this nightgown, but while I'm standing there, man, I can see through this thin thing. Without the robe, her whole body was revealed to me and as she stood with her back to me, bent over her face bowl, I could see the long hairs from her cat between her legs. She was standing with her legs spread wide apart and I got a good look.

After she finished and dried her hands, she asked me to come into the bathroom so that she could help me clean up as usual. But this time she asked me to remove my pants, and she helped me to unzip them, claiming that I had a spot on them. After Miss Boozie washed away the so-called spot she set my pants down near the electric fan to dry.

We walked into the bedroom and she sat down on the bed while I stood there in my underwear. As I stood in the middle of the floor, nervously fidgeting, and not knowing what to do, she called me over to the bed. Miss Boozie reached out her hand and pulled out my penis. Then she began squeezing it, which made it jump hard. She then leaned back across the bed with her cat at the forward edge of the mattress facing me. I was just the right height, standing there, and she inserted my penis into her cat. She placed her hands on my hips and started pulling me backwards and forwards, making my penis move in and out of her.

This was the beginning of Miss Boozie teaching me what sex was all about. From then on, it became a daily routine. First I did my chores, and then received what I would call lessons. I guess the bed was about the height of a chair. She would sit on it and lay back, then she would stand me in front of her and my little thing would stick up.

The lessons consisted of five different steps. The first step was learning to push my penis in and out without letting it slip out of her. The second involved learning how to twist my ass in a clockwise motion. After a week or so she taught me the third step, which was how to twist my ass counter-clockwise, all the time making sure I didn't let my penis slip out. For the fourth step, she taught me how to roll my stomach muscles. Finally came the hard part, the fifth step. I learned how to coordinate steps two and three and perform them all simultaneously without stopping. As an added feature I also was able to roll my stomach while doing all the other movements. That was the hardest of all.

After doing this for weeks, I finally got to the point where I began actually to enjoy it, because by then I had learned to follow Miss Boozie's feelings and movements. She would be moaning and groaning, finally releasing a loud grunt, which I realise now, of course, was her reaching an orgasm. At the time, however, I had no idea what was happening to her. All I felt was a good hot feeling.

We would always stop after that final groan. Then she would take a towel and clean me off and send me to school. No one ever knew this was happening.

I've found that Miss Boozie's teachings have been very helpful to me in sexual relationships with women throughout the years. Even now, some of the girls I know teasingly call me rota-rooter.

A few years later, my sister, Lee Ethel Knight, used to hire a babysitter to come and stay with us whenever she went out. This girl, who we used to call Little Sister, was only about nine years old.

I used to get with Little Sister and try out all the moves I had learned from Miss Boozie. I also taught her to respond to the movements in the same way that Miss Boozie did, which was great. My sister would give me 25c to pay the babysitter, but I would always keep the money because I knew that she really enjoyed the lesson I was giving her, and I just wanted to screw anyway.

Once, when I was walking home from school, Little Sister invited me to come over and play. Her house sat on pillars and had a shallow crawl space underneath it. While playing a game of hide-and-seek, we crawled under the house and over into a dark corner. Then Little Sister unzipped my pants and my dick automatically got hard. She laid down and I got on top of her. Just as I got in the right position and was about to start pumping, her mother began to call her name from outside.

We were often caught by Miss Hattie B., who still lives on the corner of Magnolia and Washington in Clarksdale. She would beat my butt. One time, Miss Hattie B. found us under Little Sister's house. I saw her big ankles, but when I tried to raise up off Little Sister I was stuck in my butt by a nail that was sticking down through the floorboards of the house.

Every time I struggled to get free the nail would poke me deeper and deeper. After a few minutes, I was able to disentangle myself and went home. My mother noticed the wound on my behind, and I had to tell her that I had sat on a nail earlier in the day. Momma put some coal oil on it, one of her favourite home remedies for minor cuts and scratches.

But it took more than a nail in the ass to discourage me. When Little Sis and I played house in the old coal-storage shed every day after school, we would also have sex. We were both too young to have an orgasm, but it felt good.

This went on for months until finally, one day, Little Sis and I went into our 'house' to play as usual not realising that my stepfather was at home. He saw us go in, and sneaked out to see what we were doing. He caught me playing with Little Sister's cat. My stepdaddy started whipping me with a piece of barbed wire while Little Sis ran home. When he finished whipping me, he carried me round the corner to Little Sis's house and told her mother and she got a good whipping, too. We were both put on punishment and given extra chores to do around the house every day. It was months before we could play with the other kids after school again.

Another incident happened later that year. When we walked to and from school we used a smooth, well-worn pathway that cut right across the front of a row of shotgun houses. A woman named Irene Woolfolk lived in one of these, and she used to sit on her porch every afternoon as we passed by on our way home. Miss Reeny, as I called her, would sometimes send me to the store to get stuff for her as I came by. She would always give me two or three cents or some candy.

Her husband died and she needed someone to cut firewood for her. At first, my friend Ernest Lane and I were doing it for free. Then Ernest joined the Army, and that left only me to do the job.

Miss Reeny was a short, very black woman, and, thinking back, I would say that she was a pretty nice-looking woman, too. She was perhaps middle-aged, her dark hair mingled with touches of grey, giving it a salt-and-pepper look. She wore her stockings without a garter belt, twisting them into a knot at the top and then rolling them over.

Miss Reeny had a big ass, so big that when she bent over to remove the ashes from the stove in her kitchen, her dress would ride up above her thighs. I used to peek up under her dress but I was afraid to approach her. Looking back, I think she knew exactly what she was doing.

One day she turned round just in time to catch me bending over to steal another peek under her dress. She whirled around quickly and said, 'Sonny, I'm gonna tell Miss B.' – that's my mother – 'on you, trying to peep up under old folks' dresses.'

I was scared to death. I remembered what had happened when I had been caught twice before. Standing there that day, I couldn't make up my mind whether I should stay or run away from home. I couldn't think of anywhere to go, so after staying out for several hours, I finally went home about 8.30 that night, afraid that Miss Reeny had already told Momma what I'd done.

When I entered the house, my momma said to me, 'Boy, where you been?'

I told her I'd been playing ball and had forgotten what time it was.

'I'm gonna make you remember what time you're supposed to be home,' she said. She also reminded me that I had no business playing ball anyway, because I was going to be baptised that Sunday and should have been going to revival at church all week. She lectured me about gambling when I should have been getting religion instead, but she never said one single word about my looking up Miss Reeny's dress. That's when I knew that Miss Reeny hadn't told on me.

The next day after school I stopped by and asked Miss Reeny if she wanted me to do anything for her around the house since she had no husband to do those things any more. She told me that she would like me to continue chopping wood for her now that Ernest had gone. She said that she would start paying me for it.

After that, Miss Reeny got really friendly with me. She was always smiling at me, and would playfully address me as 'Sonny, you little bad nappy-headed boy.'

Miss Reeny would sit on her front porch in a swing, swaying back and forth. As she swung the breeze would lift her dress up a little. After a few weeks or months went by, she no longer bothered to pull it back down when that breeze lifted it up. Instead she would leave part of her thigh exposed so that I could see her meat.

One day, after I had finished cutting some wood for her, I went in to stack it behind her stove as usual. She was sitting at the kitchen table, and when I'd finished she said, 'Come here,' and reached out to hand me a dime. She was sitting at that kitchen table with her legs spread wide apart and the bulk of her dress tucked between her two fat thighs.

As I went to take the dime, she held on to it and wouldn't let go. We found ourselves holding on to both sides of that dime, neither one of us letting go.

Then she said to me, 'Sonny, why are you so bad?' as she opened her legs wider. She never stopped smiling. My dick was getting hard but I still held on to the dime.

As she pulled forward, I found myself right between her large thighs. Then she reached up and put one of her arms across my back. I couldn't resist any more, and it was on.

This went on for years, and we were never caught by anyone. But she would warn me every single day not to tell anybody, 'cos if I did, she would tell Momma B. So I have never told anyone about this until now. Miss Reeny was the third person with whom I had sexual relations before the age of twelve.

Ike's childhood friendship with Ernest Lane was interrupted only briefly by Ernest's sojourn in the army. He had lied about his age to join up, and was soon back in Clarksdale.

I was kinda young when I first met Ernest. He had three sisters and two brothers, all of whom lived with his mother on my side of town. Ernest was liked by all the girls. He was a real fighter, too, and he became the new bully of the neighbourhood. After he beat up my old enemy Percy Parker, Ernest and I began running together. We became the best of friends and started to share everything – including our girlfriends.

We had two girls named Eunice and Ernestine. Ernest and I were both screwing both of them. We didn't mind swapping because we were such close buddies.

At that time Ernest's father, who was a painter, had his own place in a part of town called Overtown. Ernest could go and stay there when he got mad with his mom. One day after I got mad at my mother, Ernest and I ran away together and went to live with his dad.

His daddy played ragtime piano and he had a lot of women hanging around the house. He was a real whoring man, screwing everyone who had a big ass and was light-skinned. He had all the pretty women 'cos he always had a new car. One of them was a girl called Dolores. She made you want to jump up and down to look at her. She could jitterbug her butt off, too.

Dolores used to dance with a tall, skinny boy named Peewee. They would take the floor any time, and everyone else would stop dancing and form a circle. Man, I wanted to screw her real bad, but John Lane got her. Ernest and I decided we were going to get her too.

Ernest's father never demanded that we go to school, but if we didn't we had to work for him, painting, instead. One day after a painting job, Ernest and I went to visit Dolores, who lived a few blocks away in an upstairs rooming-house.

John Lane lived out by Centennial Church, about five blocks from Issaquena, which is the main drag. This girl lived right on the corner of Issaquena and Fourth Street, on the second floor.

She had one small room with only one way in and no rear exit. There was no other way down except to climb through the window which led to the roof.

That night Ernest and I went up there and we were in there tearing her up, boy, when we heard bang, bang, bang, bang on the door.

She said: 'Who is it?'

'It's John Lane, open this damn door.'

Ernest and I jumped up. We couldn't get out because there was only the one door, so we got under the bed.

John Lane said: 'Dolores, open this goddamn door.'

She reached up. I don't know how she did it, but she blew that lightbulb out. Then she opened the door and stood in the doorway, blocking it.

Ernest's dad was trying to look past her. He said: 'I know damn well you-all in here.' He pushed past her and tried to turn on the light. But it didn't work, of course, and it was so dark he couldn't see nothing. He wasn't fooled, though. 'I know damned well you're in there. I'm going to get Milkman!' he shouted.

Milkman was a redneck policeman who was also screwing a lot of black women, including Dolores. She was very popular because of her big ass and full tits. As John left to get the policeman, we raised the window and climbed out on to the flat roof where Dolores had hung out her laundry. We could hear the heavy footsteps of Ernest's father going down the stairs. We were frightened so we started running.

There was no way down from the back of the roof. With all wet clothes hanging there, we couldn't see where we were going, and we ran right off the edge of the roof. We hit the ground on our feet and kept on running – all the way back to Ernest's house, about six blocks away. We got there before his father did, so we pulled out the couch, which doubled as our bed, got in and pretended to be asleep.

Ernest Lane's dad had a piano but, to Ike, it was just another bit of furniture. There was a piano in the church, too, but it was of no interest to him. Then something changed all that.

On the way home from school, years before we knew Dolores, we had to pass John Lane's house on Yazoo Street. One day, Ernest and I were coming down the street and we heard this boogie-woogie on the piano coming from his house. Man, we was flying. We looked through the window, boy, and I saw Pinetop Perkins playing the piano. Well, that guy, he was whooping the piano to death, man. It excited me more than anything in the world; it put a burn in my mind. Anyway, that's when I was first fascinated by pianos.

> Pinetop Perkins and Sonny Boy Williamson played the *King Biscuit Time Show* on the radio station KFFA. At 11.30 every day, anyone who had a radio would have their ear glued to the set. This was the golden age of radio. There was no television around then, and acts like Amos and Andy were bigger than movie stars.

Pinetop – we called him Joe Willie in those days – was playing with Sonny Boy Williamson and Peck, who was the drummer, and another Joe Willie. They all broadcast from Helena, Arkansas, but they rehearsed in Clarksdale and took the ferry over there.

They used John Lane's house because he had a piano and a car, so he could take them where they wanted to go. He bought a new car every year, so I guess he was someone to know. John played old-time swing piano, but the first time I became aware that a piano could sound like a piano, like the boogie-woogie stuff, was the day I was coming home from school and heard Pinetop.

After that I could not wait to get out of school to run back and watch them rehearse. John Lane's was a shotgun house, like ours. But you know, we didn't go in, we just looked through the window. Finally, you know what kids are like, they ease on in. Next thing, we stopped peeping through the window and we were inside.

I was standing next to the piano, man, standing at the end of the piano, just watching his fingers. He was bad, man. The way his hands moved, I couldn't take my eyes off them.

Pinetop was just showing out, doing his left hand, doing the boogie-woogie. Then Ernest Lane and I got interested in playing. We'd be messing with the keys and Pinetop started showing us this and showing us that. Then he began trying to show us how to play. But we both wanted to play and there was only one piano.

So I went home and told my mother about it. I told her that I wanted my own piano.

Up to this point, Ike had not been doing very well at school. His rebellious nature was already getting him into trouble. Momma B., however, had great ambitions for him and his new-found passion for the piano gave her some leverage.

My first teacher at Booker T. Washington Grade School was mean. Her name was Miss Harper Paris. She taught primer grade – today they call it pre-school. She was bad, man. She whooped us with a big stick. I was glad when I got promoted to first grade, Miss Nichols' room.

Momma said, 'If you pass third grade, I'll buy you a piano.' Man, when I got home from school the day I was promoted, with my report card – she already had me a piano sitting in my house. I was up in the air. I loved that piano. It was heaven to me. I think in them days she paid $300 for it. That's when I really started playing piano.

My mother started giving me a dollar every Thursday to take music lessons. I went a couple of times to Miss Nichols' house on Yazoo and Douglas. She was teaching me the scale – ABCs and shit – but that was too damn slow for me, man.

Then she started to teach me a song called 'Drifting', which went 'la, la' – some kind of little stuff like that. Man, it was too slow for me. I was interested in what Pinetop was doing: 'boom-da-boom-da-boom.' Her song sounded like something you would learn out of a book, but I was learning it by ear. She thought I was reading the notes.

Finally, after about six weeks of that shit every Thursday, I started taking the dollar for the lesson and going to the pool hall. I got to be a pool shark. I stayed at that pool hall playing hooky from school.

When I left, I'd go by and see Pinetop. He was teaching me the piano, 'cos what I wanted to do was boogie-woogie. His right hand would be going one way, his left hand the other, man. It was just real exciting. I wanted to learn it bad. When I learned a little bit, Ernest would learn a little bit. There was a battle between us to see who could play the best, me or him.

Ernest reports that Ike's progress was remarkably quick. In no time, he could play a tune. 'Every time he learned something, he taught it to me. That's how I learned to play,' Ernest says. Ike's mother was pleased too.

When I got back home, I'd show her what Pinetop had taught me. She thought it was great. Man, she wanted all the people she worked with to hear her son play piano. So that was the start of it all.

4 Ain't Nobody Here But Us Chickens

L ET ME TELL YOU SOMETHING: don't nobody know I play piano. They think I am a guitar-player. I ain't no guitar-player. But keyboard and boogie-woogie and shit like that, that's my thing. I don't care what piano-player you bring me . . . You take this guy Jerry Lee Lewis. He gets all in and out of time, feelingwise. I understand that blacks feel two and four when they clap; whites feel one and three. I understand this. But man, I can *play* a piano.

The reason no one knows Ike Turner is a piano-player is that, despite his ebullient nature, he is in fact chronically shy.

When I was promoted into sixth grade and moved from Booker T. Washington to Myrtle Hall, a school up in the Brick Yard area of Clarksdale, I didn't think anyone up there knew I could play piano.

I was sitting in Devotion, that's a meeting they have once a week where all the classes come together in one big room. There were sixth, seventh, eighth and ninth grades there – five classes in all. The accordion walls would be pulled back and all the classes would come in. I was sitting in there, man, with everyone else and all of a sudden someone said, 'Right, now, to open up, we're going to have Ike Turner come up and play a song on the piano.'

Man, my heart went down to my toes. I could have gone through the floor. I remember getting up with my eyes closed and walking up holding on to the wall. I got to the piano and played a real quick piece of boogie-woogie – maybe ten seconds – that Pinetop had just taught me. Then I got up and I ran back to my seat. I was so ashamed, man. I was twelve.

Even now, although he has played onstage and on record with some of the greatest musicians of the last half-century, Ike Turner does not feel confident enough to sit in on a jam session. With the Ike and Tina Turner Revue, he kept himself in the background, often playing with his back to the audience. He feels that he is an organiser rather than a performer.

On only one other occasion did he play at a school – up in Lula, Mississippi – and despite his bashful performance he soon discovered that there were great advantages to being a musician.

That took a lot of nerve for me. But when I played that tune in school that day, Ernest and I became popular with all the girls. We must have screwed about 60 per cent of them in the Brick Yard area after that.

Ernest's daddy had just bought a new car at that time and we would push it out into the street at night after he went to sleep. Then we would hot-wire it and drive off into the night. We used it to go and pick up girls. Then we would stop and park in a dark spot somewhere and have sex in the back seat.

The change of school caused problems for Ike. From his home in Riverton, Booker T. Washington had been just across the fetid Sunflower River in Overtown. The town's sewers empty directly into the river. It was a long walk around by the road bridge, so the children would take a short-cut, clambering up and walking across the pipes that straddled the river.

If you fell in, you came up with a turd in your head. When we got older, we would risk crossing the railroad bridge high over the Sunflower River. We never knew whether a train would show up before we got across. We'd do anything for a dare.

But Ike's senior school, Myrtle Hall, was further away, to the north of the Round Yard. Beyond that was the Upper

Brick Yard. These were altogether tougher areas. Ike was still very much a momma's boy.

After the whipping Momma B. gave me for fighting Percy Parker, I stayed a coward for a long time and was really afraid to fight. For some crazy reason, I was always scared of any boy who had a light skin and a bald head.

It was Ernest Lane who forced me to have courage. We graduated together from Booker T. Washington School, which only went to fifth grade, and transferred to Myrtle Hall. I was glad to be with Ernest because Myrtle Hall had a bunch of bad guys who loved to beat up all the new kids coming from Booker T. Washington.

There were two boys, Frank Nathan Jones and Van Allen, who just happened to be great big kids with bald heads and light skins, just the kind of people of whom I was most scared. On the fourth day of school, I went to the store and spent 5c on some ice-cream. It was all the money I had. When I came out Frank Nathan took my ice-cream away from me. Right away, I went and told Ernest what he had done, thinking that Ernest would beat Frank up for me. Ernest knew I was afraid to fight.

But when we caught up with Frank around noon that day, instead of fighting him himself, Ernest told me that if I didn't fight Frank he was going to beat me up. At that point I forgot about Frank's bald head and his size. I jumped on him and managed to throw him to the ground. He hit me pretty hard on the head with a bottle and I started into him.

It wasn't easy, but I ended up winning the fight. This was the very first real fight I'd ever won. I beat his ass real good.

Meanwhile, there was a stand-off between Ernest and Frank's friend Van Allen. They didn't fight that day, though. Things came to a head between Ernest and Van Allen over a girl. Her name was Julia Mae. I liked her, and used to carry her books home from school for her. She was tall, high-yellow complexioned and had real nice legs. She was one of the best lays in Clarksdale, but she was Van Allen's special lay.

Because I was trying to get with Julia Mae too, Van Allen wanted to jump on me. But Ernest decided that since I had already whipped Frank, it was his turn to fight. So they fought, and after Ernest won, he and I walked Julia Mae home.

By the time we got to her house, I was really turned on by her and wanted to have sex, but I was too scared to ask her to do it with me. Her parents weren't home, so she invited us into the house. They had a piano, so while Ernest played I began to slow-dance with her. I had my arms locked around her real tight, hugging her body real close to mine.

While we danced, my stomach muscles were rolling, and my hips were moving to the left and to the right, just like I'd been taught by Miss Boozie when I was young. It was a real hot day, and Julia Mae was hot too, responding to my sexy moves nicely. But I was still scared to raise up her dress, in spite of the encouragement she was giving me. So instead I went and got a broom, and while she held the handle end down at her cat, I held the straw end over my hard penis and we kept our movements going that way.

When Ernest stopped playing, Julia went and got two pitchers of iced water. Ernest and I – just like we did with almost everything else – had a friendly competition to see who could drink the most cold water. I was the winner.

After a while Ernest, who had a job as a shoeshine boy, had to go to work. This left Julia Mae and me alone in the house together. Then I was able to lay her down across the bed. I began to work Miss Boozie's movement with my penis inside her body. All at once, from out of nowhere, came this intense feeling I had never felt before in my life. I didn't really know what it was and it just about scared me to death. I didn't know I had just had my first orgasm. I wasn't sure if I ever wanted to get that feeling again.

When it was all over, I ran to tell Ernest. 'Man,' I said, 'you gotta try screwing after drinking iced water.'

I tried to explain to Ernest just what had happened with Julia. Then I suggested to him that I should stay behind and take care of his shoeshine business while he went back to Julia Mae's house and tried the same thing. I told him to make sure he drank lots of iced water first, just like I'd done. Because Ernest and I were such good friends, I didn't mind the idea of him making it with a girl I liked.

So he did it, but later on, he told me he hadn't felt anything like what I had told him to expect.

There were also fights with the local whites. Ike can still point to the place where he and Ernest fell down the steep banks of the Sunflower River while 'duking' with the white boys. He talks without bitterness of the store-owner who used to kick the 'niggers' with his wooden leg. A tinge of sadness comes over him, though, when he remembers his friendship with a white boy at the store where he worked.

From when I was eight years old or younger, Joe Geddis, the store-owner's son, and I were friends, man. Then when he was sixteen he told me, 'You got to call me Mr Geddis now.' All my life I'd been calling him Joe. So I fell out with the Geddises and got myself another job.

In Clarksdale, such simple slights were a symptom of something much more sinister.

Denzil Turner – he wasn't a relative of mine – lived over in Riverton. He had epileptic fits. He was in a service station and fell down in a fit, slobbering at the mouth. This policeman came up, grabbed him by the arm, put his gun right up under his armpit and – bam! – killed him like he was a hog or something. Cold motherfuckers, man.

Ike's response was to start a campaign against all the service stations in town which had segregated restrooms – that is, they had toilets for whites but none for blacks. Ike had stickers printed that read: 'Don't buy gas where you can't use the restroom.'
Day-to-day life was hard enough for anyone black, but for a fatherless black boy growing up in small-town Mississippi, prospects were bleaker still. The best job a black man could realistically expect was a position at the rubber plant, vulcanising tyres. There he could make $45 a week, considered a fortune in those days. But none of this stopped Momma B. being ambitious for her son.

My mother always wanted me to be a doctor or a lawyer or something. She raised me like that. I just wasn't going to pick no cotton; I wasn't for no kind of labour like that. I liked music, but I never knew I was going to play no music – that was the furthest thing from my mind. I came up hustling, man. After working for a couple of drugstores as a delivery boy, I got a job with another one of the Geddis brothers. He used to get people to sell candy for him out in the country and then, instead of giving them money for it, he would let them pick pots and pans and dishes from his store.

I also worked at the Sunflower Laundry. I used to press clothes at the presser. Then I went out with Mr Chaney, all around the country, man, picking up laundry. I used to wrap it up with string and put the person's name on it. That was a bitching job, man. I just liked to ride.

Then my brother-in-law – my sister's husband – bought a pick-up truck. I used to go to the woods way out from Clarksdale and saw down trees and cut them up into stove wood. I would go and sell this wood around the neighbourhood in the truck.

I was real young and had no business even in the truck. But I did what I had to do in order to get by.

At nine years old, man, I bought an old laundry truck. I paid $200 for it. I sold chickens and shit to get the money to buy it. At ten years old, I had my whiskey still out in the woods. I was selling whiskey all over. That's how come I can tell you about everything in the state of Mississippi.

Give me some rye, some sugar and corn, and I'd make you some corn liquor. You set your whiskey still out there in the woods, 'cos nobody's going to be looking there. Shit, if the police found it and don't catch you there, they ain't going to do nothing but tear it up.

> Back then he was a country boy and would jump from log to log in the swamps, not worrying about snakes. These days he is a dyed-in-the-wool townie and shudders at the thought of snakes and lizards.

One time, I was in Overtown in Clarksdale on the north side of the Sunflower River. Just me, Ernest and Calvin Lane were over there. They heard the bell ringing – the fire department. Somebody said, 'Hey, that's 304 Washington, man. That's your house.'

> In the fire, Ike's beloved piano was badly damaged. So he rebuilt it using a felt hat, cement glue, shoelaces, steel from the inside of a car tyre, paper and a socket wrench. The insight this gave him into the workings of a piano was soon put to good use. He added a new sideline to his business: piano-tuning. Later, Ike learned to fix other instruments. When he formed his band, the Kings of Rhythm, he tied together broken guitar strings and overhauled saxophones using a car chamois for pads and needles to replace springs. He'd make saxophone reeds from sugar cane.

I never played piano in church during a service. But I sometimes tuned the piano for an extra $3. And if no one was listening, I would play a boogie-woogie.

When I was in the eighth grade, I got a job at the Alcazar Hotel, a white hotel in Clarksdale, driving an elevator after school. I used to sit outside on the sidewalk sometimes on my break.

One day the white kids had a school prom in the ballroom on the second floor. I was sitting on the kerb outside the entrance of the hotel, just watching the white kids driving up in their daddies' cars with their little white girlfriends. They were about eighteen or nineteen; I was maybe fourteen. I remember sitting on the kerb, just looking. They were prejudiced down there and you couldn't stare too hard. A black man wasn't supposed to look at no white women in those days.

I remember the white kids pulling up to the kerb in their cars and the girls getting out with their little minks. They'd throw it across their shoulders and grab their guy's arm. I couldn't really look too good – they'd kill you for staring at any white woman.

But I'd be shaking my head and saying, 'God, one of these days, man, I'm gonna have girls like that.' You know, just thoughts going through my head.

That was just so exciting to me, man, to see all those pretty girls coming there. I just wanted it, like a craving that wouldn't go away. I guess that's why, when I was with Tina, I was so whorish. I had so many women. I just had to have what I had wanted as a child.

I also admired the big houses on Elm Street the white people had. I thought, goddamn. When I grow up to be a big boy, I am going to have a house like that.

Other things were happening to the young Ike Turner in Clarksdale that were to form his attitude to women.

When I was a kid and went to the movies, it was a nickel. That's all it cost in them days, 5c. We had two theatres in Clarksdale, the Savoy and the Roxy. They were, of course, segregated. Whites sat in the stalls and used the front entrance. Blacks had to climb the three storeys to the back of the balcony, where they had to sit, via the metal fire escape in the alley outside.

The Three Stooges were real popular. So was Wild Bill Hickok, and Gene Autry. I used to go to the show every Saturday to catch Tarzan and Nyoka. Nyoka was this white chick who used to swing through the jungle just like Tarzan. She would fight lions and shit. And she had this little piece of leopardskin or something that covered her cat. So I'd sit in the front seat of the movies every Saturday, trying to look up under that little flap. Nyoka was real rough. I was in love with her.

I didn't know it until after Tina and I broke up, but subconsciously, I made Tina Nyoka. Tina Turner on stage is real wild, with the long hair, just like that jungle woman I'm talking about – rough the way she was rough. If Tina hit you accidentally while she was performing, man, you'd really get hurt. There's nothing feminine about her at all. There's a lot of force in her movements; everything she does is rough.

I would buy Tina $4,000 gowns and cut them up into rags. I wasn't aware I was making Tina into Nyoka until after we divorced. Then it flashed on me that that's what I'd done. Subconsciously, I'd turned Tina into Nyoka.

As a kid I was also crazy about the women in short dresses who spun their batons in the parades in Clarksdale. Those parades were something. I remember sitting on the steps of the church in Fourth Street, watching and eating my first hamburger. I'll never forget that taste as long as I am black. The majorettes excited me. I guess this is why I started mini-dresses with the Ikettes. I was thinking about those majorettes. I was crazy about legs.

Subconsciously I made the Ikettes like the majorettes and I made Tina Nyoka, but I didn't realise any of this at the time – I never really paid attention to the image I had created onstage.

After Tina and I broke up, maybe a year or so later, man, I was looking at a film of us on some TV show. There were the Ikettes on stage with their short skirts, real wild – just like the majorettes, but without the batons. Tina, in the cut-up gown, was the woman swinging through the jungle.

My job as a lift attendant at the Alcazar led to my first job in the music business. There was a radio station, WROX, located inside the hotel on the second floor. The announcer was a white guy called John Friscilla. When I got my breaks from the elevator, I would run up there and watch him playing records through the window in the control room.

Finally he said, 'Hey, come here.' I suppose he got used to seeing me standing there all the time. I went inside the room and he showed me how to cue up the records. You cued up the record to where it started and held it with your finger until the other one ended. And then you just had to lift up your finger. He also used to show me the cartridge with the commercials. Then he would go downstairs to Hager's Drugstore across the street to get coffee and shit.

After some months, the station manager came and caught me in there. I thought John Friscilla was going to get fired, but after the manager saw how well I did it, he gave me a radio programme. So now I was a disc-jockey. He would let me play records for an hour or two in the afternoons from three or three-thirty until six o'clock. We only had half a day of school and got out at twelve o'clock. I did that for a long time. I just played anything I wanted to play, man.

At the time, there weren't many disc-jockeys on the air.

Early Wright was the only one in Clarksdale. He broadcast on the morning show, playing spirituals. But there was a sensation coming out of Nashville, Tennessee on WLAC, a guy called Gene Nobles. All the black people throughout the whole South would listen to him because he played the real stuff.

The blues singer Robert Nighthawk, who had played with the legendary Robert Johnson, had his own 11–11.15 am spot on WROX in Clarksdale, competing against Sonny Boy Williamson's and Pinetop Perkins' *King Biscuit Time* over the river in Helena, Arkansas, on KFFA. Sonny Boy Williamson was more popular than Robert Nighthawk, with the harmonica and all. But Robert Nighthawk was real, real good with the slide on his finger. So was Elmore James, but Elmore James wasn't into broadcasting.

Sonny Boy was more popular because his records had had more exposure than Robert Nighthawk's.

Later B.B. King had his own show on WDIA in West Memphis, and Ike worked there too. But as a youth on WROX, Ike enjoyed a wonderful exposure to all kinds of music. In those days, record companies simply mailed all their new releases to the radio stations. There were no playlists and no specialist programmes. The DJ simply played whatever took his fancy.

I played stuff by Roy Milton and Jimmy Liggins. I played a lot of country stuff. My favourite music is country.

I remember the record labels mostly. One of them was Specialty. I used to play 'Stardust', 'Roses of Picardy', Tommy Dorsey boogie and records by Louis Jordan. I loved Louis Jordan. He was an alto saxophone-player and singer. His words were so good. He was real hot with 'Caldonia' and 'Ain't Nobody Here But Us Chickens', and all that stuff.

As a disc-jockey I had some real stupid sayings: 'Does anybody out there want to buy a duck? I got one for sale for a dollar-three-sixty-five. Right now we have Louis Jordan singing, "Ain't Nobody Here But Us Chickens".'

I started to go and see live acts too. There was a guy called Manuel who worked at the funeral home. He had a Cadillac.

Down South, people who don't have cars pitch in – a dollar apiece in those days – to ride to where the dance is in somebody's car. When Charles Brown played Chambers, Mississippi, I had no ride so I made plans to go with Manuel.

I was working over at the Checkerboard feed store. I carried my clothes to work with me and changed there. When I went over to the funeral home to meet Manuel it was still early in the evening. In the funeral home, a corpse on display used to be laid in the front office where the family could view it. At the back of the office, there were two swing doors that led into the embalming room, where the bodies were prepared. I stayed outside. I had some rocks and was sitting on the kerb playing jacks.

Then Manuel said, 'Ike, come on in.'

I said, 'You know I'm not coming in there.'

Always was scared of dead folks, man. I never wanted to go to no one's funeral. When I was young and me and Baby Sister were in bed I was always scared of ghosts. I used to walk by the graveyard coming from school. It'd be raining. And I could have sworn there was something behind me. The faster I walked, the faster it walked. And I was afraid to look back. I kept on walking faster and faster until I was running.

'We ain't got no bodies – look,' said Manuel.

He opened the front door to show me that there were no bodies or caskets in the front office. 'Man, come on in, I got something to show you,' Manuel insisted.

I went into the front office, but Manuel had disappeared out of the swing doors out back with another guy.

Meantime, what they were doing was standing up this big, tall, dead stiff; cold. He had been cut all under the arms. They propped him up against the swing doors so that when I grabbed the door to open it, he fell into my arms. It felt like a piece of ice.

I just turned him around, dropped him and took off. I ran right over the hearse parked outside. When I stopped running I was over in Riverton at my house. My Momma said she saw me coming. I was over that fence in one jump. I couldn't breathe – couldn't breathe in, couldn't breathe out. The air had just stopped. She couldn't take me to the hospital 'cos it was whites only, so she took me to a doctor who got me breathing again.

To this day, I'm terrified of dead bodies and funerals. I would like to try to put a stop to funerals. I think you put a person through a whole lot of shit. Plus it is costly. A person dies, then you keep him in a funeral home for x amount of days, so you can view the body, and then you've got to go to church and view him again while you go through the grief.

Why don't you take him away when he dies? Why isn't that the end of it? You can go to the graveyard and remember. But a funeral opens all the grief back up, man. I just know that this is cruel to make people go through this.

Man, the only things I am scared of are a snake, the Internal Revenue and a dead man.

5 The Kings of Rhythm

At Ike's senior school, Myrtle Hall, they had a school band,
but Ike could not join it because he did not play a brass
instrument. Instead, he and some other pupils formed a band
called the Tophatters, which played concerts and dance clubs.

THERE WERE THIRTY-TWO or thirty-six of us, all kinds of
musicians. Some of them liked blues. Louis Jordan was
real famous then. Some liked Woody Herman, Tommy
Dorsey, stuff like that; the stuff the big bands played.
When we had the Tophatters, the first thing I learned, man,
was Tommy Dorsey, Glenn Miller and Harry James, all of that
big-band stuff. The rest of the band was reading it from sheet
music. They thought I was reading it too, but I was playing it
by ear. I would listen to the record and learn my part at home.
So when I come to a rehearsal and they put a sheet in front of
me, they thought I was reading that shit. Anyway, I shook my
way through it.

Ike's friend Clayton Love, a trombone-player with the
Tophatters, could read a little bit and realised that Ike was
winging, but it didn't matter. 'Make no mistake,' he says.
'Ike Turner is a genius.'
    Soon both of them were fed up with big-band music.
They were into the blues, especially Amos Milburn and
Charles Brown. The Tophatters stayed together for six
months, maybe a year, and then they broke up into two
groups. The jazz faction called themselves the Dukes of
Swing. To outdo them, the bluesmen, led by Ike Turner,
dubbed themselves the Kings of Rhythm.

The other guys wanted to play jazz. I didn't know anything about any fucking jazz. We wanted to play blues, boogie-woogie and Roy Brown, Jimmy Liggins, Roy Milton – all these were the hot people back in them days. Amos Milburn and Charles Brown were extremely hot.

So they went their way and started playing jazz. We started playing whatever was on the jukebox, whatever the people wanted to hear. Then, for a while on Saturdays twice a month, we would back up two trucks on Sunflower, over towards the white folks' part of town, block off the street and have a battle between the two bands.

There was a theatre up in the Brick Yard called the Harlem Theater. When the Tophatters first broke up, we started to play there, every Wednesday, man. It was a nickel to get in.

We had this boy named Sterling. He was 5ft 10 and 160lbs with a head the size of an apple and a normal-size neck. Sterling was twenty-one years old but had the mind of a child. He wanted to be a musician, so he hung around with us. Sometimes we'd call him monkey man to make him chase us. When we worked up at the Harlem Theater, Sterling would be our dancer. When the time came to divide up the money, if you gave him a dollar bill you would have to fight him, but if you gave him ten pennies he would be happy. He was 'off' like that.

Soon we started playing gigs all over Mississippi – Marks, Friars Point, Batesville. We even played Duncan, Mississippi, the late King Curtis's home town.

The time I went down to Chambers, Mississippi, to see Charles Brown, he was hot with 'Black Night' and 'Merry Christmas, Pretty Baby'. He was real famous in his heyday. Then I saw Roy Milton, the piano-player. He was real, real big then with 'RM Blues'. Hadda Brooks had 'The House of Blue Lights'; Amos Milburn came out with 'Bad, Bad Whiskey'. Whatever was hot, that's what we would learn.

I don't want to sound egotistical, but there are times when my band can be playing onstage without me, and when I come on, and they know I'm there, the vibes from my body can change the whole sound in the room.

I also sang with a cappella group, a barbershop quartet.

The first machine that let you make your own record came

out. You bought the blank vinyl and you put it on the machine and sang in the microphone and it cut a little record. Well, Momma bought me one of the first ones to come out, man. We sounded like Boyz-2-Men, with me singing the lead.

WROX played another key role in Ike's musical development. It was only a matter of time before he hooked up with Robert Nighthawk.

Robert Nighthawk had just recorded the song 'Sweet Black Angel'. I remember how the first verse of that song started out:

I've got a sweet black angel,
I love the way she spreads her wings,
When she spreads her wings over me,
It brings joy in everything.

I could really relate to this song because it reminded me of Julia Mae. I still sing it to this day.

At night at that time I used to roll up blankets and put them under the counterpane to fool my mother that I was in bed asleep. Then I'd climb out of the window, go to dances to meet girls and listen to music. After a while I felt I was a grown man.

I left home 'cos I was 'smelling my pee', as Momma put it. I moved over to the Riverside Hotel. Robert Nighthawk stayed there and Ernest and I would help him carry his instruments over to the radio station. He didn't know we could play piano at all. We just used to carry his amplifier and guitar, just to be around musicians.

Eventually Ernest and Ike contrived to have Robert Nighthawk hear them play. At the time Nighthawk was losing the ratings battle against Sonny Boy Williamson. Sonny Boy would have only five hours at a dance, whereas Nighthawk would have to play a straight twelve.

Before long, Ernest and I both started working as musicians for Robert Nighthawk. We played the drums and the piano for him in the local roadside joints. Our hours were long. We used to play out at Marks, Mississippi, and we would start at eight o'clock at night and not get off until eight o'clock the next morning. We got $11. There wasn't no intermission. If the drummer had to pee, I would play drums until he returned. If I had to go they would continue to play till I came back. There were no breaks. We just switched around.

If either of us saw a good-looking girl we wanted to screw around with, we would have to pretend that we needed to go to the outhouse so that we could sneak outside with these hot girls and screw. Both Ernest and I managed to do this quite often.

> The youthful Kings of Rhythm were still in existence, but they were not playing as much as Robert Nighthawk. And Ike had a powerful incentive to play with the old bluesman.

I was getting more grown women playing with Robert than I would with the kids. Robert had some fine women, grown women, you know. I was still playing with the Kings of Rhythm, but I was playing more with Robert because he had most of the gigs.

> With Robert Nighthawk, Ike used to play at the Red Top in Clarksdale and the Harlem Club. He played all over Mississippi – Marks, another club in Batesville, the Silver Dollar Club in Greenville ('That's where we had to overhaul the piano every night before the gig started'), John's Nightclub in Indianola, Ruby's Nightclub in Leland and Jake's Place in Belzoni.

One morning at dawn I was coming home from a gig. I was on a gravel road that passed by a huge compress, about eight blocks long and eight blocks square, with a platform where trucks back up to unload cotton. Inside the compress you get rows and rows of cotton which has been baled up at the gin and is waiting to be pressed.

They have big presses. They sling that 1,600lb bale of cotton in and that big press comes down on it and it is reduced to quarter of the size before it goes off on the train to where they make cloth.

Inside the compress, man, it looks like miles and miles of cotton. You look down this narrow aisle and as far as you can see are bales of cotton. If you don't know where you are going in that compress, you will get lost.

There's a boiler room in there. The boiler room, there ain't but one way out – the way you go in is the way out. But on top of it there is a hole where I guess the steam comes out.

The sun was just beginning to come up and I saw this black guy come out the side of a house. He ran across the street in front of me, man – I had to slide and turn sideways to avoid hitting him. He had a shotgun in his hand and big boxes of shells.

What had happened was that this guy was having a fight with his wife and somebody called the police. The police went in there and slapped him. Well, man, no man is gonna slap me – a man slapping another man – I don't care if you are the police. That's not your job. Your job is to arrest me, man, you know? You dig what I'm talking about?

Anyway, the policeman slapped this guy and the black dude whipped his butt. Man, he knocked his dick-string off. Anyway, the black dude knew he was in trouble now. They say he ran into the bedroom and I guess that's when he got the shotgun and two, three boxes of shells. Then he climbed out of the window and ran across the street in front of me.

He jumped up on the platform where the trucks pull up. There's a huge door at the back of it. He slid the door open, ran into the compress and pulled it closed behind him. The policeman went to his car and called the sheriff.

After a while, the sheriff came along with another deputy. He said: 'Man, I'll show you how to get the nigger outta there.' And he walked up there and he grabbed that damn door, man. He pulled that door open and – boom! – that black guy blew his head off. It had to be a 12-gauge or something like that.

The other two policemen were real scared now. They got down on the ground with their guns out. One of them had the radio, talking – calling for help, I guess.

In about an hour or two, I can't really say how long but it

was light by then, white people started coming from everywhere – in pick-up trucks, cars and everything. They surrounded this whole fucking compress. This was all happening in Riverton, my neighbourhood. Believe it or not, a lot of people in Mississippi today I've talked to down there still remember the scene.

So the white guys started going in, from the other side, all round. I knew this dude inside must be scared, 'cos if he didn't know nothing about no compress, he'd be lost. We couldn't go in, so we stood outside. We heard shooting in there.

I later found out that he ran into the boiler room and they shot tear gas or something in there, down the hole where the steam came out.

When I next saw the black dude, they were dragging him on the floor by the feet. He was unconscious. By then it was real daytime – eight-thirty, nine or ten o'clock, I don't really remember. They dragged him out on to the platform where they unload the cotton, where all the blacks could see him. They tore loose his pants, took a knife and cut his penis off – the whole thing, penis and balls. Then they cut his throat and stuck his penis into his throat. You know, that was supposed to scare the niggers, man. But it didn't scare me, because he'd killed maybe twenty-six of the motherfuckers before they got him. I sat there and watched the whole thing, but it didn't put no fear in me. I don't think he felt anything because he was unconscious.

Despite witnessing such scenes, Ike does not hate white people, though he applauds that black man – in one final, defiant, heroic gesture – for killing twenty-six of them. More than once Ike has been in similar circumstances and has risked his life rather than back down. To have survived in Mississippi as a black man, you have to be that hard.

6 The Hunter

'Rocket 88' was a great success, but at the same time a huge disappointment for Ike – and not only because he made just $20 from the number 1 hit. The featured singer was Ike's saxophone-player, Jackie Brenston, and the record label was supposed to have read: 'Ike Turner and the Kings of Rhythm featuring Jackie Brenston.' Instead, 'Jackie Brenston and his Delta Cats' was printed. Ike blames Sam Phillips, who leased the record to Chess. Whoever's fault it was, by the time it was released there was nothing he could do about it.

Worse, the band's regular singer, Johnny O'Neal, had already signed a solo contract with King Records. The other members of the band – drummer Willie Sims, guitarist Willie Kizart and Raymond Hill on tenor saxophone – began to squabble.

RAYMOND HILL'S MOTHER wanted him to be the bandleader and the band started to fall apart. So I went to Memphis and found Hank Crawford, Calvin Newborn, Phineas Newborn Jr and Phineas Newborn Sr. They were the musicians Jackie and I played with after the band broke up.

Then Jackie got a big head with me and I said, fuck him, and went off to be a disc-jockey or something.

So Ike Turner had a ground-breaking hit record, but no money, no recognition and no band. But, as Ike frequently observes about his life, there is no use crying over spilt milk. He moved to West Memphis.

Just over the Mississippi from Memphis, Tennessee, West Memphis is in Arkansas. It is a tornado-ripped shanty town of trailer homes and truck stops. Memphis itself is protected from tornados by a bluff. In late spring, squalls of tornados race across the Great Plains, hit the bluff that runs along the Tennessean bank of the river and bounce up over Memphis. But West Memphis, on the Arkansas bank, has no protection and gets it every time.

Yet living there allowed Ike to stay in touch with the burgeoning music scene in Memphis. He also played with various local bands in clubs around West Memphis.

There was this white guy who drove a gravel truck. He used to park it around the back of the place I was playing at. It was a black club, and he would sneak in the side door and hide behind the piano while I was playing and doing my stuff, all that crazy shit with my legs and all.

Years later, Tina and I were playing the International Hotel in Vegas when this guy comes up to me in the hallway and tells that he was the man who used to hide behind the piano and watch me. It was Elvis Presley. That's where he got all that shit from.

Despite his influence on the development of the king of rock 'n' roll, Ike is dismissive of his one-time disciple.

In America, if you're white you can get away with anything – you can be a superstar like Elvis Presley, man. Elvis has talent but he's no Paul McCartney. He don't even come nowhere close to that dude. They talk about him being the king of rock 'n' roll, but in my opinion management manoeuvrings had a lot to do with his success. I believe Colonel Parker – a white Don King – contributed 75 per cent of it.

Ike had stayed in touch with his old friend Riley 'Blues Boy' King, who was also in Memphis at that time. One day, when B.B. was recording with Joe Bihari of Modern Records in the Sun Studios, Ike turned up. The session was not going well. Joe Bihari says the problem was that

Phineas Newborn, who was on piano, was a jazz pianist rather than a blues pianist. And after repeated attempts to get the song right, Bihari gave the band a fifteen-minute break.

I turned up on my bicycle. Joe Bihari was up in the control room with Sam Phillips. They were trying to cut 'You Know I Love You' with B.B. King and I was out there in the front just looking, listening to them trying to do it.

So they took an intermission for hamburgers or something. They had the doors open – it was hot in there – and when they took the break I came in and started playing the piano, just fooling around. Joe Bihari, who was in the control room, said, 'That's what I want, that's what I want!'

Bihari was immediately impressed by Ike's talent. In fact, Modern had been in the running for 'Rocket 88', but Leonard Chess had got in first. It marked the beginning of an intense rivalry between Chess and Modern.

Bihari employed Ike on the recording session and Ike played on B.B.'s first hit, 'Three o'Clock Blues.'

Then Joe Bihari said, 'Hey, is there any more talent around here like you?'

And I said, 'Yeah, lots of it.'

I told him there were musicians all over Mississippi, everywhere. So he went outdoors, talking to me. He wanted me to take him and show him where some of this talent was. So I took him down to Clarksdale, Greenville, Batesville and Marks, Mississippi, just a few places. And he listened to some of the groups and he said, 'Man.'

He was all excited. He said he would come back in two months and record. Then he went and bought me a car, a green '49 Buick, so that I could drive all over Mississippi, Alabama, Georgia, Louisiana and Florida and find talent, and then, he said, he would come down with the portable equipment and record it.

The Bihari brothers were giving me a salary of $100 a week, every Monday. They would mail it from California. Then every Wednesday I would get another cheque for say $125, for my expenses. Man, that's $225 a week. The top job for anybody, I don't care what colour you were, down in Mississippi was something like $45 a week. That was a lot of money, man. And I had more money than anybody – more than four people in Mississippi.

Ike and Joe Bihari hit it off immediately. Joe was a bit older – but the same size. Bihari kept Ike supplied with flash suits that he had originally bought for himself out in Los Angeles where Modern Records was based.

So I went scouting for people with talent. Some of them would be in church, different places. After Joe bought me the Buick, I would ride down through Alabama, Georgia, Florida. I would go to the barber's shop and say, 'Hey man, any singers around here?'

They would say yeah, and I would write down the names and go talk to the singer, telling him we were going to come back in the month or so and record.

In the meantime, I would get a whole list, forty people or so in different states, and addresses. Then Joe would come.

Joe Bihari and his two brothers had set up Modern Records in 1945, though they had started looking for talent and rehearsing acts in 1944. They had a factory in California. One brother handled the manufacturing and another the sales while Joe did all the recording. He would come over to see Ike every six weeks or so. Together they travelled all over the South.

Joe carried with him a four-channel Magnecord, the first portable equipment to be produced after the war. It cost around $1,000. 'We set up any place,' says Joe Bihari. 'It didn't make any difference. If you listen to those recordings today, now that they've been filtered through all the modern equipment, they're fabulously good.'

One problem was that there were only four inputs. They used to splice two microphones together and plug them both into one input, so often there would be two microphones on the baritone, tenor and alto saxophones and one on the trumpet, all coming into one input. The musicians would then have to be juggled around – some moved closer, others further away – to get the phasing right.

'Crazy the way you had to do it,' says Bihari. 'But it worked. There is an old saying: you can spend hundreds of thousands of dollars in the studio and get nothing and you can spend $100 in your garage and get a hit.'

Bihari acknowledges that Ike had a great ear for talent, but Modern Records did not have as much money to spend as he would have liked, so they had to move quickly. They had to go into a town, record, pay the artists and get on to the next call. Joe and Ike doubled up on these trips, making promotional calls on disc-jockeys and record distributors. There were not enough hours in the day, but it was a great education for Ike. He was learning the music business inside out, and his songwriting output was prodigious.

We'd leave from here to go a hundred miles to record someone. On the way, Joe would say, 'Have they got any original songs?'

I'd have just heard them sing, and I'd say, 'I don't think so.'

So I would write a song while we were driving down to the town where the artist was at. That's how I got to be creative. I had no pressures: it wasn't like I had a month to write a song – I didn't know when Joe was coming. You know how long it takes to cut an album now? Man, I cut *The Hunter* and *Outta Season* – two albums – in four hours and today they're spending $500,000 on cutting an album. I can take a mini-keyboard and cut a whole album in an hour, excluding the lyrics.

I wrote seventy-eight hit records for the Biharis – everything on their label that says TAUB. I didn't know what a songwriter's royalty was. They gave me $100 a week, and that was a lot of money for a kid, as I said. And they gave me the car. It was enough to keep me green. In those days it was not unusual to be paid a flat fee and to give away copyright.

Today Ike's songs are constantly being reissued. Joe Bihari says he gets about two calls a week from companies like Ace Records in England who rerelease old records from the Modern catalogue, many of which are Ike's. Ike gets not a penny from any of them.

But Ike's job wasn't always easy, even with his prolific songwriting abilities.

We were in Memphis, where we were going to record Bobby 'Blue' Bland for the first time. Bobby couldn't read or write, so we had to cut something he already knew. We chose 'Stormy Monday' and recorded it at Tuff Green's house. Tuff Green was a schoolteacher in Memphis, Tennessee, but in the world of R&B he was something of a legend. I got to play with Tuff. He was a real popular musician down South, but man, was he picky. When you rode in his car, you had to put paper under your feet. And if you were going a long, long way and got sleepy, you had to put paper under your head. When you rehearsed at his house, you couldn't smoke in the living room. He was just picky about every fucking thing, man – Tuff was tough.

Joe recorded at his house two or three times, and at the YMCA. We cut 'Woke Up This Morning' with B.B. King at the YMCA in Memphis, and Howlin' Wolf's 'Moaning at Midnight' and 'How Many More Years' at Sam Phillips' studio. Joe also recorded Junior Parker over in West Memphis. And we cut Rosco Gordon's 'No More Doggin''.

It was Ike who discovered Little Walter and Muddy Waters. As well as being the talent scout and songwriter, he also played accompaniment on the recording sessions and can be heard on the early tracks of B.B. King, Johnny Ace and Howlin' Wolf. Ike learned another valuable lesson during his time with Joe Bihari: how to play one company off against another. When Ike discovered Howlin' Wolf he took him to Sam Phillips, who signed him to Chess, and then took him to Modern. Both recorded him.

Modern got into trouble signing Elmore James. 'Ike and

I went to Helena, Arkansas, and recorded Sonny Boy Williamson,' recalls Joe Bihari. 'He wouldn't sing on the session. We recorded Dudlow Taylor and James Speck Curtis, and I think they told us where Elmore was. We went from Helena to Canton, Mississippi, where Elmore had a little radio-repair shop and we recorded in a nightclub.'

But Elmore James was under contract to Lillian McMurray of Trumpet Records in Jackson, Mississippi. McMurray heard about the session and sued. Modern was forced to settle the suit, and did not release the record. Elmore James refused to record for Trumpet again. Instead he waited for the remaining year of his contract to be up, and then called Bihari and signed a personal contract with him. Modern took Elmore to Chicago and New Orleans to record. They had a number of hits with him, on which Ike played piano.

Ike also recorded himself. He and his then wife, Bonnie, released a number of songs on Modern. He also recorded as a country artist under the name of Ickey Renrut – 'Renrut' is Turner back to front.

Bihari's recording trips down to the deep South were not all plain sailing. 'It ain't like today,' says Ike. 'There wouldn't be no white man and no black man riding together in a car.'

Fortunately, at that time, Joe Bihari's girlfriend was Nina Warren, daughter of Earl Warren, chief justice of the United States Supreme Court. If Bihari got into any trouble down there, he could call Nina and get Chief Justice Warren to take care of it.

On one occasion they were in Clarksdale, where Ike had lined up a lot of talent. They had rented the old Greyhound Bus Station and were recording there for a week. Joe had a red Lincoln Convertible with an extended rear end and twin antennae. While he was there, he lent it to Ike, who drove it around town.

On the last day of the recording, the men were loading the equipment into the boot of the Lincoln when two police cars pulled up right behind them.

'What you been doing here?' they asked Bihari.

'I've been recording,' Bihari replied.

'You know, you been paying the nigger too much money,' said one of the cops. They told Bihari to get out of the state, to head north and not stop until he crossed the Mississippi state line. He had no choice in the matter – they accompanied him, one squad car in front and the other behind.

In Alexandria, Louisiana the police took Bihari to the FBI, who called him a communist. He was interrogated for some time. Bihari now thinks that he must have been crazy. 'I had no fear in those days – and, remember, this was before the Civil Rights Act.'

On another trip, they had been driving in Mississippi, somewhere near Jackson, for some time and were getting tired. Bihari thought that there was a motel up ahead so he got into the back seat. 'That way, Ike could drop me off before going to find some accommodation for himself in the black part of town,' he explains.

When they reached the motel, Joe got out and went in to register. The clerk said, 'Oh, I see you have your chauffeur with you.'

Joe confirmed that he had. 'Well,' said the clerk, 'we can take care of him. We have a room for him too.'

'They gave us adjoining rooms,' Bihari says. 'That was unheard of in those days. I guess Ike was frightened. He said, "You are crazy to let me stay here." I told him not to worry about it.'

But Ike was all too familiar with the sinister mores of the deep South.

The only two people in America who've ever really had justice are a black woman and a white man. Them two can do anything they want to do. A black woman could stand up down South in Mississippi and knock your dick-string off, and ain't nobody going to do shit. But if I even look at a white woman like that, they're going to break my neck. They going to tar and feather me and put me in a barrel of hot tar. That's the way it was.

A white man can go to a hotel and rent a room in Mississippi where they don't like no integrating at all. He can pull up there with a black woman and say, 'Hey, I want a room.'

And the clerk says: 'OK, sir.'

'And I want a roll-away bed for my maid.'

They put a roll-away bed in your room for a fucking maid. You ain't going to use no roll-away bed, you going to be in the bed with her, but they let that go by, 'cos everybody's doing it.

But you let me pull up at the hotel with a white woman in the car. She better not talk about me getting no room at the hotel with her. 'Where's my driver gonna stay?' she'd better say. 'Where's the black part of town?'

In an attempt to get Ike away from this savage, stifling atmosphere, Joe Bihari took him out to Los Angeles. But Ike found himself out of his depth there.

Joe moved me to California in 1951. They got me an apartment on Harvard's Boulevard. Modern's office was on 244 Cannon Drive then. I went to the office and sat there watching those people working. Boy, to me it looked like everybody was running around like a bunch of Chinese. Down in Mississippi, life is slow. Tomorrow, you are going to plough this field. The next day, you going to cut down these trees. You stop and you go on about your business. Next day, you start back on sawing trees or whatever you doing.

Here I am in California, and this chick, the receptionist, is saying, 'Hold on, Mr Bihari, line 2 . . . Hold line 3 . . . Hey, Joe, Mr Something or other on the phone for you . . .'

I thought, what goddamn time does this stop? People doing all this shit. I thought, man, what do they do, do they pull the plug at five o'clock? I was sitting there at 4.55 pm, waiting for five o'clock to come to see how everybody was going to stop. How're you going to put brakes on all this shit?

Next thing I know, ten years on my own life is like that because I've got my own publishing company, my own booking agency, my own production company, every fucking thing. I've got all this shit going on all over the world, and I am doing it from my little den in my house. I was there before I knew it.

Clearly Ike was not too happy on that first trip to California, and he didn't stay too long. He went back to Clarksdale, where he continued to work for the Biharis. Yet one thing he saw in Los Angeles did leave a lasting impression.

On the way to the airport, this guy said, 'Ike, when you get some real money, this is the neighbourhood you'll stay in.' And he drove me up to Mount Olympus. I saw this woman opening the garage. I'd never seen an electric garage-door-opener before. I said, 'Man, did you see that?'

Man, that was exciting to me.

When a record company gave me $20,000 for 'A Fool in Love', I went back up in them hills and I bought the exact same house where I'd seen the woman open the garage door – 4263 Olympiad Drive.

7 Sweet Black Angels

T HE FIRST WOMAN I MARRIED WAS EDNA DEAN STEWART from Ruleville, Mississippi. I was fifteen or sixteen. We lived at my mother's house. That's when I got my eardrum busted. I was lying in bed with her. She was on the edge of the bed, and I asked her to lend me her bobby pin to clean my ear. She reached behind her and gave it to me. She had her back to me and I had the bobby pin in my ear. Then she turned over and she said, 'Where is my bobby pin?'

I said, 'I ain't got it.'

Then she grabbed me to kiss me and knocked that bobby pin down into my ear busting my eardrum and breaking a bone in my ear. It fucked up my whole music life. I had to learn to tune an instrument all over again. Someone could holler at me, 'Hey, Ike!' and I couldn't tell which direction the sound was coming from.

Twenty years later, Tina and I were on our way to Washington DC in a plane and my ear was killing me. All of a sudden, the ear 'turned on' – like two electric wires were touching together. I could hear. I went to hospital in Washington DC, and they told me that the best ear hospital in the whole world was in LA. When we arrived back in LA, I went to Dr House and he found that a bone had been broken down in my ear all them years ago. He put that bone back together. I think now I have maybe 40 per cent hearing in that ear.

Originally, I was playing every song off the jukebox, note for note. I used to go to rehearsals and sit there with the band and give everybody their notes from listening to a record. Then I began making it my song, doing it like the jukebox, but adding to it or taking bits away from it. When my eardrum got broke it made it real hard to do that.

After my ear was screwed up, I would sit up at night by myself and learn the record – everybody's parts – and make sure I knew it, so that when the band boys screwed you around and told you they were playing it right I could say, 'No, that ain't right, that's a lie.'

With the band boys, you've got to know what you're talking about, so I made sure I knew it. Even when Tina and I were together, I would still take songs off records.

Edna and I stayed together a while, but she didn't want to stay up in Clarksdale so she ran away. I walked all the way from Clarksdale to Ruleville, Mississippi – thirty-six miles – to get that girl and she talked to me through a fucking window, told me she wasn't coming back. That fucked up my ticker. So I let her go, forgot about her.

After her I met Thelma Dishman, who, at that time, I thought was a pretty girl. Thelma was pregnant, not by me, but I liked her. I started keeping house with her. She was from Yazoo City, Mississippi, so I moved there. That's when the white guy Jimmy Longford wanted me to play piano in his club. I told him I needed a drummer. I went back to Clarksdale and got this guy Willie, a show drummer who threw his sticks in the air.

When I moved to West Memphis I married Rosa Lee Sane. Her mind flipped on her. Her people put her in the insane asylum up there in Tennessee. I went up there trying to find her, trying to get her out, man, but it didn't work. I never saw her no more after she left.

Then I started going with Snow – her real name was Etta Mae Menfield. But I never married her, I just lived with Snow. After Snow, I went back to Mississippi, and that's where Bonnie came in.

In those days, a marriage licence in Mississippi cost just $3. If you were under age it was easy enough to get someone else to buy one for you. It was another $2 for the preacher to marry you. Nobody in rural Mississippi bothered about the nicety of divorce, so when Ike and

Tina became famous, Mrs Turners began calling from all/ over the world.

Bonnie was the next Mrs Turner.

Bonnie was a singer, She sounded like Ruth Brown. Ruth Brown was hot in them days – she had a song out called 'Mama, He Treats Your Daughter Mean'.

Bonnie played piano. It was a job staying ahead of this chick, man, 'cos she was always trying to outdo me. Meantime, I was getting the band back together and having trouble with guitar-players. They were unreliable, man. I figured there was no point in two of us playing the piano, so I picked up the guitar instead and started to learn to play by ear.

Ike was fortunate to have two of the best teachers at hand – Earl Hooker and former King of Rhythm Willie Kizart. With Bonnie, Ike slowly reformed the Kings of Rhythm, teaching his nephew, Jesse Knight Junior, to play bass. They were soon good enough to go back to Sun Studios and record for Modern Records.

Earl Hooker came to Clarksdale. He told us there was a good season gig down in Sarasota, Florida. We had no money, man, but almost enough gas to get there. Earl said, 'Don't worry, man, you can go into an orange grove and eat as much as you want to eat.'

When we finally got to Tampa we were starving. We went in that fucking orange grove and we ate up everything we could see in there. We ate till we got sick. Then we went on to Sarasota.

In Florida, Ike, Bonnie and Earl Hooker worked on and off with Billy 'The Kid' Emerson. In the meantime, Ike lost another wife.

Bonnie ran off with some other guy. She was getting her hair fixed at the beauty store and the guy there liked her. She started fucking around with him, and I didn't know about it. Next thing I know, Bonnie done run off with him to New York, and that was the end of me and Bonnie.

Ike returned to Clarksdale, dejected. But, professionally, things were going well. Raymond Hill had returned to the fold, along with former Tophatter Eugene Fox, and the Kings of Rhythm began an endless round of one-nighters. Ike also found the time to accompany Greenville artists Little Milton and Houston Boines in sessions at Sun. And besides, wives – the lack of them, at any rate – were never a problem for Ike Turner.

The next time I married, I married Alice, in Helena, Arkansas. She was the one I never slept with after we were married. She had been the singer Johnny O'Neal's girl, but I liked her so I married her.

I married Alice because she was going with Johnny O'Neal. He was a fighting sonofabitch, and I didn't want to be locking heads with him. If I married her, he couldn't do nothing, so that's why I did it. One day she thought we were going to Memphis to play, but the job was cancelled and I caught her on the porch in the swing, with Johnny O'Neal's head in her lap.

O'Neal's contract with King Records had not worked out. Willie Sims rejoined the Kings of Rhythm and even Jackie Brenston, whose solo career had foundered, was back in Clarksdale. The scene was hot enough for Ike and Joe Bihari to set up a recording studio. Clayton Love, Billy Gales, Dennis Binder and the gravel-voiced Eugene Fox all recorded there, accompanied by Ike on piano or guitar.

However, the association between black artists and the white producer was too much for Clarksdale to take, especially as the building that housed the studio was in a white area.

There weren't no niggers supposed to be across that side of the railroad track. The white folks came into the studio there and tore all the wires out of the walls and ripped them up. They told Joe Bihari, 'Don't you know that us white folks don't associate with these niggers? What the hell do you think we fought the Civil War for?'

And Joe said, 'I don't know what you fought it for, but you lost.'

After I married Alice, the next Mrs Turner was a girl named Anna Mae Wilson from Greenville, Mississippi. She played piano. And she used to do the books and the payroll. She used to handle the business part. She and I were together when we hit East St Louis.

8 The House of Many Thrills

W<small>E WENT TO EAST ST LOUIS</small> just to play one night at Ned Love's place. My sister had moved there and she was always saying, 'Why don't you come to St Louis?'

So we rode up there and went over to East St Louis, where Ned Love's place was. We just sat in and played only one song. First they wanted us to play some more, then Ned Love wanted us to play another two nights. Then he said, 'Man, I want you next weekend.'

So we went home and got some more clothes and came back. Then he wanted us Thursday, Friday, Saturday and Sunday.

Next the 2151 Club on St Louis Avenue wanted us on Monday nights and the Harlem Club in Brookline, Illinois, wanted the Sunday. Before we knew it, we were doing fourteen jobs a week in St Louis. You couldn't get in no place we were playing at.

> St Louis was a lively, prosperous town. It looked down on the blues as something poor and rural and from the South. But it hadn't heard anything like Ike – the pounding rhythm, the slick, sexy lyrics, the honking brass and the whining electric guitar. It was 1954, and the whole world was about to fall to rock 'n' roll.

We tore them up 'cos St Louis was a jazz town. Here come us from down there playing the blues, and we were just drawing a trillion people. I started playing at a club called the Fireworks Station, and we played at the Blue Flame Club and the 1700 Broadway. Chuck Berry was at the Cosmopolitan on

Seventeenth and Bond. Little Willie John wanted to hire my whole band and take us on the road, but I was scared to leave St Louis. Then I met this guy called Booker Merritt. He was more like a father to us, man. He had this brick building at 1320 Broadway. It was more like a house. Me and my band went in there and knocked all the walls out and sanded the floor. We made the bandstand, we did it all. We made the Manhattan Club, in East St Louis. Soon everyone knew about it. It was me and my band who made that club. It was like our home, man.

> Ike started to play to a white teenage audience at George Edick's Club Imperial. 'He went over so big here,' says Edick. 'He had something different besides the four, five pieces. He had horns; he gave it a little big-band sound. It had more rhythm, more beat.'
>
> Ike covered a lot of pop music, including Chuck Berry numbers. His band was slick, dressed in sharp suits and ties.
>
> 'Ike's was the band,' says Clayton Love. 'Ike had a showmanship that really captivated people, white and black. He just had them going.'
>
> They recorded a number of regional hits. 'I do believe that Ike Turner's was the best band around at the time,' says another St Louis resident of that era, Anna Mae Bullock – who later became Tina Turner.
>
> It was George Edick who gave Ike his first TV exposure, on *Party Time at the Club Imperial*. At twenty-three, Ike began making real money. But that brought its own problems.

That's when someone told me that if you bought a Cadillac, man – I was told that if you bought a new Cadillac, the Internal Revenue would start checking you to see whether you were paying taxes. At that time I had never heard of no taxes. I got all scared because I had just bought a new 1956 Cadillac.

By this time, I had already developed an appetite for women with big legs and big asses, healthy women. And St Louis was just full of them. I worked all over the place in East St Louis and Brookline, Illinois. I think we drew more women, which made the men follow. I was drawing them two to one in the crowds. I think that was why everywhere we played was sold out.

That's when I became real, real whorish. I'd go with any girl with a little waist and a big butt. Chicks started to visit me, and then women began to give me the keys to their apartments. I had keys to thirty-two women's apartments. Man, I was just doing it. I was making the rounds once or twice a week. I was terrible, but I was having fun, man.

All of these girls were working girls. There were beauticians, supermarket clerks, department-store salesgirls, even bank-tellers. I didn't have to worry about no groceries, having my hair done, beauty supplies or clothes.

When I went to a store to buy something, one of the girls would ring up a much lower price on the cash register than the value of what I was actually buying. I could purchase a $150 suit for only $35, and all kinds of other things at a big discount. One of my girlfriends was the manager of a large store. She would let me come in and buy $700-worth of uniforms for my band and charge me only $300.

Nancy and Mel Johnson knew Ike at this time. 'St Louis was real small and Ike Turner was the hot thing then,' Nancy says, 'so you went to see him wherever he played. You went there to have a good time, and he gave you a good time. He had a huge following, just huge. Sometimes you couldn't even get into places. We became friends. He was a very clean-cut person, very professional. There were no drugs, period – otherwise bye-bye. As long as you were performing – the only thing you did was perform. He had a reputation as a womaniser. He believed in having plenty of big-hipped women. And he would fight.'

Is that what they really call it, womanising? When you have a lot of women? I was terrible, man, but to me then, it wasn't terrible. I don't mean to be putting nobody down, but I was just doing what I felt, what I enjoyed. I think a lot of people might say, 'Oh, I wouldn't do that,' but I don't really believe them, man. I think it's just that the opportunity ain't presented itself to them.

Because the group I put together was so popular in St Louis, it wasn't long before a lot of men there began to get jealous. They envied us because of all of the female fans we attracted, and some of the gangs decided to challenge us. They would come into the clubs where we were playing and deliberately start fights. Sometimes they came armed with guns and knives.

My band was very close, though. We were a gang ourselves. There were seven of us, eight including me. We shared a brotherhood type of thing, so when one band member fought, well, we all helped him out. We lived as one. We didn't bother anybody, but if you messed with us we did what we had to do.

Knowing that we now had these violent rivals, and feeling that we had to protect ourselves, we went out and bought guns. All the boys in my band, including myself, began to double as bouncers, helping to break up fights in the clubs where we worked. We had to do this because word was spreading that there were a lot of fights at our gigs, and crowds were beginning to drop off. The public was afraid to come and see us play because of the deliberate violence of these jealous gang members. So we started putting them out if they started a fight – by force, if we had to.

We would sometimes start slapping them upside the head with the gun, pulling the trigger at the same time. This usually scared the shit out of them, and let them know that we weren't messing around.

After about two months, the gang violence stopped and our crowds soon went back to normal.

Some of these incidents made headlines in the newspapers, and Ike began to earn a reputation in the press as a bad guy. The headlines dubbed him 'Pistol-whipping Ike Turner' after one particularly violent confrontation during which he was arrested. The problem was that you could not live in East St Louis without a gun.

After this incident I went to see a judge in East St Louis, and a captain on the police force. They assisted me in getting special deputy sheriff badges for myself and the band. These special badges entitled us all to carry guns legally.

Another time there was an incident at an audition. One of the musicians who had flunked out was full of resentment and wanted revenge. He returned to the club where I was working armed with a handgun.

He waited outside and had someone deliver a note to the saxophone-player, who had gotten the job the musician had tried out for. He wanted us to come outside with our guns in our hands. His intention was to start shooting as soon as he saw one of us.

One of my men, Eddy Jones, went out of the front door while I went out the back way and sneaked around to the front. We had no idea how many people might have been out there waiting for us.

By the time I arrived at the front of the building this man and Eddy had already had a gun battle. They had both managed to fire all their bullets, and they were both wounded.

The police came and arrested us. The East St Louis cops didn't know that we had all been issued with these special badges, and they hassled my whole group. During the next seventy-two hours, we were charged with everything from speeding to assault, carrying a firearm, resisting arrest and even jaywalking.

I later discovered the real reason behind this period of harassment. The girl I was married to, Anna Mae Wilson, left me and moved in with this policeman called Jackson. This was his way of getting back at me. Anna Mae wasn't only my wife, she also played piano in the band. Everybody all over St Louis and East St Louis knew her. Because she'd left me and moved in with him, this notoriety really boosted Jackson's ego.

One week he made seventeen arrests among the band. I wrote a letter to have him brought before the police board to try to get him off us. He never showed up at the meeting.

I was coming home one night with another girl, Audrey. Audrey was married, but she and I just loved to have sex together. That night, as we were driving down Broadway looking for a good place to park and have sex, I was pulled over by this cop Jackson. I had already seen him in the rear-view mirror when he got behind me at Fifteenth and Broadway, and he followed me almost to Seventeenth Street. We were in a 25mph zone, so I was careful to keep my speed down to 20mph.

Nevertheless he pulled me over and arrested me, claiming that I was driving at 55mph. He made me leave my car parked with Audrey still in it, so she was later able to drive it down to the police station to pick me up. When Jackson and I arrived at the jailhouse, I was marched out of the police car with my hands cuffed behind my back. Jackson opened the door of the station for me, and then – bam! – he hit me from behind. That blow was a pretty good one. He used his fist and hit me on the head around my left ear. So now I was completely deaf – for a while, until it got better.

In East St Louis I developed another lifelong habit: I became a gambler. I was always real lucky. One night I won enough money to fill a beer crate to the top and over. I guess word got round about my winnings, because later some guys tried to rob me. I was climbing the stairs to my small apartment on the third floor. I didn't pay much attention to the fact that all the lights were out in the stairway that night. I had no idea that these guys were waiting for me.

Suddenly they jumped out of the darkness and made a grab for me. One of them had a knife. He managed to stick it through my left hand, pinning it to the stair. With my free hand I reached into my suit coat, where I carried a pistol in a shoulder holster. I drew the gun and fired a shot, and my attackers fled down the stairs.

Because my body was numb from the struggle, I wasn't aware that my hand was skewered to the floor. All I felt was a stinging in that hand. In a hurry to get up, I snatched my hand from the stair, pulling on the knife and making the cut deeper. I still have the scar today.

I bought a house over in East St Louis on Virginia Place. They called it 'the house of many thrills'. It doubled as a studio, and 'Boxtop' was recorded there.

We had ten bedrooms. Man, at night, when we got off work at the clubs, we would invite all the girls, married or not, to come over to the house, and just party all night. There were eight of us, me and my band. And boy, we had a house full of women.

Guys used to come by and they'd know their women or wives were in there. They'd be mad, and take a shotgun and – boom! – shoot at the side of the house. After they drove by, they'd have to come round the next street to get back. So we would come out of the back door, jump the back fence and stand on both sides of the street with shotguns. As the guy drove by we'd shoot out all four tyres, leaving his car flat on the ground. Then we'd drag him out and beat his ass. We used to do some stupid shit.

Bebe, one of the guys who set up our equipment – today they call them roadies – was caught alone when none of us were around. They took him out to the park and cut his balls out. He bled to death. East St Louis used to be really rough, man.

Sometimes it was good, though. Through the alley at the end of my block was the Kroger Grocery Store, which didn't open until 8 am. Their supply trucks would leave the groceries sitting outside from 3 am to 6 am. I used to have Jimmy Thomas and DeLarry go out to the store and steal enough supplies for a week's partying. We were never caught. The only thing we ever had to buy was drinks.

I had this guitar-player called Jimmy. He was a real good player, but his problem was that he liked gimmicks. In those days there was no balance line to balance the volume between a wah-wah pedal, a fuzz tone and a neutron. So every time he switched from one pedal to another, the volume would go up or down, mostly into feedback. I told him four or five times that he was gonna have to mark where the knobs should be on each pedal, but he never did. He would fuck up the whole solo to the song trying to stop the feedback or bring up the volume. So I cut him loose and rehired Willie Kizart.

Later I heard about a new superstar called Jimi Hendrix. You guessed it: it was the same Jimmy I'd fired.

In 1959, just as Ike's career was taking off, his mother died.

It was the greatest disappointment I ever had in my life, man.

I'm a momma's baby – I guess you can tell that from the way I am. I always wanted to do things for my mother. I wanted to make her hopes and dreams come true. But before I had a chance to do it, she died on me. I guess that's the reason why now, when I meet girls and friends, I'm always giving to them. I guess I'm trying to make up for what I couldn't do for her. That will always be with me, but you can't undo the past. I don't think no one can disappoint you: you can only disappoint yourself by over-expecting.

In St Louis, I had my first experiences with white women. I had a real problem with this one white girl, whose name was Jane. She and her little sister were rich. Their parents had died and left them a lot of money. They lived alone in South St Louis. Jane was real crazy about me. She was supposed to have been a virgin, but I never believed that because I never had any trouble inserting my penis into her cat.

Jane was so much in love with me, but she was real possessive about me too. She bought me two new cars: one was an Oldsmobile stationwagon, the other a brand-new '59 Cadillac with big fishtails. Boy, I was happy.

When my mother died, I told Jane that I would have to go down to Mississippi for the funeral and that I would be gone about two weeks. I left her in St Louis, promising that I would return.

After about two weeks had gone by, Jane became impatient and travelled down to Mississippi to search for me. When she was seen in the neighbourhood where I had grown up, the police started inquiring about who she was and why she was there. The woman had no idea of the danger involved in a relationship between a black man and a white woman in the South. Her actions almost got me hanged.

I was real relieved to get out of Clarksdale and back to East St Louis, which was much more relaxed racially.

In Memphis, Tennessee, it was better than Mississippi as far as prejudice was concerned. If I was outside a white hotel or nightclub waiting for somebody to come out, nobody would harass me. A cop might ask me, 'Who are you waitin' on?' but as long as my answer started with 'I'm waiting on Mr . . .' I'd be OK. In a similar situation in Mississippi, you could end up being killed if some whites came by and saw you sitting there. They probably wouldn't waste time asking you why you were there, they'd just start heckling you, and if you responded any way other than humble, then you could get hurt.

St Louis was more open. In St Louis, I could go stay at a downtown hotel, though you still could feel the racial tension if you were black. There wasn't a lot of mixing, not a lot of black guys with white chicks, but if you wanted to go with a white girl, you could. They were still prejudiced there, but it wasn't like Mississippi. In Mississippi, you'd better not even look at a white woman. And if one lied on you and said you stared at her, they'd hang you.

Nevertheless, blacks had their nightclubs and whites had theirs, cut and dried. It was totally black at the Manhattan Club in East St Louis, the Harlem Club in Brookline and the Kingsbury up in Madison, all in Illinois. The white clubs were the Club Imperial in St Louis and Johnny's Lounge out in South St Louis. After I gained a heavy following among both blacks and whites, I started demanding that blacks should be able to go to white clubs and whites to black clubs.

In East St Louis we gained the popularity among the blacks, and then I started playing the Club Imperial, which was for white teenagers, on Sundays. We were real popular there. Soon we were drawing in white kids and the police started harassing them for following us. We were not messing with these kids, believe me. They were eight to fifteen years old.

The police would raid the club on Sunday evenings. They would arrive with two or three squad cars and one big bread truck. Like I said, this club was only for teens and there were no wrongdoings going on, but the police didn't like these kids mixing with blacks. So they loaded up the truck with the white kids, took them to the police station and called their parents to come and pick them up. They'd tell the parents that their kids were hanging round blacks and so they'd been brought in before they got into trouble.

Then Wally Olson started a club for older white kids where my band would play. But our fans there would want to follow us over to East St Louis afterwards. We used to line up, man, like maybe fifty cars of kids. As far as you could see was cars

– and it cost 15c to cross the toll bridge to East St Louis. Man, we would get up to 50, maybe 60mph, and all of us would just go straight through the toll. Nobody paid.

So we'd ride over to the black clubs with these white kids. I wouldn't play at the black clubs unless they let the whites in, and I wouldn't play at the white clubs unless the blacks were allowed in.

Today those kids, I'm proud to say, are the people who run the banks, the laws and everything in St Louis.

> This racial integration through music had its casualties. Ike heard that a young white fan, Sandie, had been put into a convent by her father, who told her that if her forefathers knew that she was even looking at a black guy they would turn over in their graves.

And there was a little white boy called Jimmy Hendal, who changed his name to Rubin. He copied my guitar playing note for note. He stood onstage the way I stand onstage. He was Ike Turner – only he was white. His daddy disowned him, man – he didn't like him copying off no nigger. He eventually became an arranger for Ray Charles.

> While Ike was responsible for integrating the fans among his black and white followings, any improvement in the racial tension in St Louis that came about as a result may have been short-lived.

When I lived in St Louis you couldn't pay a white cop to call you no nigger. I went back there in 1971–72, twenty years later. My son, Ike Junior, was driving, and the police stopped him, pulled him over and said: 'Hey, nigger, where the fuck are you going?'

I swear, I couldn't believe what I was hearing.

9 A Fool in Love

Before Tina came along, Ike did not have girl singers in the band. Jackie Brenston, Johnny O'Neal, Willie Kizart and Ike himself did most of the singing.

MET TINA IN EAST ST LOUIS. My drummer, Eugene Washington, was going with this girl named Alline Bullock, who was Tina's sister – Tina's real name is Anna Mae Bullock, Little Ann.

We were playing over at the Manhattan Club while I was going with this other girl called Pat. You worked five hours onstage in St Louis – forty-five minutes at a time followed by fifteen minutes' break. That was the union rule.

Sometimes I would just sit onstage at the piano during the break, just be messing around you know, playing whatever songs were on the jukebox or some other song I wanted to learn. This girl Alline used to ask me, 'Hey, why don't you let my sister sing?'

So I say, 'Yeah, OK.'

She did this for a month or two, but I never did call her sister – everybody say they sing, but they can't.

One night, I was just messing around on the piano and the drummer took the mike out of the mike stand. It had a long cord on it, and he reached down to a table at the front and gave it to this girl.

All at once I heard this voice singing.

'Damn,' I said, 'that girl can sing.'

It was Tina – Little Ann. We all called her Little Ann because she was very skinny then. She was singing a song that was popular in those days – I think it was 'Love is Strange' or

'Darling, I Love You', I don't remember. But she sounded real good, I remember that.

Little Ann started going with Raymond Hill, my sax-player. Raymond could be described as high yellow with wavy hair, and he liked to fool around with a lot of different ladies. He and Eugene were renting rooms in my house and Tina and Alline would come over to see their boyfriends.

Tina and I got to be very good friends, and sometimes I got mad at the way Raymond treated her.

At night, when I wasn't partying, I would sit at the piano writing songs. Tina would be there with me and I taught her singing and voice control, and a number of the songs we did then. So she was learning maybe two or three songs a night.

Back in those days, people weren't that crazy about women singers, but I let her sing at the club 'cos the people liked her. I never paid her any money, but I gave her gifts instead and I wasn't charging her for any of the tutoring or singing lessons I gave her.

For four years, Tina and I were close personal friends. We did everything together except have sex. Whenever I went to buy Lorraine – the girl who was living with me then – anything like clothes, coats, shoes or jewellery, I would buy something for Tina too.

Eventually, Tina got pregnant by Raymond. She and her mother had an argument about it and her mother put her out of the house. So she went and rented her own place, a small room on Taylor Street in St Louis.

After Craig was born she got a job at Barnes Hospital as a nurses' aide. Even so, she was short of money after paying for her room, the bus fare back and forth, the babysitter, baby things and food and stuff. So she called me. She said she was running $3 short and would I give her $3 a week. She would work. I said I would give her the money, but she didn't have to work. I didn't need no singer. Everybody in my band sang.

Then I found out her real circumstances. She was living in a fucking garage, a car garage – a little old dumpty place in an alley, man. I felt so sorry for her living in that goddamn place, man, I went over and moved her out and into my house. I never said nothing to Tina's mother – I never even knew her mother. There was something in that movie, *What's Love Got to Do With It?*, about me giving Tina's mother $300. That's bullshit. There was no reason to ask her mother anything. Her mother had already put her out.

She got back with Raymond briefly, but his attitude hadn't changed. Tina wasn't my woman – I never did nothing with her then – but because I was tight with her, I didn't like that, man. So I confronted him. I told him he'd better get himself a place somewhere else.

In the end Raymond got to wrestling in the house with Carson, a saxophone-player, and he broke his leg. While he was sick, he went to Mississippi to stay with his momma. He never came back to St Louis.

It was about this time that I met the singer Art Lassiter. He sounded like the Ink Spots, and so I told him, 'Hey, man, what you need to sing is something like this song, man, something with a beat to it. I'm gonna write you a song.'

So I wrote 'A Fool in Love' for him. Tina was there when I put all the music together and she sang it over and over. She sat in when I was teaching it to him and the background group – I got Robbie Montgomery and three other girls.

Now this guy Lassiter was going to beat me out of $80, man. He borrowed $80 from me to get some tyres for his car until after we did the recording session, then he was gonna pay me back. Anyway, I rented Technosonic Recording Studio, which cost maybe $25 an hour – that was a lot of money back in 1960. And man, we're sitting at the studio waiting on him and he never showed up. As we were waiting there for an hour or more, and we had to pay for the studio time anyway, Tina suggested, since Lassiter was not there and she knew the song, should she just sing it? Then when we found him all he had to do was put his voice on. We could lay down the backing track and just put her voice on as a guide.

This was the first time I got hip to two-track stereo. You can put the band on one track and the singer on the other. So when this guy finally showed we would be able to erase Tina's voice and put him on it. I went and asked the guy who owned the studio – Ed, his name was. He said, yeah, we could do it, as long as we was paying.

Anyway, this guy did nothing but commercials in this studio, man. He didn't know anything about no limiter. After we got the background down, Tina starts singing, 'You're just a fool, you know you're in love.' Then she hollers, 'Hey, hey, hey, hey!'

Ed goes crazy. 'Goddammit, don't holler in my microphone!' The reason she was hollering so loud, straining, on the record, is because the song is not in a woman's key. It's in a man's key, for a man to sing. I was recording the key for Art Lassiter, and that's why the song is so high. But Tina, she don't sing like a woman, she sings like a man.

On Tuesday nights, I was working at the Club Imperial over on Goodfellow Street. When I played the tape of 'A Fool in Love' with Tina's voice on it for the white kids in that club, they all thought it sounded pretty good. They said, 'Man, why don't you put it out with her singing it?'

Dave Dixon, who was a disc-jockey with radio station KATZ, heard the tune and asked me to let him send it to Juggy Murray over at Sue Records in New York. He was real great about it. He flew down there right away. He wanted the record. He came down and asked me to sign the contract. I told him $20,000 and we would sign.

He wanted to put it in Tina's name – Little Ann. I said, 'Hell, no.' I told her: 'Hey, I'm not gonna do it like that, 'cos I know what's gonna happen later on.' I was thinking, if the record's a hit and Raymond recovers from his broken leg and comes back from Mississippi, he'll snatch Tina away. She was so in love with Raymond, and they had a baby together. And Raymond and I had been having problems ever since we was kids: his mother always wanted him to be the bandleader instead of me, but he didn't know enough about arranging. All he knew was just blowing the saxophone.

It had happened before, remember. When I cut 'Rocket 88', as soon as we had a hit record – boom! – Jackie Brenston, he gone. I had written, arranged and produced this entire tune by myself. How many times you got to get bumped on your head before you get sense?

Anyway, I told Tina, 'I'm going to make up a name for you so if Raymond snatch you I'm just going to get me another girl in your place.'

So I sat down and started writing down names like Sheila – even Nyoka. I was trying to think of names that sounded like they was jungle. I wrote down a whole bunch, and then I came up with Tina. I patented the name so that if Raymond Hill ran off with Little Ann I could find myself another Tina and keep on going.

At first, we were going to use 'Ike Turner and Tina'. Then Juggy said, 'Why don't you have Ike and Tina Turner?' It sounded better. I told Tina why I was doing it and she agreed. That was the beginning of Ike and Tina.

Later, I thought up the name The Ikettes for my all-girl backing group. This name, too, was registered – I wasn't going to have people running off with my shit again.

Juggy Murray gave me the $20,000 and I signed. The record was a big hit. That was when I bought my first house out here in California, with the money I got from the first record.

Joe Bihari had looked over the contract and added key words such as 'forthwith', and specified that payment should be made by 'cashier's check or cash'. There were some bad reputations around in the music industry at the time.

But things had already changed between Ike and Tina. When Little Ann became Tina Turner, she was already pregnant with Ike's child.

Tina and I were like one pea in a hub man, even though Raymond was her boyfriend. People used to say we were brother and sister. I would pretend to be a fag and say, 'No, we's sisters.'

Tina always knew what kind of guy I was with women. I would tell her, 'Hey, see that girl over there? Go get her for me and tell her to meet me over the house.' Tina knew everything I liked and disliked in a woman. If I took a chick to the house, I would tell Tina, 'Man, I can't stand that chick. In the morning she get up, she don't even brush her teeth, man.' Or I'd say, 'This chick, man, when she get up in the morning she don't even make up the bed. She don't even offer to cook you no food.' I'd tell Tina, 'I don't like this girl because she can't screw,' or 'That girl is too possessive and jealous.'

Tina knew everything about every woman that I was going with, because she was my buddy. She met all my girlfriends and was friends with them.

One night we played at Turner's Hall. I went out and bought Tina a blue sequinned dress. I think that was when they first started coming out with sequinned dresses. At Turner's Hall, the stage is way up high and I was looking down on the dancefloor. I saw Tina dancing with this white guy named Teddy Cole. Teddy was a good dancer, and Tina could really jitterbug, too.

All the other people had stopped dancing and formed a loose circle and I was looking down at Tina in that blue dress. She looked real sexy to me. Each time she got down on that floor and moved, she looked just like a snake wiggling around. It was the first time that Tina began to appeal to me in a sexual way.

I don't drink, man, but that night after work I decided to take a whiskey while I waited for the owner of the club to pay me. 'Cos I wasn't really a drinker, I began to feel bad. I drank maybe two shot glasses of Old Charlotte and, boy, I got sick as a dog.

You know they say whiskey got three bloods in it? And I was on the third blood, the hog's blood. I just wanted to lay down and wallow. So Tina and my driver, Stennis, put me in the back seat of the car. Tina rode in the back with me, trying to comfort me while I was vomiting and stuff. So we get to my house in East St Louis and they carry me upstairs. She's pulling off my clothes and gets me into bed. Then she goes to change and make me some coffee.

She came back into the room wearing one of those sexy nightgowns I had ordered from Frederick's of Hollywood. That gown barely went down to her hips and you could see right through it. She's up there trying to make me drink black coffee – I guess to bring me down from this drunk I was on – and, man, I remember looking down at her legs. When she reached over to set the coffee cup down on the night stand, my dick got as hard as Chinese arithmetic. Then Tina and I began to wrestle around playfully on the bed and the next thing I know, man, I done had sex with her.

When I woke up the next morning, Tina was still in bed with me. I felt embarrassed and ashamed. It was like I just screwed my sister. All I knew was that I didn't want to do it no more, man. So I left her alone for about five or six weeks. Then she came and told me that she was pregnant.

This was a real headache – and not just because they had recorded a hit record and needed to get out and promote it. To make matters worse, another girl, Pat, was also pregnant by Ike. Pat was a singer, and she and Tina used to compete. So when she told Ike that she was pregnant too, he didn't believe her. That difficulty resolved itself when Pat suddenly disappeared. The real problem was Ike's live-in girlfriend, Lorraine Taylor.

Before all this happened, I was living with Lorraine, the mother of our son, Ike Junior. Her parents owned the Taylor Sausage Factory in St Louis. She had run off and moved back with them for a while, taking our son with her.

But about a month after Tina and I had sex, Lorraine decided to come back. She didn't know anything had happened between Tina and me, but she soon found out that Tina was pregnant. She asked me about it but I always managed to avoid answering her questions.

One morning I was real tired after playing a club and staying up all night gambling. I went home and got into bed with Lorraine to get some sleep. Lorraine tried to ask more questions about me and Tina, but again, I didn't answer her.

While I was sleeping, Lorraine got out of bed and went to Tina's room. She had my .38-calibre pistol and a poker from the fireplace. She went in and said to Tina, 'Bitch, are you fucking Sonny? I'm gonna kill you, whore.'

Tina told her that if that's what she felt like doing, she should go ahead and do it. There was a stand-off. Tina got out of bed, and, rushing past Lorraine, came to wake me up. She shook me. She was screaming, 'Ike, wake up, wake up, Lorraine's got the gun!'

I was struggling to clear my head while Tina told me what had happened. I got out of bed to go find Lorraine. As I went up the hallway, I heard the bathroom door slam shut and the lock go 'click'.

I went to the door and yelled, 'Lorraine, give me that fucking gun!'

There was no answer. I was just about to go around to the balcony, from where you could reach the window to the bathroom, when I heard the door lock click again, followed by a loud pow!

Lorraine had unlocked the door, then put the gun to her side and pulled the trigger. She had shot herself. The bullet went through both of her lungs and punctured her heart.

I panicked. The first thing I did was to pick up the gun, leaving my fingerprints on it. I took it to the bedroom and set it on the table, then reached for the telephone to call the hospital. My hands were shaking so bad that I couldn't even dial the number.

Finally, I got the operator and told her that a girl had just shot herself and gave her the address of my house. A few minutes later, the police arrived with an ambulance. They took her to St Mary's Hospital in East St Louis, a place where blacks still had to go through the back door. Meantime, the police were asking me if I was the one who had shot Lorraine. When I told them no, they said that I was a damned liar.

Things were looking pretty bleak for Ike. He and his band already had a reputation for violence and involvement with guns. And by now Lorraine was lying delirious in hospital, moaning, 'Sonny, don't shoot.'

Worse, his fingerprints were all over the gun. It looked as if they would put him in jail and throw away the key – if he was not sent to the electric chair, that is. Then he got a break.

Police Captain Trainy Polk, who I knew, showed up and called me over to one side. He told me not to lie, then he asked me if I had shot Lorraine. I told him the truth about everything, even how I had picked up the gun, leaving my prints on it. He believed me. Captain Polk then drove me to the hospital in his police car so that I could be with Lorraine.

Miraculously, Lorraine survived. If she had died, Ike would have almost certainly been indicted for murder and his conviction might well have been a foregone conclusion.

I helped nurse Lorraine back to health after she came home from the hospital. She already had two other kids, who were living with her mother. She always said that she didn't like kids. But once our records began to hit, she stayed at home while Tina and I went out on the road. Once a week or so, she would come out to wherever we were and spend a few days with us.

Out on the road, though, I started to have sex with Tina again. As far as that side of our relationship is concerned, I've always felt that Tina was attractive, but not really sensuous in bed. She felt more like my sister, not my wife. To be honest, I felt that having sex with her was almost a duty.

A lot of times I had the impression that she didn't want me to touch her. I could feel resentment coming from her. As we went through the motions of sex, I felt that her actions and responses were mechanical. I don't know if she was that way on purpose, thinking or knowing that I had just left some other woman or one of the Ikettes' rooms.

But there were many times when I enjoyed having sex with her. She is not what the public thinks, though. She is a very clean-cut 'one-man woman' with relatively little experience of sex.

10 I Idolise You

In August 1960, 'A Fool in Love' climbed to number 2 in the R&B charts and the tour launched on the back of it took Ike and Tina all across America. In Los Angeles, Ike saw his dream house with its automatic garage door and bought it. When the tour ended and they got back to St Louis, Tina, who was four or five months' pregnant, came down with yellow jaundice. Ike had his problems too.

HAD THIS THING WITH THE BANK. I was charged with interstate transportation of forged cheques and conspiracy. Meantime, I need $2,000 for a lawyer. I told the man at the record company. He said he needed an album. If I wanted to borrow some money, I had to cut him an album. Tina was in the hospital. She had yellow jaundice and she was pregnant. But still this dirty sonofabitch said, 'I ain't going to loan you the money unless you give me an album.'

I said, 'Tina's in the hospital. How am I going to give you an album?'

'That's the way the cookie crumbles,' he said.

I went to the hospital and told Tina. She slipped out of that hospital and we went to the studio. I had all the music and ideas together and we cut that whole album in one night. That was the first album I cut on Sue Records, *I Idolise You*.

But I was mad at this guy at the record company now. He done made me take Tina out of the hospital, 'cos if I don't get no lawyer I am going to jail.

The trial ended with a hung jury, so now I faced the expense of a retrial.

Meantime, we were touring again, travelling across the

country. I met this guy Wilson Watson in Berkeley, West Virginia. Wilson used to manage Lloyd Price. He had this big old stretch truck, man, which used to belong to Lloyd Price, up on blocks, its tyres all rotted. I told him about my troubles. He said, 'Man, don't worry about it. I'll take care of it.'

I have met some great people, man, who've been good to me at the time I needed it. Wilson, he gave me $2,500 and bought me a round-trip ticket to go back to St Louis to court that month.

> The tour climaxed, some four months later, with the Ike and Tina Turner Revue, which opened at the famous Apollo Theatre in Harlem.

The Apollo Theatre in New York City is a slave-house, man. We did four shows a day, seven days a week, six on Sundays. And we were thinking that Tina was only eight months pregnant – in fact she was nine months gone. She really wowed the crowd there, jumping off the stage down into the pit and dancing. The owner of the theatre, he was scared she might fall, so he told her not to jump down there no more. It was about 5ft from the stage to the floor.

After Tina and I got together and my career started going up, I started going with every girl I saw with a little waist and a big ass. I wanted to try them all, man. When we were playing the Apollo Theatre, I was messing around with three girls: Wilhelmina, Eloise and another girl named Martha.

We planned to return to Los Angeles for Tina to have the baby. After the Apollo, our next date was in Las Vegas – not on the Strip, but over at the damn black-ass club which I think Sammy Davis owned a part of.

Tina and I flew there; the band drove. We played only one date and then continued on to LA. We still thought Tina was in her eighth month.

I had found a girl in Detroit whom I had trained to take Tina's place when the time came for her to give birth. This girl looked like Tina – same height, same complexion – and we had trained her well enough for the public not to be able to tell the difference.

What I didn't know was that she had been working as a

hooker. This girl had been travelling and practising with us for five or six months and had been secretly turning tricks on the side.

After closing in Las Vegas, I flew Tina to Los Angeles, while I rode in the car with the driver and a few of the Ikettes, including the girl I was training as Tina's stand-in. Man, we partied and orgied all the way to Los Angeles with those girls.

In LA, we checked into the Booker T. Washington Hotel on Adams and Western. We had a gig to play there but we got to town early. I had to leave that Thursday to go back to St Louis to appear in court on Monday. I left Tina at the hotel in LA, still believing there was a full month before the baby was due.

She went into labour when I was on my way to the airport, and our son Ronnie was born that Thursday night.

I was making calls every few minutes to check on Tina's condition. I was also worried about how the show would go on Saturday night with neither one of us able to be there. Tina told me not to worry. This new girl was well trained to take her place and Tina would make sure everything was all right, even if she had to sneak out of the hospital to see for herself.

That Friday, one of the Ikettes went out to the hospital and told Tina that this girl was turning tricks in the hotel under Tina's name. The guys thought they were fucking Tina.

Boy, when she heard about that, Tina signed herself out of the hospital and went back there and beat that girl up, gave her a good ass-kicking and fired her. Tina went onstage herself that Saturday. So my son was born on the Thursday, and Tina beat up that girl on Friday and she was back onstage on Saturday. I wasn't aware of any of this until I got back on the Monday. And that's when they told me that Tina had taken only one night off, given birth and gone back onstage. Is that strength, or what?

At the retrial, Ike was found not guilty of all the charges against him.

He and Tina established their home base in Los Angeles. Ike had intended to move Lorraine Taylor and his family over to California, but before he could make adequate arrangements, Lorraine rang him to say that she was leaving the kids in St Louis and he had better come and get them.

After a flurry of frenzied phone calls, Ike managed to get someone to take care of them until he could catch a plane to Missouri. Then he brought Ike Junior and Michael, his two children by Lorraine, back with him to Los Angeles. With Tina's son, Craig, by Raymond Hill, and their own son Ronnie, the freebooting Ike Turner and his sexy stage wife now had a family of four.

The only way to provide for them was by working constantly.

I wasn't charging but $300 to $600 per gig. I kept my fees at that level for a long time, until I cut 'Bold Soul Sister' with Bob Krasnow. He told me, 'Man, you ain't never going to make no money hanging around here in town. You could make as much as you make in a week in one night if you just got out on the road and travelled.'

So we started to tour for eleven months a year. I'd get home on 31 December and take January off.

Robbie Montgomery, a former Ikette, says, 'We had a bus in those days. Sometimes it would break down, and we would have to stay somewhere until it was fixed. We would rehearse on the bus, get to the hotel, rehearse, try to find something to eat, go to the gig, back to the hotel, back on the bus, it was a constant thing.'

The kids were looked after by a series of childminders, supervised by Mel and Nancy Johnson, friends of Ike's from St Louis who had moved out to LA around the same time.

For Ike and Tina, the pace never let up. Even when they became famous the world over, they still had to keep up this relentless schedule.

Rhonda Graam, who became the Revue's road manager, adds: 'We played clubs, even here in LA, and even in the later years, which held like 100 people and the stock room doubled as a dressing room. You brought your own mirror and lighting. If you didn't, you did it in the dark. The black clubs were small, holding maybe 150 to 200 people. Sometimes they would rent a hall which held 400, 500, 600. If you played a 1,000-seater that was very big. It had to be very special.'

At the same time, Ike and Tina had to live with the uncompromising situation where the bigger they got, the more people they had to employ.

By then, because of our first record, I was able to maintain a seven-piece band. Gradually, I was becoming a perfectionist, and so I got more firm with the band members, especially in the areas of dynamics and phrasing. Occasionally there would be musicians who didn't like me because I felt they didn't make the grade. In those days, I had very little patience with musicians who couldn't get it right. And if you couldn't get it right, you had to go.

I got a reputation as a tough boss. I'm very dominating about what I want onstage. You always get arguments from musicians about what you're playing, but I want it played the way I want it played. I always kept up with the top records and what was hot on the jukebox. For example, maybe a song you heard on the jukebox was just a one–four–five change or something. Well, when I hear it, maybe I wanna put a ninth in it, or maybe I wanna do something else to it. I'm not gonna sit up and argue with the band boys about it, I just say, 'We're gonna do this the way I wanna do it.'

Just say, for instance, that we are having a band rehearsal, and even though I've always told the band members not to bring people to rehearsals, some guy will bring someone with him anyway. Then I'll give him a part to play, and he plays it once the way I want. But then, just to be contrary, he will deliberately play it again the way he wants to play it.

Because our rehearsal times were limited and I felt that we had to get it right quickly, I would say something like, 'That's not the way I fucking want you to play it!' Then this person would start to carry a grudge and maybe feel that I was disrespecting him in front of his girlfriend or guest. But if he were to think back to other rehearsals, he would have realised that I always have the same attitude to my arrangements, and that I liked to maintain strict discipline.

So I don't really think I'm a tough boss. It's like this, man. I would go out and orgy with you; I'd do anything with you, man. We would party. We would go gamble together. We'd fight together. But when it comes down to what we do onstage, man, this is something we're going to give our all to. I don't just think of the glamour of the stage. You have to give. To me, anything less is bullshit. If you're sitting up there thinking about how you look not about what you're playing – well, it don't happen with me, man.

> The result was a high turnover of musicians in the band. If people did not toe the line, they were out. Ike's autocratic attitude meant that some of the band boys were frightened of him. But that, as he points out, was their problem.

My image has always been that of a serious man with a stone face. This stems from my intense concentration on what was going on during a show, and from being critical of each performance. I was constantly looking for ways to weed out faults and to make each show better.

I've always known what it was that I wanted, and I knew just what I had to do to accomplish it – and I always looked until I found it. I feel strongly that by doing all of these things to get ahead, I helped those around me. It's amazing to me that I could ever have been classified as a pimp or a user of other people.

> One way to maximise the income for his family and his growing band of musicians was for Ike to take on more and more of the business side of running the band, cutting out the middlemen. Booking agents who had the band under contract soon found that they were no match for him.

My contract covered the Ike and Tina Turner Revue. That didn't mean Ike Turner or Tina Turner had to be there – it meant that you got the Revue. It didn't say Ike and Tina Turner, so Ike and Tina was extra. If I didn't go on, no promoter could make no deductions as long as the Ike and

Tina Revue performed. Similarly, if you booked Ike and Tina, the Revue – the musicians – was extra.

I decided to be my own booking agent. I didn't have a secretary then, but I did have a housekeeper. On tour I'd call the housekeeper when I arrived in a new city. I'd give her the name and phone number of the hotel I was staying in, so that whenever a call came in to book a performance date for Ike and Tina, or to order records, she could forward it to me. That way I was always available to anyone who needed to reach me. This is how I was able to generate business and earn a living for Ike and Tina, the Ikettes and the various band members. All told, there were sixteen or more people in those days who were looking to me for their livelihood. They were my employees, my responsibility. I knew they had to survive, pay their bills and take care of their own families.

I had one of the first mobile phones – it was the size of a suitcase – so that I could book ahead from the car while I was travelling.

From the very beginning, I was kept busy, designing uniforms for the band and costumes for the girls – including wigs and make-up – creating dance steps, selecting the repertoire and making up skits for the stage. I had to handle all of the choreography, lighting, sound and stage effects.

I was the person who first pioneered the strobe-light effect. The idea came to me one day and I took two pieces of cardboard and had the light man wave them in front of the light to achieve the effect.

I developed the idea by connecting an old album to an egg-beater. The album had two slits in it, and when it was held in front of a spotlight and cranked up you got an increased strobe-light effect. The crowds really enjoyed this, and I toured all over the US 'chittlin' circuit' using these devices.

When I returned to California the following year, I saw that whitey had taken my idea and made an automatic electric strobe light.

We also used fog on the stage. I had a formula that worked pretty well, but it produced strong kerosene smells. Later, I discovered those fire-extinguishers that use carbon dioxide, and we began to use them instead.

There were other tricks Ike used to draw in the crowds. He would advertise that, for every dollar taken at the door, 50 cents would go into a barrel to be raffled at the end of the evening.

Or he would announce that he would be giving away a Cadillac at every performance. Before he went on tour Ike would send someone out to comb used car lots for old Cadillacs and buy them up for $100 to $200 apiece. 'Of course, everybody be thinking they going to get a new Cadillac, but the audience don't see nothing but you handing over the pink slip,' he says. The only person to see the car was the winner, and he didn't see it until the next day, in the car lot.

Little Richard was Ike's idol. His influence coloured Ike's writing, giving his songs a powerful male point of view.

I would put Little Richard with anyone. He can feel it and sing it. He's great – and I am talking about what's real. The system – the white man, that is – can take a white act, a male or female who can't sing or perform half as well as an artist like Little Richard, and raise them to superstardom. Look at Elvis Presley; look at the Rolling Stones: they are super-super-big. Elvis even claimed the name of the king of rock 'n' roll, but Little Richard is really the king. He's an original who should have claimed the title before Elvis even started. The mistake Little Richard made – and Fats Domino, Chuck Berry, Sam Cooke and Jackie Wilson – was to be black.

Another good example of superstardom today is Bruce Springsteen. The world knows him as the boss. I would feel better if they had given that title to Eric Clapton. He deserves it more.

I'd be writing songs with Little Richard in mind, but I didn't have no Little Richard to sing them, so Tina was my Little Richard. Listen closely to Tina and who do you hear? Little Richard singing in a female's voice. Little Richard taught Tina how to sing my compositions, so Tina concentrated on singing like a man while I honed her stage performance. I gave her attitude; I gave her movements to make on stage. For example, when Tina or the Ikettes step back, if they tread on your feet by mistake, man, it hurts, because when they dance they are not feminine at all. They are trained to be wild and rough onstage, yet feminine offstage.

> Despite the popularity that 'A Fool in Love' had garnered, Ike began to feel that he was losing his audience.

We had a record so we were drawing a lot of people. Things were smooth for us for a year or so as we travelled across the country playing all these little 200- or 300-people clubs.

I had a problem with women, though. Women didn't particularly like Tina and the girls. There was a kind of jealousy thing there. That's what made me write all the songs for Tina to make women like her, to fit the new image I had created for her.

In those songs, I had Tina saying what women everywhere wanted to say to their men. This gave the impression that Tina was a ruler and always spoke exactly what was on her mind. I would have her walk onstage and do songs like 'The Wedding'. Tina starts off singing:

> All I could do was cry.
> I heard church bells ringing.
> And I heard a choir singing.
> I saw the only man that I ever loved
>   walking down the aisle.
> And on this girl's finger he placed a ring.

Then it softens down and she starts talking. This is what started women liking Tina, 'cos she tells the guy she's had enough of his bullshit and that gets sympathy from women. She says, 'Back in my home town not too long ago, the onlyest man I ever loved got married to my best friend. And on the day of the wedding, when I finally decided to go to this affair, I took a seat in the back of the church so that none of my friends could see the hurt that I was feeling in my heart . . .'

And as she'd be saying this, the women would be looking at me, like, 'You a dirty sonofabitch.'

'. . . And as I sit there, an organ was playing "Here Comes

the Bride". And I heard the preacher look at her and say, "Young lady, do you take this man"' and Tina points at me – ' "Do you take this man to be your lawful wedded husband, to love him and obey him, to cherish him until the day you die?" She looked at my man, and she said: "I do." Then he turned to my man, the only man I ever loved, and he said, "Young man"' – Tina walks over and points her finger at me – ' "Young man, do you take this lovely young lady here to be your lawful wedded wife, to love, to obey and to cherish her and forsake all others until the day you die?" And you know what that bas–' She starts like she is going to say bastard.

'You know what he did? He said, "I do." It was so hard for me to sit there and watch the only man I ever loved get married to another woman. But that ain't all of it. As they were walking out of the church, as people were throwing rice all over their heads, he has the nerve to walk up to me and say, "Tina, my darling, you know I will always reserve a certain little spot in the corner of my heart . . ." A certain little spot in the corner of his heart! What did he think was in the corner of my heart? There was nothing I could do, nothing I could say. So I did what I knew best. I fell down on my knees and I called out' – then we go into James Brown – ' "Please, please, please, baby, please don't go".'

Then we would kick out with that song. And then she said: 'Is there anybody in this house who has ever been hurt? I want to hear you say, "I! I! I!" '

And boy, the women would stand up and be calling me 'You dirty sonofabitch.' They believe her, man. This shit ain't never happened, but they believe it, man.

She relaunched her career in the same way. What she did in writing that book *I, Tina* and with the movie, *What's Love Got to Do With It?*, is the same thing on a bigger scale. Before we were just doing it onstage for 300, 400 people. When she wrote that book, she was trying to get sympathy from the public. This really explains it, man. And then she turned round and did a movie and got more sympathy.

During our one month off a year from touring, we would have to record. I was with Sue Records, who started giving me shit. I would give an album to the Modern Record Company as well so that when I was getting ready to go out on the road I'd have a record out. I'd give a live recording to Modern Records, and cut it in Fort Worth, Texas, and one to Warner Bros. I wanted to make sure I had a record out when I toured.

> This was vital, because having a record released gave you valuable airplay which would draw the crowds and, for Ike and Tina, label-hopping became a regular thing.

If I was on my way out on the road and didn't have a record out and the record company said they didn't have time to release no record – well, I would go give one to another company who would get it out right away. I'd tell the company I was signed with that this was an unreleased old recording made before I signed with them.

There was another way around this problem: I started my own record labels, Teena, Sonny and Prann, which I owned completely. I released records by the Ikettes and other groups under these labels. To do this, I had to improvise and set up my own distribution system. I assembled a mailing list of over 3,000 disc-jockeys who broadcast on R&B, pop and middle-of-the-road-type stations.

I would personally type up a letter asking them for airtime, and I would tell them which distributing companies had the record in their area. As part of the package, I would also include a sample record for them to play.

Then, every day, five days a week, I would call these distributing companies and take their orders for my records. I was dealing with about forty-five distributors throughout the United States.

RCA had three record-pressing plants in those days, and they would do the shipping, so I would also have to call them to tell them where to ship each order I received from the distributors on a daily basis. The whole system worked well for me, and I was able to market successfully many millions of records.

Incredibly, I somehow managed to find the time to play around with women, too.

Touring meant that we were constantly coming up against racial problems. Even in California, where it was supposed to be OK, you would walk in a place and they would refuse to serve you.

One night my band and I walked into a restaurant in San Francisco – something like a Burger King, although they didn't have no Burger King in them days. This white guy said, 'What are these niggers doing in here?'

I got someone in my band, Eddy Jones or someone, to be as smart as he was, and say, 'Fuck you, honky.'

Now there's a fight – and this is in San Francisco, which ain't supposed to have no race problems. None of these places was OK really.

In the deep South, meanwhile, as a black act with a growing white following, the band had to cope with total schizophrenia.

Nat King Cole or Chuck Berry, for example, they are black artists who appeal to whites. Blacks don't care about Nat King Cole; they don't give a shit about Chuck Berry.

But take an act like Little Walter or Jimmy Reed – 'You got me running, you got me hiding' – we buy that. That got some black in it. But Chuck Berry – 'Way down in Louisiana, down in New Orleans' – blacks don't give a fuck about what he's talking about.

Now, among the white people in the South, where they're totally prejudiced, the Ku Klux Klan like Chuck Berry. If Chuck Berry is going to play in Mississippi and Chuck walks in the club, the guy going say, 'Hey, come on in, Chuck Berry, through the front door.'

If some other black dude come knocking, he say, 'Hey, boy, what you want? Come round the back door.' They don't want you knocking on their front door. You have to go to the back. But when you play music, you ain't black no more, you white. And they treat you as such – as far as they can.

But we'd never know from one moment to the next whether we were going to be treated as a kind of 'honorary' white or as black. The whites accepted us as Ike and Tina, but at the Holiday Inn and the downtown hotels, they didn't give a fuck. I was just another nigger. They wouldn't give a shit about Chuck Berry, either, unless he came in with a whole bunch of white folks.

They wouldn't even see me, so my secretary, who was white, would go in and make the reservations. Then they'd get so mad when they saw all us blacks come in there.

Having a white woman along brought its own problems, though. We were riding down near Louisville, Kentucky, and my secretary was in the front. Me and Tina were sitting in the back. These white folks got alongside of us and tried to run us off the road. I say, what the fuck's wrong with them? They were following us all the way out to the expressway, hollering, 'Drunk motherfuckers!' So I took my gun, held it up and rolled down the window, and they cut off down the side of the highway, thinking I was gonna shoot. And then I realised what the problem was: my secretary, riding in the front was white and my driver, Jimmy Thomas, was black.

> Later, the national chains such as Holiday Inn adopted desegregation as company policy. Even so, Ike would still run into managers in the deep South who tried to exclude him and his band. A call to head office usually straightened out such problems: after all, a seven-piece band, three or four Ikettes, roadies, a secretary, a driver and Ike and Tina themselves – sixteen people in all – who were on the road eleven months a year, spent a lot of money in hotels. There were similar difficulties in the South finding something to eat.

You be in a bus all day, travelling, and you get off nights when all the restaurants are closed. If there was a Greyhound Bus Station, you could go to the black side and eat. When there wasn't, the only place to eat at was the truck stop. But if we stopped at a truck stop in this big bus with all these blacks on it, they weren't going to serve us.

So a lot of times we'd go to a place and cut the telephone wires down from the telegraph poles. We'd take a rope, throw it over and pull the wires loose so they couldn't call the police. Then we'd go inside and they'd say, 'We ain't serving no niggers here.'

And we say, 'You ain't got to serve us, we serving ourselves.'

Then Tina and the Ikettes would go into the kitchen and

cook. By the time somebody went to get the police, we'd be finished eating and going on about our business.

Often, though, we were in real danger. One time, this had to be 1961, I was riding a new Cadillac in the town down near Vicksburg in Mississippi where Emmet Till was killed. He was the little nine-year-old black boy who went into a grocery store to buy some bubblegum. The white woman in the store said he winked at her. They took him out, tied him up and tarred him. They killed him and threw him in the river, weighting him down. When his body was finally found it was so swollen it looked like he weighed 400lbs. They showed a picture of him in *Jet* magazine.

Tina and I were riding in the back seat. Our driver was Jimmy Thomas, and maybe one of the girls was riding in the front. This particular night we'd played in St Louis, Missouri, and after we got off work we didn't eat because we had a long ways to go – to Biloxi, Mississippi. We got in the back seat of the car after the gig and later on we woke up hungry.

Well, we'd got accustomed to the fact that down South there ain't no place to eat, especially for blacks, except for a bus station, where we could go to the black side and eat. But this was at the time the freedom-riders and all that shit got started, and blacks began to go into the white side of such places.

When I woke up, I told the driver, 'Hey, man, at the next town pull into the bus station so we can get something to eat. I'm starving.'

When we got there he found the bus station, but there weren't no signs saying white or coloured, 'cos that shit was going on. As soon as you walked in the door of that bus station, there were two restrooms to the left – women and men. I went into the men's, and Tina went into the women's. When I came out, I couldn't see Tina sitting on what used to be the coloured side. I walked on round through the bus station to the other side and I didn't see her there. So I sat down at a table. There were three white people sitting way down the other end, talking and drinking coffee, reading the paper – older people. I sat down near the door, close to the cash register where you pay the woman when you're ready to leave. There was one white lady there at the till.

When Tina came out of the restroom, she didn't see me on the coloured side, so she came on round the other side, the white side, saw me and sat down.

Meantime, a little young white guy came through, about twenty-two years old. He come and say, 'What the hell is all of this shit, this goddamn nigger here in the white folks' side? Boy, what you doing round here in the white folks' side?' I just ignored him. I said nothing, 'cos I didn't want to get in no conflict with him down in Mississippi, no way, at that time.

He said, 'Nigger, you hear me talking to you? What you doing in the white folks' side?' And he was talking real loud, trying to get them other people down there to get involved with him. But they completely ignored him.

I had one of them rat-tailed combs with a steel spike on the end of it that you use to pull the waves up – I had a conk in them days. It was in my coat pocket. I also had a .38.

So then he say, 'I am going to show you about eating in the white folks' side. You northern niggers don't come down here trying to start no motherfucking trouble.'

This young white guy picked up a sugar-shaker and began to motion like he was going to hit me. I had my hand on this comb with this rat-tail in my coat pocket. I was going to hurt the sonofabitch, hurt him and stick his ass to death.

We started going round in circles, man. The white woman come out from behind the counter. She called the guy's name and said, 'Don't start no trouble. We don't want no trouble in here.'

Meantime, Tina says, 'Please, Ike, they just kill that boy down here.' She's standing in front of me, saying come on, Ike, and pushing me back. I got this steel spike in one hand and the .38 in the other. And I'm thinking, if this sonofabitch has some guys outside and I'm outnumbered, they will probably try to kill me. I could take five of them with me with the .38, but they weren't just going to get me like that, like they did Medgar Evers.

Tina said, 'Let's just go, let's just get out of here.' So we went on outdoors and got in the car. But it wouldn't start – a brand-new fucking car. Jimmy got out and went up to the guy with the bread truck who was delivering to the bus station. He said, 'Sir, could you give me a jump, please?'

The guy says, yeah.

Then this white boy come out there and said, 'Don't give them goddamn niggers no jump. They just some northern niggers trying to cause trouble down here.' But the man ignored him and went on giving us a jump. And we got out of there fast.

Yet things were changing down there. We were playing down South, in Savannah, Georgia, in a football stadium. The bandstand was in the middle of the field and the audience was sitting in the bleachers, the blacks on one side, whites on the other.

Well, that ain't no good. When you play, you got to be able to see the people's faces to judge their reaction. You got to have them close.

There were all these police in blue shirts and one in a white shirt. I guessed he must be in charge of all of them, so I went over and told him that the kids were too far away and asked him, 'Can they come down on the field?'

He refused. So I sent my secretary to find the manager and I went to see him. He told me that the field had been marked up for a game the following day, with the white lines and all, and if the people came down on the field they would spoil it.

So I gave him $10,000 to get those lines repainted and the field fixed if the kids messed it up, and told him he could send any overpayment back to me later. But the cop with the white shirt said he had to check with the mayor.

Well, they couldn't get the mayor on the phone, but the manager said to the police, 'If this boy is willing to risk his $10,000, I am willing to risk my job.'

Now I never go on a microphone, but that day, back on the bandstand, I went on the microphone, apologised to the audience and told them what had happened. Man, they were so happy, they started climbing over that fence on to the field.

'Stop,' I said.

And they stopped like somebody pulled a switch.

I explained to them about the game the following day and reminded them not to drop their rubbish on the ground.

Anyway, they all sat down on the field, Indian-style, black and white together. And afterwards, man, those kids picked up all their rubbish.

Later, we's up in the party room when the police come.
Man, there is all this cocaine and shit. And this police with the
white shirt, he says, 'Man, you taught me more in one hour
than I learned my whole life. I never thought white folks and
niggers could get along.'

After Ike and Tina started getting real big, Mrs Turners
started calling from all over the world, man. 'I'm Mrs Turner';
'I'm Mrs Turner'; 'I'm Mrs Turner.' But all of them other
women I married didn't mean anything. When my lawyer, Al
Schlesinger, checked all the marriages I told him about – eight
or nine of them – he found none of them was valid except this
one girl, Alice Bell. I *was* legally married to her. She was the
only one I had to get divorced from.

We got a detective agency and found her in Chicago. I sent
my secretary there to get her to sign the papers that the lawyer
drew up. They gave her, I think, $2,500 to sign them papers.
She signed them and took the money, then came out here to
California and tried to file a divorce on me in Torrance. But
when it came up before a judge and I explained the situation,
the judge just had me give her her bus ticket back to Chicago.

Ike is unsure exactly how many times he has been married
– ten, maybe twelve times. But he is sure of one thing: he
was never married to Tina.

There was a joke marriage. After I bought the house in Los
Angeles, a bunch of us went down to Tijuana, Mexico. It was
my first time down there. You know, we'd heard about the
donkey making love to the woman and all this kind of stuff.
Well, we went down to see if it was for real.

While we were down there we went to this restaurant. There
were seven of us – me, Tina, my bus-driver Bobby John, one
of the Ikettes and some others – seven of us, all sitting in this
big booth in the restaurant.

A guy came up and said, 'Hey, you-all want a picture taken?'

We said yes, so he shot the picture.

When we got the picture back it was in a little paper frame
with 'Marriage Licence' written on it. He says, 'You guys want
to get married?'

We said, yeah. We were all sitting there in the booth. I had on one of them big old Spanish hats and we was just acting stupid, man. So I gave him the $2 or whatever it was for doing the picture and he said, 'OK, I now pronounce you man and wife.' Just like that.

That is the marriage that Tina is talking about in that book, *I, Tina*, and in the movie *What's Love Got to Do With It?* It never happened.

Even if Tina's story were true, we were still not legally married. At the time Tina claims I was married to her, I was still married to Alice Bell. But me and Tina never went through any type of marriage ceremony, no kind of way, nothing legal.

I was not a great believer in monogamy anyway. I wanted my cake and eat it, too. I want my home woman and other women outside to run with – that's the dog in a man. I'm sure we all have a little bit of that in us somewhere, whether we respond to it or not.

In fact, Ike can sum up his sexual philosophy very succinctly.

Everything is based on a hole. You got a hole in the head of your penis, where you pee from. The penis and the vagina, another hole, get together and out comes the baby.

The baby comes out of a hole into a whole – the whole world. You see out of a hole, hear out of a hole, smell out of hole, breathe out of a hole, eat out of a hole, pee out of a hole, shit out of a hole.

If you get too much money, you gonna be in a hole – because you can't go nowhere. If you don't get enough money, you definitely going to be in a hole. And when you die, where you going? Right back in a hole.

So the best thing to do is to stop trying to stay out of the hole. Get in the hole and find out what's happening with the hole and then you know how to handle the hole.

11 Peaches and Cream

The Ikettes were formed from the backing singers Ike used on 'A Fool in Love'. It was the first time he had used female backing singers, but they soon became a stable element of the act. The redoubtable Robbie Montgomery was the backbone of the Ikettes for many years, but, as with Ike's musicians, the rest of the line-up changed regularly.

WE HAD SO MANY IKETTES. When they came onstage, men would just holler and stuff. So I got the bright idea of putting together some real pretty girls, natural beauties.

There was one set of Ikettes that looked so pretty, boy. There were two sisters I hired up in Ohio, beautiful. Another girl, Martha, I'd been messing with at the Apollo. She was high yellow and pretty. Man, they looked so good, it seemed like if they walked in rain, they would melt.

When these girls walked onstage, the men in the audience creamed their pants. But when they opened their mouths, they couldn't sing worth a shit. Everybody would put their hands under the chins.

I went through a whole ninety one-nighters with these damn girls. They couldn't sing a note, so I started getting the band boys to play the notes they were supposed to be singing. The horns were playing their parts to try to make them sound better.

So I made up my mind not to find no more pretty women – not just pretty, at any rate – they had to be able to sing. And they had to be able to dance.

Just as I controlled every note of the music, I controlled

every step of the dancing. Although I never danced myself, I was very creative with choreography, I was the innovator of many new dance steps, such as the robot, for example. It started from the old thing of having my band members all move in synchronised, coordinated steps while playing their instruments.

Ike hadn't always been static onstage, though. In his St Louis days, he used to do back-flips while playing the guitar. He cut that out of the act after appearing at the Apollo. He realised that if he was going to be touring, everybody, everywhere would expect to see him do it – even when he was old and grey. Otherwise, they would be disappointed. And Ike was a showman; he knew that the last thing you do is disappoint an audience.

We kept changing Ikettes until I got Pat Podril, and another girl named Marsha Thomas, who was about eighteen or nineteen years old. And then there was Adrianne – she had big, fine legs; she was nice – and Paulette Parker, who I hired on the road while we were touring.

I used these girls for a number of years, but man, then I started having trouble with the Ikettes. The band boys started going with them and stuff. If I fired one of them, I had to fire her too. And if I fired her, I would have to fire the horn-player she was going with – or at least, he was going to quit if she went. And if I fired him, she was going to leave.

So I passed a rule that none of the band boys could go with the girls. They took the attitude that I was jealous and didn't want them to fuck the girls because I wanted them all for myself. But that wasn't the idea at all. Soko Richardson was going with an Ikette, and the trumpet-player was going with another. They was real pissed at me. But I was strict – I am still strict.

There were other problems, too. To give you an example, one night in Las Vegas I was at the dice table, me and Pat Podril. We were tight. I put $100 on the line for her, $500 for me. In an hour, she was up to $3,000 or $4,000 and I was up to $30,000, $40,000. Pat was so excited, she didn't come back onstage no more. She went back to LA – didn't even think about the rest of the show. She took her $4,000 and went straight to LA. Fuck me, fuck my show, fuck everything. She went home to take that money to her boyfriend.

And sometimes there was trouble between Tina and the Ikettes. I don't know whether Tina was jealous of the Ikettes, but some of them would mess her about, especially Claudia Lennear. She was another real good Ikette, one of my picks.

Tina told me in Las Vegas, 'Claudia is doing something to me onstage. I can't put my finger on what it is. I wish you would talk to her.'

Well, I didn't know what she was talking about. I couldn't put it together. I watched her every show to see what she was doing, 'cos I knew Tina wasn't going to lie on her.

In one part of the show, they got in front of each other. I could see Claudia from the back, and as far as I could tell her body was moving the way it was supposed to be moving. So what was Tina talking about? Maybe Tina *was* making up something, 'cos she knew I was tight with Claudia.

Then I picked up on what Claudia was doing to Tina. When they got in front of each other, they were supposed to be looking into each other's eyes and having fun. But Claudia was looking over Tina, not at her. There wasn't no visual contact. And she was doing it purposely. Because I was looking at Claudia from the back, she knew I couldn't see it.

Tina and the Ikettes naturally attracted a lot of excitable men and fights often broke out. One time, we played in Vallejo, California. There were a lot of soldiers down there in the 1960s, and we were playing on a tall stage. The Ikettes were singing background.

This song 'I Know' was real big then. When they were singing that song, one of the guys reached up to grab their legs when they ran onstage. I bent down there and told the guy, 'Hey, man, if you want to see the girls, you wait till after the show is over and I will take you to their dressing room.'

He said, 'Fuck you.'

This sonofabitch reached up there, grabbed the mike stand and hit the guy playing the solo on the trumpet and bust his lip. And boy, I kicked at that man so hard I fell on my back.

When me and my guitar got up off the floor, he said, 'Come on here, you motherfucker.' He had a knife.

I didn't even think. I jumped right down there. And when I jumped offstage, everybody in the band jumps off with me. And it was a free-for-all in that auditorium, boy. The Ikettes held down one guy and beat him with a shoe. It was a good fight.

There was another fight in Paducah, Kentucky. They had a little stage that wasn't even six inches high. You could sit at a front table and Tina was right up there in front of your face.

There is some army town right around Paducah, where all the soldiers are. And they go out to brawl with everybody. Tina was singing and this guy kept reaching his hand up under her dress. I said, 'Don't do that.'

But he kept doing it. So I had Tina tell the audience on the microphone. 'Ladies and gentlemen, we're trying to give a good show and we can't concentrate with things like this going on.'

At the start of the next song, this nigger put his hand up Tina's dress. She took the butt of that microphone stand and knocked his pooh-pipe off. He fell back, got a bottle, broke the bottle – bang! – and was fixing to come at Tina with it. I took my guitar and slapped it right down on the centre of his head. Bam. And boy, that was another free-for-all.

You see, Tina ain't no weak thing, and she ain't going to respect nobody who is weak, either.

When we were up at Buffalo, New York, I walked into the dressing room and there were some guys who wanted to come into the dressing room. I told them the girls were getting dressed to go onstage. Anyway, this guy, man, he walked his ass into the dressing room. Tina grabbed him by the collar, picked him straight up off the floor and banged him against the wall and jabbed him. It was good that I came in just then. And then my bus-driver hit the guy – bam! – busted his eyeball. The shit out of his eyeball was running down his cheek.

In those days it was very easy for the industry to find ways to criticise an act or a group. To be banned or censored was reason enough to keep a show off television. If that had happened to my act, it would have prevented us from getting the better bookings in the exclusive clubs and the main showrooms of Las Vegas. Even though ours was a sexy show, I did manage to get me, Tina and the red-hot Ikettes on the TV pop programme *Shindig*.

An English guy named Jack Good used to have a show here in America, in LA. Sam Cooke was the first somebody on his show; the second somebody on his show was Ike and Tina.

I brought Tina and the Ikettes onstage on TV with these mini-skirts on, real short skirts. I didn't know what sort of stockings they needed to wear with these mini-skirts – I didn't know you could wear just plain stockings, so I had stockings made of the same thing I had the blouses made out of.

So the Ikettes were onstage with the short skirts, real wild. And Tina Turner was onstage, real wild, with the long hair. I don't wanna keep going back to the race thing, but then, being black, you had to be careful about what you did and the way you did it. Because Tina and the Ikettes were black, we had to be especially cautious about them wearing such short mini-dresses. You had to make sure that the television cameramen didn't zoom in on the girls' butts while they're dancing.

This is why no one ever saw Tina or any or the Ikettes do bumps to the front. I had the girls make all of their motions to the side, shaking their hips from left to right. Without a doubt, they did have a lot of sexual appeal, and that was just the way I had planned it, but I always had to be careful not to go too far onstage.

So I had the Ikettes onstage with these long wigs on and they was throwing their hair everywhere, and they was real, real wild, man and this is what I wanted. Even the producer, man, they had fans going to help blow their hair.

Right away, the producer had a call from the network headquarters in New York telling him not to have us back on there – Jack Good wanted to have us back on there in two weeks' time. I made about ten phone calls to Jack Good and he never returned them, so I went out to where they were rehearsing with Billy Preston. Jack showed me the letter he got from New York about how wild we were, too wild for his show. I said, 'That's all you had to tell me, and I would've toned the show down some. But at least answer my calls.'

After we had been travelling for about two years, performing and doing television shows, Channel 9 started putting on white girls doing their hair like Tina and the Ikettes, and all this wildness started on TV. Then all the networks began to imitate us with white girls in very short skirts with long hair flying all about, dancing onstage and doing bumps to the front. In no time at all this became the new fad nationwide. They eventually called them go-go girls.

But still you never saw Tina or an Ikette bump to the front like that, because in those days it was considered vulgar. If you're black and you do that, you may not be able to get on another TV show, and the TV was important to us. Whenever we had days off, to make sure that I earned steady money for the band, I would book our act on to the popular shows of the time, like *The Johnny Carson Show*, Dick Clark's *American Bandstand*, *Shindig* or *Soul Train*.

> Ike and Tina continued to come up with hits. The real problem for their records was crossover – how to get out of the black R&B market and into the white pop mainstream.

We came up with 'It's Gonna Work Out Fine' and 'Fool, Fool' with me and Tina, and 'I'm Blue' for the Ikettes. I cut 'Peaches and Cream' for the Ikettes. It was a smash-hit record, but it might easily not have been, because, in white America, it was what they called a black record.

Man, I don't want to sound like I'm hung up on race and shit – I'm not – but there are certain things you just can't get around. It's just there, it's a fact.

Chuck Berry is not black: his skin might be black, but his music is not black at all. For Chuck Berry to have a hit record, he's got to have a real good promotion man with the gift of the gab.

Back then they had radio stations called KRLA and KFWB in Los Angeles. These were the two top pop stations in LA. KGFJ was the black station. The two pop radio stations, what are they, 100,000 watts or something? KGFJ, the black station, is 5,000 watts. You lose it if you coming down Route 405 when you get to the hills, but you could hear KRLA or KFWB all the way to Bakersfield.

So you recorded Chuck Berry and got a promotion man like Don Graham or Bob Krasnow, who is now the president of Elektra. Back in them days, Bob Krasnow was a talker, man. He could make you think that a boogie-woogie was a slow drag song. He would take the Chuck Berry record to the radio station and talk this guy into playing it. The guy would play it, so the record would take off and be a hit. So Chuck Berry was a hit.

But if that song was recorded by a company that didn't have somebody who could get it played on the pop stations, the record would get lost because it wouldn't get played.

The only other way to get it airtime was to get it into the Top Ten of the R&B charts. Then the Top Forty radio stations would pick it up. So if you released 'Johnny B. Goode' and the record didn't make it into the Top Ten on the R&B charts in *Cashbox* and *Billboard* – which it wouldn't: you can't give a Chuck Berry record to a black person – the Top Forty radio stations wouldn't play it. Therefore, 'Johnny B. Goode' wouldn't be heard, and it wouldn't be a hit.

Anyway, Modern told me what we needed on the Ikettes was a pop song. So I got this little white kid named Steve Rennee to write this song 'Peaches and Cream'. He wrote the words and I put the music to it.

> Mama told me that love is not all sweet,
> Watch out for all the boys you meet,
> But if you find the right boy to marry,
> Life can be a bowl of cherries, like peaches and cream.

Well, blacks don't want to hear no shit like that. Blacks want to hear shit about 'my woman is gone' – we dealing with more real shit, man, than the other stuff. But Jules Bihari – Joe's brother – at the record company told me that he wanted a pop record, so I cut this one.

At that time, Modern had a black promotion man. They released 'Peaches and Cream'. After a month and a half, no play on the radio. KGFJ, the black station, are not going to play it because it is not a black record, and the black promotion guy can't get it on the white stations.

I called Jules and said, 'Hey, man, what's happening with the record?'

Jules said, 'Man, the record ain't happening.' 'Man, it's not being played,' I told him. 'How you going to tell if it's any good or not?'

He said, 'Ike, don't you know we're in the business to make money out of records? If there was any way we could get the record on, we would get it on. We're about money.'

So I said, 'I bet you $2,000 I get the record on.'

He said, 'OK.'

There were these two guys, who owned the California Distributing Company. They distributed Motown records and a lot of the pop labels in the area, and so they had power at KRLA and KFWB.

I flew into Los Angeles and went to see the two guys. I told them I would give them $500 apiece if they got 'Peaches and Cream' on KRLA and KFWB.

They got the record on – KFWB played it as their 'Discovery' and KRLA as their 'Pick of the Week'. In one week, we sold 250,000 copies in the Los Angeles area.

You can get a record on KGFJ and go to Dalton's in Hollywood, which is a black record shop, and they haven't sold ten. That shows you how records can get lost, man.

With a couple of successful records under their belts, the Ikettes decided to leave Ike and Tina and try to make a go of it on their own. They were offered a record deal in London. But Ike owned the name Ikettes – he had had it registered. When they tried to play, using the name, he sent over a sheriff with an injunction. 'That's what Berry Gordy of Motown should have done when there were Supremes playing all over the country,' Ike says.

The one Ikette who stayed faithful was Ann Thomas.

I met Ann Thomas when we played Bakersfield. She was a little ole girl standing in front of the stage with this false hair and her face all painted up. I couldn't tell whether she was Spanish or Japanese or what the hell she was. I didn't know that she wasn't but seventeen years old. Anyway, I knew I liked her – boy, I really liked her.

I gave her $50 to come up to LA the next night to play Ciro's, a place on Sunset Boulevard, right next door to the Hyatt Hotel. I got her a room in the hotel, and she came. That was the beginning of us.

I introduced her to Tina and Tina thought she was very pretty. Anyway, when we needed some girls to play Vegas, Tina suggested that I send for Ann and she tried her out.

Ann had the looks and could dance, but she couldn't sing. She couldn't carry a note in a paper sack, man – she's tone-deaf. But Tina wanted to put her in the band. She said, 'She's pretty enough, she don't have to sing.'

That was great for me. She and Tina hit it off real good. So now we had four girls instead of three – three girls who could sing pretty good, and then Ann for looks. That worked.

We trained her to do the act. We took videos of the Ikettes to show them what they were doing wrong. Ann was with the Ikettes for some years. People thought she sang, but she never did sing. Whenever I heard something out of tune onstage, I knew it was Ann Thomas who had done started singing. She could sing in between keys, man – it was horrible. And she didn't even know it.

One time we were recording in the studio. We had about seventeen people in there singing one night, and I had Ann Thomas singing with them. They were singing 'Irene, Good Night'. Boy, Ann Thomas was all out of key. If I had sent that to a radio station they would have paid me to keep her off the radio.

But, boy, Ann Thomas was my kind of girl. She was sensuous. She had a lot of sex appeal and I loved her. For a fact, I loved her and I loved Tina. I loved them both. I loved Tina, but I was in love with Ann Thomas.

Having two Anns around was, of course, a little confusing. Ike called Tina by her real name, Ann, or Little Ann, until they split – after all, Tina Turner was only her stage name. Now he calls her Tina. Back then, Tina tolerated, if not encouraged, this *ménage à trois*.

They both got the name Ann but they knew the difference. When they were both together, I said Ann and whichever one I was talking to would look round and the other one wouldn't. I guess I put a different accent on it.

There was no rivalry between them. I never seen no arguments between them or nothing. I would hear Ann Thomas and Tina talking in the dressing room. Whenever Tina said something to put me down, Ann would tell her no, no, that ain't Ike, what he does. If Ann T. said something about me, Tina would tell her no, no. They had a pretty good hook-up.

Ann Thomas is a real beautiful, beautiful woman. In LA she was living at the house with me and Tina. She slept in the games room, where the piano was. That's where I would write at night.

When we got home from work ... You know the long gowns that hang all the way down to the floor but you can see the cat through the gown? Shit, Tina and Ann would have them gowns on and be walking around and my dick would get as hard as Japanese arithmetic. Tina would say, 'I'm going to bed,' and kiss me goodnight. And she would leave Ann in there with me, 'cos Ann was supposed to sleep there on one of them couches which were as big as a bed. One night, I stopped playing the piano and started messing with Ann. We started making love. The lights was out. At almost the point of climax, there was a click and the lights were on. It was Tina. She said, 'Oh, I'm sorry,' turned the lights out again and went back to bed. She never to this day said nothing to me about that. I don't know what she said to Ann Thomas. She and Ann were very, very tight.

Finally, man, Ann got pregnant by me. We was in Houston. She thought I was going to make her have an abortion and she ran off back to Bakersfield. I didn't go get her, but before the baby was born, Tina told me, 'Ike, you should make some kind of arrangement to take care of that baby until it is eighteen. You'll save yourself a lot of problems later on. There is probably going to be some problems if you don't.'

So I asked her, 'What do you think I ought to do?'

She said to tell the bookkeeper to send her something every

month, so Ann wouldn't have any reason to take me to court.
I started doing that. I don't know whether I gave the baby $50
a week or what, I forget. I did that all the time. I ain't had me
no problems with Ann Thomas.

Tina accepted the situation. After the baby was born, she
suggested that I get Ann Thomas back. So I asked the secretary
to call her and get her to come back to the group.

I got a big cheque, for $50,000, and I gave Ann Thomas's
mother $11,000. So Ann's mother kept Mia, my daughter, and
Ann started travelling with me again.

Then some guys over in London were crazy about Ann
Thomas. They tried to get her to sign up with them for
recording. But she couldn't carry a note, as I said. I think they
was into some pussy, right? Ann didn't go for it, but the other
three Ikettes quit. They were going to go over and sign with
these people in London. I replaced all three of them, man.

In the meantime, Tina was teaching Ann to cook what I like,
the way I like it; how to do everything the way I like it. Tina
was training Ann to be her. I don't know whether they
discussed me when they were on their own, but I do know they
were very open with each other.

At that time I had another woman, too. When I first saw
Rhonda, I was playing at the 54 Ballroom in LA. It was a
predominantly black club, and Rhonda was the onlyest white
person in there. I noticed her from the stage. She was doing her
neck real funny.

I asked her why don't she come on ride up to the house with
us when we got off. She said yes, so she followed me and Tina.
She had a cream-coloured convertible, I think it was a '56
Chevrolet.

After she came up a couple of times, I said, 'Why don't you
spend the night?' And she stayed all night. Finally, I started
messing around, screwing her.

She was working at the Prudential Insurance Company. I
would ask her, 'Why not take the day off work tomorrow and
come with me to the record company?' or wherever I had to
do business. She would take off and in the end she got fired.
So I told her, don't worry about it; I would take care of her
bills and I would give her money until she found another job.

But she never did get another job. She just continued to work with us and helped with whatever we needed.

She was very, very loyal. But like all women, she could be devious too. I had her and Ann T. living together for a while. She would cook Ann's food and take it to her in bed, giving her the royal treatment. And then she would tell Ann, 'Ike came to my room last night, man. I hate for him to come into my room.'

She told Ann all that shit, and Ann would come to me and say, 'Why don't you tell Rhonda to stop telling me what she do with you?' I talked to Rhonda about it, but naturally she denied that she'd told Ann anything.

But Rhonda was a good girl for me. She handled all of our business A1, man. I could tell her to do anything and she would do it. The only bad part about Rhonda was that she would never make a decision about anything. She was always afraid to make a decision.

12 River Deep

WHEN PRESIDENT KENNEDY WAS KILLED in 1963, we were on our way to Peoria, Illinois to play. I was lying in the back of the car. Jimmy Thomas was driving. He had the radio on. All at once they broke in with a special bulletin saying that Kennedy had been shot.

Down inside of me, I was hoping that he would live. It wasn't that long afterwards they said he died. I just couldn't believe it, man.

I never did meet John Kennedy, nor Bobby, but I love Ethel Kennedy. Ethel Kennedy is, like, really my friend. When we played at the Sheraton, Hyannisport, Ethel came to hear us play and took us out to their plantation.

They got guards there. They got big farmhouses, they got little farmhouses, they got chickens, they got dogs – they got everything. It's like a huge estate. Ethel took us out on this boat which had four Rolls-Royce engines.

I had real good feelings about John F. Kennedy and I had good feelings about Bobby. John F. Kennedy was taking America in the right direction, I felt – not that I am a political man.

I don't give a shit about politics. It don't make no fucking difference who gets in. They going to do what the fuck they want to anyway.

The only time I vote was for . . . Who was that, Nixon? It could have been Eisenhower, I don't know. Whatever president it was who said, 'I will bring your sons and husbands home. I will stop the war.' Because at that time I was right at the age where I would have to go to war. So I went and voted so that I wouldn't have to.

Ike would have been thirty-seven in 1968, when Richard Nixon won the presidential election on the promise of ending the Vietnam War, too old for the draft. But he was just twenty-one when Eisenhower ran on the pledge to bring American boys home from Korea. Yes, Ike voted for Ike.

His love for the Kennedys was not confined to Ethel, John and Bobby.

I had the same kind of infatuation for Jackie Kennedy as I had for Nyoka in those *Tarzan* films. I would never have tried to approach her, but, at the same time, it was a little heart's desire.

I had the same kind of inner feeling for Lena Horne when she did the movie *Stormy Weather*. You long for that woman, you want that woman so bad, but you never do anything to get her. It's a kid's infatuation.

Early in 1964, everything in the music industry changed when the Beatles took America by storm. Ike understood the English invasion because he knew what they were playing – the blues.

I thought it was just some kind of a fad. I just couldn't believe that people were so crazy about some group. I didn't know anyone could be that big. I really admired them, 'cos they were just four little people who were really really together. They paid a lot of bills and they were very creative.

We done heard blues ever since I can remember. I started playing with Robert Nighthawk and Sonny Boy Williamson when I was a kid. But in 1964, when the Beatles and the Rolling Stones came over, B.B. King couldn't get arrested here in America.

America is followers, man. Blues – B.B. King, Sonny Boy – has been in America all along. But when the English started playing the blues, the Americans said, 'Hey, these are white people.'

Then they started playing blues over here. B.B. got real real hot, with no record. And Chuck Berry. They came out of nowhere and they don't know how they got hot.

Despite his appeal to whites, Chuck Berry's career had nose-dived in the early 1960s, and he was in jail in 1962–63, leaving the charts safe for the likes of Pat Boone.

B.B. was living in Pasadena. All at once, man, he gets to be real famous again. But it didn't come from America. It came because the English people were into blues. You go to England, they can tell you more about what is happening in America as far as blues and stuff is concerned. But now in America, there are people trying to understand it.

So the Bob Krasnows and the Don Grahams – the promotion guys who could really get a record on the radio – they went to England to see what the English people were dancing to. They come back and say, 'Hey, man, blues is what is happening.'

So then they start grabbing in their boxes. It's been there all the time, the B.B. Kings. This is how it crossed over in America. Blues had been in America all the time, but in reality, it flew back from England. England woke America up to the blues.

Ike soon got to see the blues scene in England for himself, after having a huge hit in the UK and the rest of the world – and a huge flop in the US – with a record that he neither wrote, arranged, produced nor performed on.

I did a TV thing, *The TNT Show*, with Phil Spector. I think it was the first time I met him. It was certainly the first time he saw my show. I was aware of him through the Ronettes and the Righteous Brothers, whom he was producing at the time. He had his secretary call me to say he wanted to produce a record on Tina himself. He came over to my house and said he wanted to do it all on his own. He didn't want me to participate in the session, in producing it.

I said, 'Great.'

All I wanted was a hit record – I didn't care who did it. I got no attitude. I don't care who produce a hit record on me today, man. All I care about is success. It ain't how you win, it's did you win? I'm not interested in the glamour of it. So I told him, OK, and he had Tina come out to his house to sing.

It is a funny situation with Phil Spector and Tina Turner,

man. He seemed to know an awful lot about what is happening with Tina. He make nice gestures to me, but he don't never follow through on it. He also act like he is a friend of mine until it get down to really showing that he is a friend of mine. What I mean by that is, he don't owe me nothing but I don't ask him for nothing, either.

Overall, I really like Phil. But that don't mean nothing to him one way or the other, because he ain't put no money into this project. And he ain't put none into my pocket even to talk about it.

I like Phil as a person, but when he drinks, I can't stand him, 'cos he always embarrasses me when he drinks. He is a little dude and undoubtedly he has a complex about it. Being small, he has the urge to be big or something. Anyway, when he gets drunk, he wants to boss everyone around him.

And the people he has around him! I guess I was the same way at one time. I had a lot of 'yessirs' round me, just kidding me, just yessing, man. I hated that they were like that with him. I don't think it is fair to him.

In my opinion Phil Spector is a genius. I don't know if he play an instrument or not, but I got respect for that man. He made ten times the money I made in this business. He is a sharp dude. I would kinda like to do something with him. He doesn't know my talent; he doesn't know nothing about me.

So I stayed out of the studio and let Phil and Tina get on with recording 'River Deep, Mountain High'. I didn't hear it until it was finished. I thought it was a great record. I also thought that it was the kind of record you might not like if you played it low. You had to play it loud to like it.

Tina told me he had seventy-eight broads singing: 'De-do, de-do, do, de-do, de-do, do'. Seventy-eight voices. You don't even hear them on the record. But Phil did a great job on 'River Deep'.

Despite the international acclaim it commanded, 'River Deep, Mountain High' peaked at number 88 in the US – and Ike knew why.

It stayed in the charts for twenty-one weeks in London. All over the world, the record was a great success, but in America, it never did nothing. The black stations said it was too white, the white stations said it was too black, so the record had no home here. They shouldn't have put my name on it like that.

In Europe, man, they don't give a shit what colour you are. If the record's got it, it's got it. All over the continent the record made it to number 1. If they hadn't tried to categorise it, maybe we'd have made number 1 in America.

Man, I was never crazy about whether my name was on it or not, or where I stood onstage. It didn't mean nothing to me. All I'm interested in is getting the audience off. I've never been interested in the front part of it.

Look, say there's this guy out there. He's got a problem. He just lost $100,000 and he's got to sit there with his wife and kids. He don't want to be there, he wants to be out getting that money back or whatever. Hey, man, onstage I can feel that. My whole thing is to get his mind off it and make him enjoy the show. That's where my head is.

Some people say that 'River Deep' is the reason Phil Spector quit the record business, but I don't agree with that. I just think he has a hell of a talent in the studio. He did wonders in the record business with people like the Ronettes.

'River Deep' wasn't Tina's only solo effort. This guy Bob Crewe produced all the hit records for the Four Seasons. I got me an idea that I would see if I could get him to produce a record with Tina. When I was in New York I made contact with him and got him to produce Tina. It wasn't a hit, and I done forgotten what the song was. He had a technique like Phil Spector. I was actively pushing Tina as a solo act: it wasn't like Ike Turner was a singer and Tina Turner was a singer; Ike Turner was the music and Tina Turner was the singer. That's what Ike and Tina is.

Although Ike had nothing to do with the recording of 'River Deep, Mountain High', he had the job of reproducing onstage the sound Phil Spector had created with a thousand overdubs and limitless numbers of musicians and backing singers. And it was the Rolling Stones who gave him the opportunity to do it abroad.

When the Rolling Stones were first here, we were playing a place called PJ's on Santa Monica Boulevard. They came there to hear us play and we got acquainted.

Mick Jagger can't sing. He's all right, but he ain't no singer, man. If Mick had to start all over today, he would never have made it. He was lucky. He hit it just right. They got big coming from England, he got big. And, man, he is still going. Maybe I should have taken up singing. At that time, I met Brian Jones. We really got to be tight brothers, man. When Brian got drowned, I got close to Keith Richards. Man, Keith and Eric Clapton are the two guitarist-playing people I seen in my whole fucking life.

Keith Richards don't know how good he is. He don't know what he can play 'cos he don't never repeat himself when he plays.

I never did get close to Mick, though, and I never met any of the Beatles.

The Rolling Stones were so impressed by Ike and Tina that they invited them over to England for the 1966 UK tour. But Ike had problems with the promoter. At first, they wanted only Ike and Tina. Then it was Ike and Tina and the Ikettes. Ike, however, insisted that his whole band came over, and eventually, he got his way.

We only played six days with the Rolling Stones. The rest of the time, we played tiny places – pubs with sweat running off the walls. The big promoters were surprised by the reaction, but there wouldn't have been such a reaction if I had not brought my band.

We were front page in the *Mirror*; all of the newspapers, for that matter. They said the show was a bomb. When I saw the word 'bomb', man, it scared the shit out of me because I thought they were saying that our show was no good. In America bomb means no good – you know, 'the show bombed out'. And boy, I got all nervous. But they say, 'Hey, that's great, man.' If they say that, that means the show is great. That was the beginning of our thing in England.

I was impressed by the music scene in England, especially the

London venue Middle Earth. They had a band here, a band there, another band over there, all around. All the bands were playing at one time. And man, they would play the fucking blues, and they'd make you cry. They loved the guitar. This guy, you could feel the charisma from his body. The English people, they were really into blues.

I met Eric Clapton in Manchester. The Yardbirds went on first; Ike and Tina were second. The Rolling Stones were headliners. Ike and Tina had to go on three times 'cos the Rolling Stones were late. Girls was screaming – man, I was afraid. I thought there was going to be a riot.

Between the first and second set, I was walking down a corridor backstage and heard a guitar – man, it was crying. It sounded like B.B. King or Elmore James. This guy could take a note and bend it, make that guitar cry from the heart.

I hadn't seen any blacks in England, but I was sure the man behind that guitar was black. I walked into that dressing room and there was Clapton sitting on the table, just playing. I said, 'You're one bad motherfucker, man.' That sonofabitch plays from the gut. He can grab a string and make it cry; you can feel the vibe from it. He plays the blues.

This guy now, Springsteen is supposed to be the king of rock 'n' roll guitar. I saw him at the House of Blues a little while back. How did he get that reputation? I don't believe, today, man, what's real and what's not, but I'm just into music, man – I wouldn't just do the thing for the dollar. It's got to be real.

Man, in England the Ikettes went crazy. You know how Americans act all big in England, like everything's so cheap. That's not it at all. They just thought a pound was a dollar, when it was $2.40 in 1966. And those pounds, shillings and pence they had. Them girls could not figure it out at all. The Ikettes just gave all their money to the taxi-driver and he would take the lot.

We came back home for a couple of months and then we went to Europe, all over Holland, Germany, France, all those places. After that we went there every year in October and came back in November. Finally, we went to Australia. It was as if they had never seen nothing like my show. There was nothing like my show, though, and I don't think there is today.

Even so, I was surprised by the reaction we got abroad. I just didn't expect to be that big. People were just overwhelmed by our Revue.

> In many ways, although it was gruelling, playing abroad was easier than touring back home because there were other people to do the organising. But they had to travel every day, and that was never entirely without its problems.

I had trouble in some parts of England. In Bristol we had reservations at a hotel. Rhonda Graam, my secretary, a white girl, went in and the woman behind the desk said, 'Yes, we have rooms, come on in.' When she saw all the black folks get off the bus, though, she said, 'I'm sorry, we're full.'

It shocked me, because I hadn't run into any prejudice over there in England.

> Ike says that the Bristol incident was an isolated one, but Ronald Bell from EMI, who used to accompany Ike in Europe as translator, reports that the band also had problems in an hotel in Rome.
>
> Bell toured Europe with Ike and Tina for years. He used to hold Tina's dressing gown when she came offstage and would admire her magnificent body. Despite the recent repeated allegations that Ike beat Tina, Bell says he never saw a mark on her. He also says that, while Ike was something of a martinet with the band, he was a kind and generous man – and not only to those around him. Ike, Bell says, was also given to anonymous acts of charity.

With Ronnie Bell one time we played in Berlin. On the airplane, I put my bag in the back of the seat in front of me. There was about $26,000 in there. We got to Berlin, got off the plane, I forgot the bag and went to the gig. While I was in the dressing room I remembered my bag. I told Ronnie Bell, 'Ronnie, you know I left my money on that airplane.'

He went flying off to the airport. It was about seven o'clock when I missed it, and he got back around eleven. I was onstage when he got back and he waved up at me. The airplane had been to four cities and had come back with the bag still in the pocket of the seat.

Man, I was so grateful. He could have come back and told me he hadn't found it, but he didn't.

A similar thing happened in France, except that time the ending wasn't so happy. My contract said that the promoters had to pay me in American dollars. They couldn't pay me in no English money, no francs, no nothing – American dollars only.

We was getting $10,000 a night back then. So I had up to $80,000 or $90,000 in my briefcase when we went to Paris. When I walked into the dressing room, I set the briefcase down behind the door. I got dressed, did this TV show, came back, changed into my street clothes, opened the door and looked around the room. I didn't see nothing so I got into the limo. Twenty minutes away from the TV station I say, 'Where is the briefcase?'

Tina said, 'Ann, you got it? Ike, you got it?'

The driver turns around and flies back to the TV station. That money gone.

Tina believes in psychics. She said, 'Ike, Peter Hurkos can find that money. I know he can.'

I said, 'I bet you $10,000 he can't. If he find it, I give you $10,000. If he don't, you don't spend any money for the next . . .' I don't know how many months I told her.

She said, 'OK.'

So I called up Peter Hurkos in Amsterdam, Holland. He flew to France. He was touching things, talking about he feel this, he feel that. Then he went to Amsterdam to see some of his people, and then he came back again.

He ain't found shit. That shit ain't about nothing, man – like I said, there was $80,000, $90,000 in that case. Someone had a real good Christmas.

I think that the police recovered it and never gave it up. I called them two or three times. I had a police friend here who was checking on it for me, too. He told me the international police had tracked it down, 'cos that was a lot of American money, and it was all in 100-dollar bills. That's hard to get rid of. I never got it back, though.

Peter Hurkos's failure in France didn't shake Tina's belief in psychics. Another psychic told her that she was going to meet this foreigner and fall in love with him and that we were going to break up. This foreigner she would be going with had a pond in his garden, the psychic said.

I sent Tina to do the movie *Tommy*. I didn't go myself. After filming was finished, they gave a party at Robert Stigwood's house. He got this pond in the yard of his house, so she's thinking he is the one.

When she saw that pond, Tina started throwing herself at him. But he didn't respond, no way. Then she came back to America and started calling his office in New York. He wouldn't even return her calls. The secretary would put her on hold and never come back to the phone.

They never told me nothing about it until after we broke up.

We had a big following in Germany. Once we were playing Cologne, Germany, and the press were down front. I know they want to hear 'Nutbush'. I know they want to hear 'River Deep'. I know they want to hear 'I Been Loving You Too Long'. These are the songs they came to hear.

I climaxed that show without playing those songs. So what is the audience going to do when you go off and they ain't heard what they came to hear? They going to clap you back on. So I go offstage and come back. I still wouldn't do those songs. I came back for thirteen encores.

Boy, the next day, we were all over the news: 'Ike and Tina couldn't get offstage . . . a complete show in encores.'

That was the only time I did anything devilish like that.

Ike is especially fond of Germany and intends to live there eventually. The contacts he made there while touring were vital.

I always felt that Gerhardt Augustine was the real key to Ike and Tina's success in Europe. Gerhardt was working for United Artists in them days. He had connections all over Europe. He also spoke eleven languages. He went with us everywhere.

I always liked to buy Gerhardt suits. If I buy me a suit, a derby, man, a walking cane, then I buy the same thing for Gerhardt. He was my buddy. We had a lot of fun.

Having introduced Ike and Tina to Europe, the Rolling Stones then exposed them to millions of young white fans in America by taking Ike and Tina on their 1969 tour of the States.

We played in LA at the Forum. B.B. King would do his show, then we would come on, then the Rolling Stones. While B.B. was on, Mick Jagger and I – sometimes Keith Richards and I – would walk through the audience out there. When Mick went out among the audience, don't nobody bother him. They only bothered him when he was onstage. Then we'd go backstage. Tina and I would practise or show one of the girls some steps. Mick would stand and watch us. I guess that's when he got interested in dancing, because he wasn't dancing before that.

Then we went onstage, man, and lifted that audience up to the moon. Ain't nobody could follow that. The Stones were only supposed to do an hour-long show or something. Shit, they'd be onstage an hour and a half, two hours, trying to get the audience to move. But they'd just be sitting there with their heads propped up, looking. Coming on behind us like that was rough. So what Mick did was to put us on first, then B.B. King, and then they went on.

I also know Joe Cocker. I went by to see him 'cos I liked that song 'With a Little Help From My Friends'. I walked in and he was singing, 'What would you do, if I sang out of tune . . .' I really liked him, man. That mother can sing. First time I saw him, I didn't catch nothing but the end of his show. I always kept a .45 with me in those days, a pistol. We came out of those side doors in the Fillmore East and got into the car and there was a bunch of white guys whipping on a black dude. This black dude was trying to defend himself. They were throwing bottles at him and he was backing up between cars and stuff. They had him cornered. He jumped down into the walkway down by a basement apartment and they were beating him. I said, 'Tina give me the gun.'

She gave me the gun and I got out of the car and – pow! pow! pow! pow! – and they took off. Then I got out of there, 'cos I thought all them gunshots would call the police. I never did know who that black dude was. But maybe if he reads this book he will know that it was me who saved his life.

When we started going out on the road we met Janis Joplin and Big Brother and the Holding Company. Janis used to come up to LA and I would show her different things about singing. And I met Kathy MacDonald. She was a bitching singer, boy.

Janis, she was just an average person. She wasn't stuck up or nothing, man. I don't think she died the way they said she died. I don't believe she was on no heroin at all. I know she drank Southern Comfort like it was going out of style, but I don't think nobody I knew was using needles. Maybe they were.

I never thought Janis overdosed on no drugs. I always believed that the Mafia had something to do with her death, or the politicians in some kind of way. She had started being very bold onstage, talking about fuck the government and fuck this, fuck that. Real bad. In Beaumont, Texas or somewhere, I saw her and I told her that it wasn't good that she did that. They don't like you when you are doing shit like that.

I respect the way Janis and other white kids of her generation stood up and spoke out. She had a lot of white followers. Janis drew 90 per cent whites. Same thing with Clapton. Ike and Tina drew 85–90 per cent whites – we had his kind of pull.

Because of people like Janis, the Rolling Stones, Clapton, and other groups, things changed. You had a younger generation that was not hooked on race. It was free everything, free women. They didn't care how prejudiced or biased their parents were, they came out and said, 'I want to see for myself. I ain't going by what my parents or my grandparents did.'

It was complete change, and it was the younger generation that brought it about. That's why today, man, our young blacks don't know about shit. They don't know what blacks – and not just blacks, there are whites on the black side – went through to get to where they could stand up and do the shit they do today. If they'd done this shit in the 1950s they would be hanging from a post somewhere, or shot like Martin Luther King.

Ike did not know Dr King, but he thinks he shook Malcolm X's hand once, at the Apollo Theater, or possibly in Chicago.

But Stokely Carmichael, I knew him. He was just another black dude who believed in what he believed in. As far as I was concerned, he was another dude like Martin Luther King or Malcolm. Stokely was really just trying to bring his race out of poverty.

Despite his impressive record of standing up to racial prejudice, especially in the deep South, where he frequently risked his life, Ike fell foul of the Black Panthers.

In the seventies, one of the Black Panthers was running for mayor in Oakland, California. They had booked my band and signed the contract under another name, 'cos I don't get mixed up in no racial shit, man. They were thinking race; we just thinking of music and having fun.

My views on racial shit are this. If you got 80 million whites and 20 million blacks, blacks ain't got nothing to fight with. The power is among the white majority. For a black to have any power, he has to get some of those whites on his side. If he gets 20 million whites on his side, then he's 40 million strong, and he weakens them other 60 million whites.

See, the white man in America could shoot into a crowd of blacks and not give a damn who he hit. But if the blacks have got whites with them, the white man can't shoot 'cos his own kind is in there. That gives you another strength.

So in my opinion, man, when you're black and you get up there talking about 'down with the whites', what you're doing is turning against your own people. I don't think that's right. I don't believe in being militant; I don't believe in saying fuck whitey.

Whatever we use to get those 20 million whites on our side, we use the same philosophy to get 20 million more of them whites on our side. So then we got 40 million whites and 20 million blacks – that's 60 million strong. Now we are a majority. I feel these are the tactics we should use.

This is what I had been saying, and I guess maybe my attitude got back to the Black Panthers. I don't think they liked that, man.

I can't be against blacks – I just don't belong to no black organisations. I don't belong to no white organisations, neither. But if I walked into some hotel and there was some prejudice shit going on in there, or they were mistreating blacks, I made my stand – wherever it was, man. My band and I had a whole lot of fights with a whole lotta whites.

Travelling down through the South, they wouldn't let us check into them hotels. We had to sleep on the fucking bus. And we had to change and wash up in the goddamn Greyhound Bus Station. So I paid my dues just like Stokely Carmichael and all the rest of them. But I did it my way. And I ain't prejudiced – my secretary was white.

Anyway, when we got to this place in Oakland to play, something was wrong. I could just feel it. When we pulled up there at the kerb, this guy called Fred Boggin, the engineer who used to work at my studio, said, 'Man, this is a rough joint. They took my pocketbook when I first got here.'

He was white and Oakland is predominantly black. So I said, 'I'm sorry. If you had any money in it, I'll give it back to you.'

In the dressing room, I was sitting there getting kind of worried about Rhonda, my secretary, going up the front there to get the money. So I told Eddy Burks, my trombone-player, Mike Johnson, the trumpet-player, and Soko Richardson, my drummer, and someone else to go with her.

But what the Panthers planned to do was to go into the dressing room while I was onstage and take the money from Rhonda. I felt it.

Normally, when we came offstage, because we'd be wet, we'd go back to the dressing room to dry off and settle down, cool out before we got dressed to leave. That night I told Rhonda that when we came offstage we were not going back to the dressing room. We'd go straight out that back door, get into the car and leave. I told the roadie to go pack up my shit and put it in the car.

So Tina and I went onstage and started to do the show.

There was a 30ft gap on either side of the bandstand where people could come up. The bandstand itself was 5ft high, with the dressing-room door on the right-hand side, so I could see the top of the door.

After a while, I heard the dressing-room door go bam. I could see it opening from the stage. They were surprised, 'cos there wasn't anybody in there. They're mad now. I was worried about Rhonda going back there, so I told Jackie Clark, my guitar-player, to make sure those guys had left the dressing room, 'cos I didn't want her in there with them. When Jackie went down the steps of the stage, they grabbed him and started beating him. I saw, and jumped down off the stage. And then they started to beat me. Then Tina jumped in.

These guys were beating the shit out of me, beating and stomping on me. One of them had this big old metal coatstand. He picked it up and I saw him coming down on me. I put my hands up and jammed my elbows against the floor. It came down and numbed both my arms. I had no feeling in my hands. So, my arms is dead, and I can't feel nothing. Even so, I tried to pull one of them down on me, to give me some protection. I was flat on my back with them stomping and kicking on me from everywhere. When I did that, I gave one of them a chance to hit me right on the top of my head. He knocked me out and they thought I was dead.

When I regained consciousness, Warren Dorson, my bass-player was there. His shirt was tore off and his back was blue. And Tina – they'd snatched her wig off. It is hard to get Tina's wig off, man. You can pick her up by that wig. But she didn't have no wig on. They put eight of us in the hospital.

That's when I made up my mind I wasn't playing no black clubs no more in a predominantly black part of town. As well as the incident with the Black Panthers, Rhonda got beat up in the dressing room one time over the ghetto. If I was going to play a black club, it had to be a club everybody could go to. I wasn't going over no ghetto and playing no more dates, man.

In 1971, we went to Ghana to perform at the Independence Day celebrations. I'd never seen nothing like it before. We were over there with Wilson Pickett, Santana, who were just starting then, Roberta Flack, Les McCann and the Staple Singers. There were ninety-seven of us on this one old raggedy airplane. And on the way over, there was a lot of stuff going on, everybody telling stories about what they expected when they got there. They were saying things like, 'Whitey took us away from over here on the boat, now they bringing us back on a fucking airplane,' and that started some racialist shit on the journey.

I didn't particularly like the people who ran the hotel. They seemed to think that American blacks were stupid and they treated you accordingly.

Anyway, Wilson Pickett, he's temperamental. At Black Star Stadium, there weren't but two dressing rooms. They used one for the Red Cross, the other for the artists, so each artist would get a chance to use it before they went onstage. But Mr Pickett wanted his own fucking dressing room. So he arrives and he gets pissed off. We were in the dressing room getting ready 'cos we're next onstage. So he gets all pissed off and says he ain't gonna play.

I went onstage and did my show, and tore the audience up. If you ever saw that movie they made of the concert, *Soul to Soul*, you'll know it. When I came offstage Wilson Pickett was still refusing to go on. I said, 'Man, you know what? Let me tell you what the real deal is. The real deal is' – I knew how to get to his ego – 'the real deal is you scared to go onstage behind me, that's what it really is.'

Now, normally I would never have told him no shit like this, 'cos I'm not the type. But all these people had driven for miles with oxes and stuff, and there were people as far as you could see. Black Star Stadium was so big you could have had four football games going on there at the same time and they wouldn't have conflicted with each other. That's how big that place was. As far as you could see was people, and he was talking about not going on.

They knew Wilson Pickett. They knew nothing about Ike and Tina. Wilson Pickett was the headliner, because he was the only one they knew over there. Boy, if he hadn't gone on, there would have been a riot over there. So I told him that to get to his ego and get him onstage. And he went on. That was good.

In Ghana, they showed us the places where they used to hang up them 9ft black slaves. They used to hang them up on these tall things. They would hang them up there for two weeks and not feed them until they were weak enough to get on the boat.

They had rides to take you out and show you these caves and things. Out there Tina sang and danced with an African lady and I started dancing with them. I thought those Africans were wearing their usual clothes, but in fact they were dressed in traditional costume, the things they used to wear years and years ago. They had a king sitting up in there, and I thought that was the way Africa was. I don't really know about Africa. That was the only time I've been there. They were all dressed up, like in a movie. Old, old, old people dressed up, doing different dances for the king – like Nyoka, only they were all black.

It was fun, but I wouldn't eat no African food. I wouldn't eat that food over there, man, 'cos I didn't know what I was eating. I'd heard that they were dirty people, this was the shit they had told me. The only thing I ate over there was cornflakes. I ate cornflakes that whole fucking week.

The maid who cleaned our room didn't have a broom with a handle on it. Instead she took a handful of straw and swept the floors and put the straw back in this vase. It was an experience, man.

When we got ready to check out of the hotel, they done charged our bill double. They really think that Americans are stupid. We went up there and spent three or four hours getting our bill straightened out. It was really less than half what they were asking.

To this day, we ain't never got a dime from that movie they made of the concert, that *Soul to Soul* movie. They had it on at all the hotels we stayed in in Europe and I think it must have made money.

At one time, they had it in America. Maybe they still do – I've been trying to find it. I think it was a good movie they cut out of there, man. I really liked our part, 'cos those Africans had never heard of us, and the change from when we come onstage to when we go off – well, it was a complete turnaround. They was just waiting on Wilson Pickett, that's all they knew. They chanting, 'Wilson Pickett, Wilson Pickett.'

We got whatever we were charging per night, but we were expecting to get a percentage out of the movie. What happens is you don't make any money doing the movie, but they say you're going to make a lot of money from it if it sells. You've got some artists today, like Fats Domino or B.B. King, who are regular sellers. Whatever they put out there, they sell. It ain't like an Elton John record – you put it out, it goes way up to a peak, then it drops down, it's dead. Fats Domino sells it steady. That's like this movie, *Soul to Soul*. It never really went high, but I'm sure it sells steady.

13 Mountain High

HE STONES TOUR, that was the beginning of us doing well. We were playing Vegas and stuff after the Rolling Stones. That's when I cut 'Proud Mary' in the studio at Vegas. On 'Proud Mary', where you hear my voice – and that's a rare thing for an Ike and Tina record – that's me telling Tina the words. My voice was supposed to have been erased. I didn't mix that record. I had to leave and go to Australia and we were one song short on the album. I thought the engineer knew he was supposed to erase my voice, but he left it on – and that song was a hit.

After the Rolling Stones tour, we played in North and South Dakota. It was freezing cold. Tina and the Ikettes were out there throwing snowballs at each other and playing in the snow. When we got back to LA, Tina got sick. She never missed a show or got sick onstage, but this particular night we were playing in some club and she almost passed out.

Ester Jones, one of the Ikettes, was one of the great dancers. She stayed in the Ikettes longer than anybody. We were at the climax of the show, on the last song, when Tina was taken ill, and Ester took her place, moving over to where Tina was supposed to be. It was the only time Tina ever failed to complete a show.

Tina had pneumonia and tuberculosis. Then there was something else. She had a lymph node come up right by her collarbone, and then another big one came on the right-hand side of her neck. It got to be the size of an egg. Dr Thomas, our doctor, said, 'Ike, you need to let me take that lymph node out of her neck. There are three of them there. Then I can tell whether they are malignant or not.'

Meantime, I had booked thirty days with Fritz Rolf over in
Europe. We were charging $240,000 and would be working
twenty-five days out of thirty. We had fixed the dates and he
had sent me the $120,000 deposit. It was two weeks before we
were due to go. The doctor wants to take this thing out and I
know Tina is not going to be well enough to go. So I am
thinking about waiting until we come back. But Dr Thomas
talked to me again and I said, 'OK, take it out and I am going
to call Fritz and cancel the dates.'

I called Frankfurt and told Fritz that I had to cancel the dates
because Tina was real sick and I returned his money. And I
paid him the money it cost him to tell the audiences that the
shows were cancelled, so he wouldn't be out of pocket.

So the doctor took that thing out of her neck. Then Tina
said, 'Ike, I can still sing.' But she had stitches there, and when
Tina sing, her neck swells out.

I said, 'If you think you can do it, I will ask Dr Thomas
about it.'

Dr Thomas said she could sing but he would have to take
out these stitches and strap a gauze around her neck, so that
when she sang she would bleed on to the gauze.

So we did the Europe tour after all. Tina had a cut several
inches long in her neck and when she sang it opened up. She
went onstage for every one of those twenty-five fucking days
with that cut on her neck. Tina is a strong woman.

We also got to play Las Vegas – this time the Strip. When
they opened the International Hotel, we opened up in the
Lounge with Redd Fox and some white guy called Cochran.
Elvis Presley was in the main room and he had the Sweet
Inspirations singing with him. This was when I found out that
the white boy I had turned on to rock 'n' roll in West Memphis
was Elvis.

I had it put in my contract that they had to give me two
two-bedroomed suites, one on the twenty-ninth floor and
another one somewhere else. The one on the twenty-ninth floor
would be just for partying. The other one would be for me and
Tina and whoever handled our clothes, Ann Thomas or
whoever.

I kept seeing this white guy around the hotel every day. The first time he was clean shaven. Next day, I see him with a little bit of stubble; the next day, with a whole lot more. I thought, this guy is sick.

I found out that he had some air-conditioning company in Pennsylvania somewhere. I hope he read this fucking book, so he can send me my damned money. It's OK. That's a joke.

This guy owed $500. He'd been staying at Caesar's and we were staying at the International. He had been trying to win $500 to get his clothes, because they had locked him out of his room at the other hotel. He just went down and down. He kept calling and getting money sent to him, but he kept on losing.

I got to meet him and liked him. So, me being as lucky as I am, I said, 'OK man, we ain't got a problem. I can win you $500.'

Most times, I can win $500 like popping your fingers, man. But this time, I put $500 down on the line and boom, craps, I lost. Another $500, craps, I lost again. Now I'm $1,000 under.

Then I put $1,000 on the table, thinking that if I got a hit I'd be even. I ended up losing $30,000 in an hour and a half. I just reached in my pocket and gave the guy $500. I left to go onstage and I said, I am through gambling for today.

That night, around three o'clock, I left the party room and came downstairs to the coffee shop – me and Mac Bride, the guy who runs my spotlights. I was walking through the casino after I finished eating at the coffee shop and this lady said, 'Mr Turner, Mr Turner, can I have your autograph?'

So I felt in my pocket for a pen man, and there were three green chips – $25 chips. I asked the guy over at the dice table if he had a pen I could use. He gave me a pen and I signed the autograph. The lady had $5 – five white chips, so I said, 'There is no point me going to bed with these three green chips.'

I put them down and – bam! – there was a hit. Now it's $150. I left it down there. Now it's $300. I left it there, now it's $600. I put down the $600, now it's $1,200.

So then it is my time to shoot – there ain't nobody there but me and this lady – she up at one end of the table and I'm at the other. Next thing I know, man, I had won so much money that I stopped shooting black chips – $100 chips – and started shooting $500 ones.

I had $500 chips all around the whole table down to her end in two rows, and another row on the top. That night I won $470,000 with $75.

After the thing was over, I didn't put the money in the cage, where you normally put it. I took it up to my room, where I filled the drawer up with it.

Tina had her wig on a dummy head on the dresser and there was a TV at the foot of the bed. The bed had a canopy hanging down and curtains, and you had to take three steps to get up to it.

Tina's mink coat was right there on the chair and her wig was on the dummy. My .45 was lying right on the dresser and there was all this money in the drawer.

Then the maid came in. She didn't see us lying in the bed behind the curtains. She propped the door open. She saw Tina's wig and she picked it up and put it on her head. Then she reached for Tina's mink coat and put it on. She stood there in front of the mirror, and then she saw the gun. She picked it up between two fingers, by the handle, and set it down out of the way 'cos she was scared of it, I guess. She was doing all kinds of poses in front of the mirror. I said, 'Are you looking for something?'

She screamed and the wig fell off her head on to the floor. It was so funny, man. That night, I was in the dressing room telling the security officer about it, just 'cos it was real funny. But, oh man, he went and told the head of security and they fired that maid. So I had my secretary find out where she lived and I sent her $15,000 to hold her until she got another job. It wasn't my intention to get her fired.

Around this time, we did this TV show with Andy Williams. Tina and he did a song together, and Sammy Davis was also in the same show. We took pictures and shit together.

Then, when we started playing Vegas, Sammy set up there. He was doing this movie, *Bill Baker,* and he wanted us to do some songs for it. When we got through, he gave Tina a white Jaguar car as a gift, I think that was the last time I seen him. Everybody always said we look alike, but he was just a little-bitty dude, man – his head only come up to my shoulder.

Meantime, we were drawing in England and we were

drawing in America – and we were attracting the older whites, young whites and older blacks. We did *The Ed Sullivan Show* in them days. When you playing in Las Vegas you got to do *The Johnny Carson Show*.

Today, I appeal to the young blacks. I don't know what to attribute that to, except perhaps Tina's movie and kids being curious: what about Ike? What is Ike? What did he do? How did he get to be so popular? Kids are inquisitive. On the whole, though, back when Ike and Tina were beginning, I never appealed that much to young blacks. When I was thirty years old, all the black kids in the audience were eight to fourteen years old. I could please them by playing the shit that was on the radio, but I didn't like the kind of music they liked – I never liked that bo-bop shit. I knew I could get over to a black audience but that wasn't my main music.

I am now double that age, so now those kids are aged thirty-two to forty-four. That generation don't know that much about Ike and Tina. Between thirty and forty-five, they've heard about Ike and Tina from their parents, but they don't know nothing about us. People of that age are the people I associate with mostly these days. And the ones who really were my fans back then, and still are, are forty-five to seventy-five. That is something for me to think about, man.

> After the early rip-offs, Ike established himself as a real savvy businessman. The problem was, as always, the number of employees he had to support.

I bought a lot of property and shit. I had enough money. No one never knew what I had 'cos I was not the type to go borrowing money off people. God has been kind enough to me to allow me to maintain my independence without relying on nobody. I have always been fortunate like that. People always thought I was rich, even though I wasn't.

I am probably better off right now than I was back then, because then I had twenty-six people to worry about – how they were going to eat, and how I was going to keep them in some kind of work so that they could pay their bills. It was a big headache. But now I ain't got to worry about shit. If there ain't no big deal, there ain't no mental strain.

132

If I show up with a record, great, but I ain't licking nobody's ass to get a record deal. I am just letting fate do it on its own. During that time, though, I was under a great deal of pressure.

I was very, very, very lucky with gambling. I went to this gambling club one night with about $2,000 and I lost it, in under half an hour. We had recently played this place the Haunted House on Sunset Boulevard, and the promoter always paid me off in $1 bills. I wasn't charging but $650 a night, but even so, that's a lot of $1 bills. So on my way home I called Tina from my Rolls-Royce and said, 'Hey, I need some more money right quick. Look over the dresser and give me that money.'

I wasn't gone from the gambling house but fifteen minutes. I went home and came back with two big old envelopes full of money. This made the guys at the gambling joint think I had money at my house, so now they're getting ideas to come to my house and rob me.

Soon afterwards, some robbers came to my house, robbed it, tied up Rhonda and stayed there until six in the morning, waiting on me to come home. I was in the recording studio. It was a live recording and there was leakage on the other tracks. I was trying to get Tina to say the words in the same spot where she said them before. I was there all night until about seven o'clock in the morning.

My secretary finally cut herself loose and came over and said, 'Ike, they just robbed the house.' Man, I had just bought Tina some new boots and maybe $3,000 worth of clothes.

When I got home the TV cameras were there. It was all on the news that Ike Turner's house had been robbed.

I told Rhonda tell me everything that had happened. They even shot in the room the kids were in. What made them do that? Rhonda told me that one of the girls who was there with the robbers had said: 'You didn't tell me that you was coming here to do all of this. I don't want no part of this.'

I picked up the phone and called the radio station, and I offered $5,000 to whoever would tell who these guys were. Soon as they put it on the radio, it wasn't five minutes before the girl called and told me who they were. She said they were supposed to rob some other place the next Thursday. I told the police, and the police got a helicopter. I went up there with them and we circled up over that house. And those stupid bastards went into this joint. The safe was locked and those stupid sons of bitches were trying to get the safe out of the front door.

They had stolen my car too, and they were using my stationwagon to do this robbery. The police followed them with a nightlight back to where they had all the stuff stashed, and I got all my shit back.

14 It Starts to Snow

Ike was not a drinking man. He had had some bad experiences with alcohol. Just a couple of shots of whiskey had made him really sick that first night he slept with Tina. Grass suited him no better, and he banned drugs from the band, too. The band boys were allowed to drink only after a gig. Ike was a professional musician, strict and businesslike when it came to work.

TRIED SOME MARIJUANA, MAN. The woman said, 'Ike, this is some good weed, the best. Try it, try it.'

I took but one draw. By the time I blow the smoke out, I am unconscious. I am unconscious for two or three hours. I just can't handle it.

I would fire you, man, from the band if I thought you had grass, cocaine – any kind of drugs. I thought they were all the same. You know, there's a difference between heroin, grass and cocaine, but I didn't know the difference. All of it was drugs, and if I found you with any I would fire you instantly, man.

When I was in Las Vegas playing the International Hotel, which is now called the Hilton, some of the other well-known entertainers who were playing in the main room there gave me some cocaine and a dollar bill. Two of them became very big in the entertainment world. Today both of them are dead.

I cannot reveal their names because I feel they were not trying to do me any harm by giving me cocaine. Later, I used to do the same thing, give away coke to people with good intentions, not knowing what the end result would be. Anyway, the guys in Las Vegas, they would say, 'Man, you just put it in your nose, do it like this.'

But I never did do it. Instead, I took the cocaine home in my pocket. I took it to the doctor and asked him about it. He explained the pros and the cons. I kept it around the house for maybe two weeks. Finally, one night, man, I went home and I thought about it. It was about eleven o'clock and I decided to try it. I went in there and got the stuff out of the drawer.

I was sitting in the living room with the piano, with the recording equipment. I was gonna record and just create songs and stuff, and write. I put some in my nostril, like I had seen the other people do. And I didn't feel nothing. Then later on I took some more in both nostrils. I still didn't feel nothing.

You see, I had no idea what to expect from it, except that the doctor had told me it could burn a hole in your membrane – I have one I can put a pen through now.

So anyway, I was looking to feel drunk, like when you drink whiskey and you begin to get woozy and feel yourself getting heavier and heavier. I was looking to feel something like that from cocaine. But cocaine has the reverse effect: it makes you feel like you just woke up in the morning.

Next day at one o'clock, I'm still sitting right there at the piano doing the same thing, putting the cocaine in both nostrils, writing songs and saying, 'Man, I don't feel sleepy.'

Then, man, I say, 'Wow, I sit up all night and I'm not even tired.' I wasn't thinking that cocaine could give you all this false energy, or whatever – I don't know what to call it.

Then the drummer came over. I say, 'You gotta try this stuff, I've been sitting here all night long. I don't feel nothing but I ain't even sleepy.'

When I realised that this was what it was doing, giving me all of this fucking energy, I went and found somebody who had some and started giving it to all the band boys. 'Man, this stuff keep you awake, make you horny, make you want to fuck – man, you got to try this shit' – that's me turning the band boys on to this shit, right?

Then I started buying for the band boys, and that's something I regret, man. But it's like finding something other than somebody you love – that you like to have sex with. If you find something that good, you always want to share it with your friends.

I thought this was good so I told my band boys, and they all liked it. We played, man. We were having so much fun playing music on stage, man. This is the beginning of it, before you get hooked. When I say hooked, I don't care if it's mental or whatever it is, man – either way, you'll be wanting some more. It starts out as fun; in the end you are a slave to it.

Man, I don't want to sound like I'm promoting drugs or none of this. I'd say everyone got their own mind to do whatever they want to do, but think about it before you do it.

With me, I've had a lot of fun with a lot of women and I did a lot of drugs, which at the time felt great. Later on, I wanted to stop, after thinking back on how it had brought down my career and my livelihood. It start off fun and then it end up . . . Man, you live for it. I used to hurt so bad with snorting and stuff. My nose would be bleeding and I would be trying to get my finger behind my eyeball when I went to sleep, because it would get so dry behind there.

Cocaine-dealers, don't shoot me, I'm just telling it like it is. That's the real deal here. This is what Tina and I really broke up about in the end.

The cocaine I used came straight from South America. This lady friend went to Peru and brought me back some pure cocaine. She brought it back in hangers, man, in those wooden hangers. The cocaine was inside the wood. I never saw nothing like that before. You bust the hangers open, slashed them with a knife or something, and the cocaine was inside there. It looked like rainbows, the pure stuff. I guess she used her kids and stuff to do it.

I used to rent a party room for the whole band whenever we went on tour. I would rent the biggest two-bedroomed suite I could get in the hotel and we would use it to entertain the people from the music business – disc-jockeys, radio-station programme managers, promoters, record-distributors and other guests. I would get another suite – two-bedroomed also – for Tina and me to sleep in.

In the party suite the musical instruments were in one of the bedrooms – usually just a piano, guitar and a small practice drum pad. They were set up so that we could do some entertaining. We would sit around and create songs.

In the living-room area was a table set up with catered snacks and dishes and liquor. I would spend at least $400 per day on whiskey to stock the bar. We usually kept a small record-player in the corner. And we would use one bathroom to snort and freebase with cocaine, always with the choice girls. I started setting out the cocaine in the party room in bowls, everywhere I played.

In Germany, they didn't even know what it was – 'Man, what is this?'

I said, 'Try it, try it. It's great, great, great.'

So then they started trying it. Then I went to England and started giving it to everybody. See, at first I didn't think you could be arrested for cocaine, anywhere we worked in the United States, or in London, or in Germany.

In Munich I had a four-bedroomed suite and we had the cocaine out in big bowls in the living room – I'm talking a whole pound. We wouldn't hide it. I would just give it away. I was giving away $52,000 worth of that stuff every six weeks and, man, whatever I wasn't giving away, they was stealing. It would have been impossible for me to do that much. I didn't think about being arrested – it wasn't even on my mind.

I had cards printed up that we would use as invitations to these after-show parties. They were like blank forms, so that all we had to do was fill in the time, date, hotel name and suite number. I would give each band member eight little cards to give out to invite people. The men were told only to give the cards to women, and the girls to hand out the invitation to men. Any person who received an invitation could bring along a guest of their choice, male or female. I didn't know who they were inviting. Any one of them could have been the police.

In the Waldorf in New York, for instance, I put out the cocaine on the table – pounds of it – and when you walked into the party it was there for the taking. Anyone could have come in. I could have been in jail a long time ago, but nothing ever happened to me. That was the beginning of my coke thing.

However, for the band boys, there were some rules that were strictly enforced. No members of our group were allowed to take any of the booze from the suite back to their own rooms, neither were they allowed to put their personal room numbers on the cards and use them to invite people to their own private parties. If they were caught doing any of this, I would impose a stiff fine, anywhere from $100 to $500. In reality, the fine would be only $100, but with the added Turner tax, it could be pushed up to 500 bucks. One of the band was caught breaking these rules on a number of occasions. He would put his room number on the cards to get the girls into his room, and was fined $500 each time, but he never seemed to mind much.

He used to trick girls by telling them, 'Ike wants to meet you in his room.' He would let them wait there for hours and then have one of the other band members fake a call to him, claiming to be me on the phone. After he hung up, he would then say to the girl, 'That was Ike. He said don't leave, just get undressed and go to bed. He will be here.' When she had done this, he would leave and return a short time later saying, 'Ike and Tina just had an argument, and he won't be able to make it.' Most of the time, since the girl was already naked in his bed, he would get from them just what he wanted. That guy was what I would call doggish.

There were times when girls would come and tell me that he had taken their money from them. I would usually ask them how much had been taken and give it back to them out of my own pocket. I found out later what he was doing. He would take a girl to his room to have sex, and afterwards, when she went into the bathroom to wash herself, he would clean out her purse.

Sometimes, he would see a girl with me whom he wanted to be with real bad but with whom he couldn't make any progress. So I would take the girl into one of the bedrooms in the party suite. Once she and I were in bed, he would call me on the phone, pretending to be Tina. I would say something like, 'Hello? OK, I'll be right there.' He would always walk into the room just as I was leaving, while the girl was still in the bed, nude. From there the rest was up to him. We did that a lot.

Another trick we used was to get two bedrooms with an adjoining door. After I had finished having sex with a girl, I'd run the water in the bathroom. This was the signal. When he heard it, he would meet me at the door and we'd switch rooms. He would then continue the sexual exploits with the unsuspecting girl.

When I stayed in the party room and didn't go out to eat with Tina, she would bring me food. A few times when we were in the middle of an orgy, she knocked at the door and I would have one of the girls open it. Tina could see me from the door, lying in the bed. She would reach in with the food and say, 'Give this to Ike.' Then she would leave.

Sometimes, when the girls saw her they got nervous or scared, thinking that Tina might cause a big scene. I would tell them, 'Don't worry, she's not going to do anything.'

She never did.

Tina did not participate in these parties. She turned up at functions for the press, the media and to help our career, but she never came to the party rooms after the shows and never participated in any of the sexual acts there.

Nor did she use drugs – she didn't even smoke. She never could or would do drugs. The only time she ever did alcohol was if we went to some social gathering where everybody was drinking socially. She would take a glass, fill it half-full, hold her nose and swallow it straight down. And that happened maybe three times a year.

Slowly, the drugs began to cause problems. We were setting it up all over Germany in these suites. There was a black German who used to have five girls who rode with him. He used to follow us all over Europe and I would just give him cocaine.

About the third time I went over there, this motherfucker had started selling heroin or something. I didn't know nothing about it, you understand. He had snitched, told the police that we had drugs and that he had bought his drugs from us. We hadn't even been over there at the time: we didn't go till the end of October and he'd been caught in June.

We were staying in a hotel around forty miles from Düsseldorf. When we went to work, the police went into our room and went through all of our stuff with a fine-tooth comb. Tina's clothes were thrown everywhere, my clothes were thrown everywhere. They looked down all the soapboxes, everything. They just ransacked that hotel room. They didn't find nothing but two grass joints in the trumpet-player's bedroom. They didn't find nothing in mine 'cos there weren't nothing there.

Meantime, the police came into the dressing room at the auditorium where we were playing and showed these little badges with their pictures on them. They told us they were there to search the premises and that they were looking for cocaine. They searched and searched and searched.

I had cocaine sitting in a little box that held an ounce. I had it in the shoulder pads of my suits. I had a dressing gown hanging there with an ounce in the pocket. It was in the jars on Tina's table, just sitting there where I could dip into it. And do you know, they searched that dressing room and they never saw it.

So they apologised. They said this black German guy had told them that I was supplying him with heroin. That was why they were there. And I said, 'Why would he lie like that? I ain't never sold him nothing. One time we had some cocaine, and we gave him some.' They told me he'd been busted for heroin and had fingered me so that he could go free.

Touring Europe for thirty days, we had to carry a lot of cocaine, usually a couple of pounds. I don't want to let on how I did it, but I'll give you a couple of instances. We had dummy flashlight batteries you could put cocaine in, and the false cones at the back of the speakers where we would put a pound of coke. I had wah-wah pedals you put shit in and we had false heels on our platform shoes, which you can turn and put in an ounce or two. We had shoulder pads with zips on the inside and we filled them shoulder pads up with coke; we had phoney belts, man, that held it – we had everything. Any kind of way you can name, we were doing it. I shouldn't be telling all these secrets, 'cos now customs are going to be checking out other musicians.

There was a close call in Japan. We were there around the time they arrested Paul McCartney with a roach or something. In Japan, if they catch you with drugs, they put you so far back in jail they have to pipe you sunlight and shoot you biscuits with a slingshot.

Anyway, we played somewhere in Tokyo. I had this little overnight kit with a zip on it, and I had a little brown box, round with a top you wedge on. It held an ounce of coke. That night it was raining so hard that I couldn't go out. I wasn't going up to the party room, I was going to stay in with Tina that night. Ann Thomas was in the other bedroom in our suite, on the other side of the living room, because she handled our clothes. She always stayed with us.

When I got into bed that night, Ann took the coke out of the little brown box, washed out the box and put it away in the overnight kit so that it would be clean when we went through customs the next morning.

For some reason I forget, I got mad at Tina when I got into bed. So I got up and put on my clothes, looked in the stash, filled the box back up with cocaine and went up to the party room.

I only stayed there about ten minutes, 'cos there weren't nothing happening. Then I went back to my room, took out the little box with the cocaine in it and just set it down and washed my face and went to bed.

The next morning Ann Thomas come in and saw the box sitting there. She thought maybe I'd just taken it out when I was looking for something, so she didn't open it and look at it, she just threw it in the overnight kit. Now we were going to Osaka.

Ann Thomas is a very, very, very, very pretty girl – all the verys. She was my woman also, and the mother of my daughter Mia, who is now twenty-three years old. Ann has oriental features but she's got a nigger booty and a nigger waistline. A big butt, nice legs. For a fact, man, I used to like to have sex with Ann and take her out because she was so attractive. She looked like Tina, but she had sex appeal. She just looked sensuous all the time. Anyway, when she around Japanese, her oriental features made her look Japanese. She had big, slanted eyes.

These shirts had just come out, these real thin shirts they make for women, which you can see through – you can see the titty and shit. She had one of these shirts on with the sleeves rolled up and had tied it up where you could halfway see the titty.

When I first got to Japan I had a press conference and I
talked to the press from all over the country. When they
interview you they don't ask you where you started and all that
shit like they do in America. They want to find out what sort
of person you are, what makes you tick.

So anyway, when we got to Osaka, Ann Thomas, Tina,
Rhonda and I – we were always together – were coming down
the steps of the airplane and this old man walked up and he
bowed at Tina and Rhonda, and he bowed at Ann Thomas,
and he said, 'Mr Turner, I read about you in the paper. Very
ripe tomato, very ripe tomato.'

He was calling my head a tomato, so 'ripe tomato' means
I'm smart.

I said, 'Thank you, thank you.'

He said, 'Have a good show, my grandson's coming.'

I said, OK.

We gone on inside. Now, Ann Thomas, Rhonda and I – and
Maseiyama, who brought us over to Japan – we all used to go
through the same line in customs because they didn't usually
stop me; usually they let me go on through. But with the band
members and things, sometimes they spot-checked them,
sometimes they didn't.

Ann Thomas was over there talking to one of the Ikettes. She
ain't in my line where she is supposed to be, and she's got my
overnight kit. So when she get up there to the customs, the man
look, trying to see her titties through this thin blouse she's
wearing. He ain't thinking about my overnight kit, he just
ramming in there.

Now he's got the box in his hand. He's still looking at her
titties. He's just fucking with the box but he is trying to see her
titties. All at once this damn thing's top came off. Coke went
all over the customs counter.

And this guy says, 'What's this?' He put his finger in it.
'What's this?'

'Ann,' I shout, 'it's BC.'

She goes, 'It's BC.'

He said, 'BC?'

'Headache powder.'

He put his finger in it again and put it on his tongue, so I

143

knew his tongue was gonna be dead in a few minutes. Then he flicked on his red light, and all the red lights above all the customs tables flick on. He is calling his superior. So that old man who'd read about me appeared. He was head of customs, and I didn't know it. He came down and put his hand in the cocaine, waved it aside and said, 'Have a good show, Ike.'

When we got to the hotel, we had maybe a pound of cocaine left. I called a meeting for all the band. I told them what I thought we ought to do: get Ann Thomas out of the country. I said, 'Rhonda, you call and find out what time the next train is leaving for Tokyo and what plane she could connect with from the train, where she could be going to America.' I was expecting this young dude to go to his superior's superior and try to make a name for himself.

To make Ann less noticeable, we took off her wig. Now Ann don't look oriental. She look like a gypsy without her Tina wig on. Leon Blue, my piano-player, we took his wig off – he's bald on top. When he wears a wig he looks something like me.

I gave them $4,000 and told them, 'You catch the fast train and when you get to the airport, if they don't have enough seats on the airplane, here's $4,000 – $2,000 each. Give someone that $2,000 for their seat. Make sure you get on that plane out of here tonight.'

Meantime, I took all this cocaine we'd got out of all these different hiding spots and told a roadie, 'OK, flush it all.' And boy, he sat there scooping it out, putting it in the can and flushing it away. Then he'd put some up in his nose and say, 'Lord have mercy, what you got to throw all this away for?'

I said, ''Cos the police could come down to that place tonight and that little boy trying to get rank, he could have told on that old man.'

I don't know whether that old man knew it was coke or what. He just said, 'Have a good show, Ike.' Anyway, the next day, I gave my secretary $20,000 to give to him. When we got to the airport it was his day off. I ain't been back to Osaka since.

The drug thing just got bigger and bigger until finally it was totally uncontrollable. As long as I had money and knew where to go and get the stuff, I would go. It is my belief that every

Starting out: artist photo from the Spud "Nik" Booking Agency

Ike and Tina with the first Ikettes; Ester, Claudia and Edna

In Pompeii Records days

Swingin' Sixties
with the Ike &
Tina Turner
Revue

Ike: lean
and mean
in the late
sixties

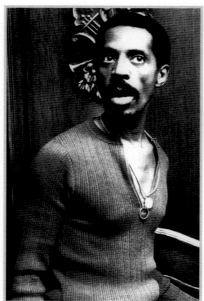

Ike & Tina at
the Hungry-I,
San Francisco,
1967

A courageous
man, backstage,
1971

Ike Turner Revue backstage
at Carnegie Hall; Vera
Hamilton, Ike, Jimmy Reed,
Warren Dawson, Ester Jones,
James MacBride, Tina.

Live in London, 1973

Ann Thomas,
Ike's wife, 1981

Ike in the studio,
late seventies

Ike Turner, 1999: alive and defiant

drug-abuser really wants to stop, but subconsciously he dreads what he will have to go through and the time it will take to accomplish it.

You see, when you do drugs, it's a totally destructive thing. When you start it's OK, but the next thing you know, you start living for the next hit. I can only talk about crack cocaine, man. When you start, it is fun, but after three or four times, it becomes a priority. When you get up in the morning, man, you're not looking for a plate of food to eat, you're looking for drugs. You're not living for anything but that.

It got to where my nose was getting real sore, then started bleeding. We were playing somewhere in Europe and Tina was sick. A doctor came to see her and I told him about my nose. He put a light up there and said, 'Well, you got a hole through there.'

It was a little hole then, but it started to bother me. It began to hurt me so bad, man, that when I woke up in the morning I had to go get me another hit. I had to put more cocaine in there to deaden it. And then I used to pray, man, 'Lordy Jesus, if you just let me go five days without doing this shit, I'll never go back to doing it no more.'

But I never did go five days. I would always lie to myself, make some excuse to do it. It was the same thing with whiskey when I was young and I was drinking. I would go get real drunk then say, 'Lord, if you ever let me get sober' – because I'd be vomiting, whiskey makes me drunk – 'Lord, if you ever let me get sober, I'll never drink no more.' But about the third time of that, man, I didn't drink no more. And with cigarettes. I said if I could just make it without smoking for five or six days, I would never go back to it. When this woman taught me how to stop smoking – how to reprogramme your subconscious mind – that's when I got my five or six days in, and after I got past that, I never looked back.

That's why I don't ever have to worry about ever doing drugs again. Because, man, I'm clean now. I feel great. And I don't regret that I did it. It was an experience. I learned, and I think I am healthy today. I'm in good health, good spirits. I think I can save a lot of other people from going down that route, but I don't put them down, 'cos I understand why they do it. I also know that they don't want to do it. They done got trapped in a situation they can't get out of. The ones who wish to get out of it, I can give them the tools to do it.

> But it was to be twenty years before Ike stopped taking drugs. By that time, cocaine had destroyed his relationship with Tina, lost him the love of the beautiful Ann Thomas, ruined his relationships with several other women, damaged his children, devastated his career, squandered his talent, wrecked his business and consumed everything he owned.

When I first started doing drugs, boy, cocaine wasn't but $250 an ounce. When it went up to $275 an ounce, I told them I wouldn't buy no more. Finally it got up to, what, $2,500 an ounce? And I was still doing it.

15 The Pleasure Dome

The idea of Ike setting up his own studio, Bolic, began with a chance meeting with Louis Jordan, the star of the 1940s whose career, ironically, had been overwhelmed by the advent of rock 'n' roll.

I WAS A FAN OF LOUIS JORDAN'S when I was a kid. He was my idol. When I grew up and bought my house out in California, I didn't realise that the real-estate woman who sold it to me was Louis Jordan's wife. When she told me I was really thrilled. She brought him to meet me.

Louis gave me some advice. He said, 'You have to get it while you're hot, 'cos when you die down it is impossible to get anything from anybody.' At that time I hadn't bought the building on La Brea where I set up Bolic. I had offices on Buckingham Road, the first offices I ever had. Two secretaries, in the office and the back. I screened it off, made it real nice-looking.

Downstairs under this office was a nightclub called the Bill of Fare. They had live bands down there, and when they were playing it sounded like it was right on top of my desk.

One night about nine o'clock, I was sitting in the office. One of the secretaries, Ann Cain, was still there. I heard this music start. Soon as I heard it, I knew it was Louis Jordan down there. I jumped up and flew down them steps. Sure enough, it was Louis, and all the Tympany Five. I was so excited to stand just inside the door and listen.

Then, man, I got really tore up. He was this guy in his sixties and he was playing in a place where he ain't getting but $10 for the side men and $15 for him. This guy had made movies

147

and did everything you could name. And boy, this was as depressing as shit to me. I didn't even say anything to him.

I went back upstairs to my office. Ann Cain asked me what was wrong. I was so full inside with emotion, I couldn't tell her nothing. I went inside my office and shut the door so she couldn't come in. And I started to cry.

Then I got angry. I hit my fist down on the damn desk. I had some books there, and when I hit my fist down, the Musicians' Union byelaw book fell out.

I picked it up and started riffling through it. This is God acting through me. And there, where it opened up, I saw – I ain't never told this to anybody, except Tina and my secretary – bang! This thing opens up on article 6, section 25, where it says: 'No agency is allowed to take their commission from the top. Their commission comes after transportation and Union dues are paid.'

To me that means that all booking agencies were breaking the law. They book a job for $1,000, they take out 10 per cent. That's illegal. When I saw that, man, I was pissed off.

The agencies and the managers have the money, man. The artists don't end up with shit. I don't think that is right. Somebody's got to put a stop to them.

I never told anybody about this, man. I guess it was selfish. I used it for Ike and Tina, but I never told nobody else. Man, I don't want to damage the agencies and managers; I don't want to hurt nobody. But this is also why they don't want me back in the industry. I quit school in the eighth grade, but I ain't no fool, man.

I typed a letter to the international union in New York. I did it on plain white paper. I said, 'Sir, it has been brought to our attention that the agencies licensed by the Musicians' Union are taking their commission from the top. And in accordance with the Union's byelaws, this is illegal. If it is illegal to do so, I am sure that you are aware of it.'

If they were aware of it, that meant they were getting some sort of kickback.

Now, I had my own booking agency, and three or four days later I got a letter from the Musicians' Union by special delivery. They sent it out to all agencies. The letter read, 'It has been brought to our attention that booking agencies are taking their commission from the top. And if we find any agency taking their commission from the top, we will revoke their licence immediately.'

That's heavy. There ain't no artist who is satisfied with his agency. They take the bookings, but they always think that there is another agency that can do better.

So what I done found out now, man, when all agencies are taking their commission from the top, is that if their artists find out and report them, they all have to be reissued licences to stay in business. So now, man, I have got a stick to fight with. But I didn't use it selfishly.

I didn't have money to fly to New York like I can now. This was the early 1960s, and we were working for $350 a night, $500 a night or something. We were on the road. Before we left California on these ninety one-nighters, I wrote a letter to the agency in Chicago that was booking Louis Jordan.

I said, 'Louis Jordan is having income tax problems and we would appreciate you giving us as much help as you can to straighten them out. Would you send us a breakdown of the last four or five years? We are sure that you have the information stored on microfilm or whatever. We will pay for it.'

So they sent it. Now I knew exactly what they had taken out. The documents showed they'd taken money from the top.

When we played St Louis, I had this letter in my briefcase. When I got off work, I left Tina and drove up to Chicago, which is only 300 miles away. I went into this guy's office – the president of the agency – and said, 'This is not blackmail nor nothing, man. I am not trying to hurt nobody. But here's a man in his sixties and he ain't got no fucking money, he ain't got nothing. I am sure you've made all kinds of money off of him. All I'm asking is for you to give him $20,000 or something, man. I am sure you can do that and it won't hurt your company. Here's my hand on my heart you won't hear from me no more. I wouldn't even publish no letter like this because it would hurt a lot of people. It would do a lot of musicians good, but it would also hurt a lot of people if my findings were published.' And that wasn't my intention.

I told the president, 'How would it look if you don't give Louis Jordan the money and I published this letter? What would the other agencies think about you, when you could have stopped it before I published it?'

He sent Louis Jordan a cheque for $20,000. Louis died not knowing where that $20,000 came from. He never knew that I was the one that got it for him.

That was the end of it. I never used that any more. Because if someone reads this book and has signed with a top agency, he is going to say, 'Fuck you. You been taking commission off the top, so I am going to sign with this other agency here.' Or, 'I don't want no booking agency.'

And there wouldn't be a fucking thing the booking agencies could do about it. That's why I never said it, man. I never wanted them trying to put no needle in my arm and kill me like Janis Joplin. It has been selfish for me to hold on to it all these years, but now I don't give a fuck. I think something needs to be done about it, what all the agencies and managers are doing is strictly illegal. It is in the union byelaw book. So every contract between every artist and every booking agency and every manager is invalid. The Stones, Elton John can just walk away.

I want to put this in big, bold, black print, man. I am not saying it to start any confusion or anything. I am saying it so that the managers and agencies will try to be more considerate with their acts.

The only reason I am saying what I am saying is because I hope it brings a better relationship between the artists and the managers and agencies, so that the artists will be protected, and when they get old, in their sixties like I am, they will have something, man. They won't have to be worried about getting welfare or this kinda shit. This is why I am saying it. I'm not saying it to hurt nobody.

I ran my own booking agency from early in my career, because I knew they were a scam. I understand business ethics, too. If you sign with a booking agency, this is what happens. You're with a company whose got a hundred damn acts. They ain't thinking about you. You can have a hit record and everybody else working off your hit record. It may be good for the business, but it ain't no good for the act.

Say an agency has ten acts signed up. One act has a hit record. He is so happy, man. Finally, he has got something that will get him work and make some money. He can get out of the soup line because he has a hit record.

But it don't work like that in the beginning, when you first get a hit record. If their other nine acts don't have hits, they're going to move their whole office off yours.

What they gonna do is this. When a promoter calls in and says, 'Hey, I want Ike Turner, man. He got that hot record out. I want him and his band down in my town,' the agent, being a good businessman, is going to say, 'Hey, look Ike is booked on that day. If you take John Doe that day and you play Jane Doe on the next date you got, then I am sure that I can get you Ike the third time.'

Meantime, on the first night the promoter wanted me, I am not even working. The agent's got a job for John Doe on my name, he's got a job for Jane Doe the next week, and I am not even working. It makes good business sense for the agent, but it is no good for the act.

When a lot of acts start out they don't know nothing, and the manager takes advantage of them. They know the guy's green. They stick him with a lifetime contract for some ridiculous fee, and by the time the act gets wise it is too late. It's like they used to do blacks. They used to say you should give a black guy enough money to buy a car and some flashy things to keep him happy, but not enough to get him educated.

They've also got to find a way past the entertainer's ego. A lot of entertainers have big egos and are real temperamental. The jew guy – I don't mean jew like Jew, I mean the manager guy – has got to figure out how to tell him he needs to take a bath without saying, 'Hey, man, you need to take a bath.' 'Cos he's going to say, 'Fuck you, I don't need to take a bath.' So the jew guy going to say, 'Man, you know what, that water is so warm. You don't know how good you going to feel when you get out of there. Man, you don't know how good it feel.'

Now the jew has got him to take a bath, without telling him he needs one. He's found a way to get past the entertainer's ego. That's why they say when a jew and a nigger get together they go straight to the top.

I reckon the whole of the music business is rife with rip-offs. Artists' royalties, publishing and stuff like that. People are supposed to be trillionaires and shit, and these new acts don't know a fucking thing. Even the biggest acts don't know how much money they don't have. They don't know how much they are really entitled to, and they don't know how to get it. They think just 'cos they got a couple of million, three million or something like that, they really got money and they really living. They don't really know, man, that they got twenty times that much money already made. They're getting publishing 'cos they're writing the songs. They're getting their writer's royalty, but they got so much more than that coming that they don't know they already done made. If they knew how to get that money, man, they would be super-super-super rich.

That's why the business has always been hard to me. I think I know too much. I ain't talking about getting back the rights to the early songs I wrote for all the companies. It's about getting the money they made, 'cos they already done made the money.

I thought my inside knowledge of the music industry systems could be put to good use, so I set the studio up to help musicians. Entertainers get all of the fame and end up with nothing – the manager got all the money.

It was the 1970s and I was really doing well. Ike and Tina were famous abroad. We were drawing the older whites in Las Vegas and we had the younger whites with the Rolling Stones tour. That's when I decided to open my recording studio.

I looked around and I found this building at 1310 La Brea in Inglewood. It was a furniture store and I really, really liked it. It weren't nothing but a shell. I bought the whole half a block there and put up Bolic Sound Recording Studio.

A lot has been made of the similarity between Bolic, the name of Ike's studio, and Tina's real name, Bullock. Ike can put an end to any such speculation.

I didn't want to wait to get my cards made and my billboard to go on top of the building printed up, so I just came up with a name that I hoped no one else had got, so I could go ahead and patent that name.

I got an architect and told him how I wanted it built. From the outset, it was two studios with twenty-four-track boards – a big one to hire out and a smaller one for myself. I showed him how I wanted the studios and how I wanted the office, the games room, reception area and living quarters in the back.

It was supposed to be the living quarters in the back, but it turned out to be the orgy quarters.

Rhonda Graam handled the details. I showed her the colours I wanted and the way I wanted the couch and the coffee table made, like a guitar, and the curtains over the bed in the living quarters. I just drew it all up – and I can't even draw. Then Rhonda would draw it again and say, 'Is this close to what you want?'

I would say yes, and she'd go and get it done.

Rhonda also ran the studios. She was the one over everything, under me. Some people call her Sergeant Graam. She got it done. She is with Tina now, I think.

The grand opening of the studio in 1970 was a huge party. 'There were banners outside,' says Nancy Johnson, Ike's old friend from St Louis. ('We be ace spoon coons,' says Ike.)

'You couldn't walk for people,' Nancy remembers. 'There were people from all walks of life – music-industry figures, VIPs from Inglewood. And there was a huge bowl of cocaine. People were coming in, the ones that indulged in it, and stealing it. It was unreal. People would be coming in with packs of cigarettes, emptying out the cigarettes and filling the packs up with cocaine. Thousands of dollars' worth. Everything was just wide open.'

It was a huge place. You walked in the front door and to the left was my office. It looked like a Mafia office. We had a big white bear rug on the floor. On the right was a games room with a pool table in it and old-time Seeburg. You put a nickel in the jukebox. We had one of those sitting in there.

The reception area was straight in front of you as you walked through the front door. Then there was a hallway.

Down the hallway to the right was the entrance to the big studio. To the left, the first door was my bookkeeper's office, the next the door to my private studio.

If you came in the front door and went straight down the hallway to the end, to your left was the maintenance room. Across from that was the refreshment room. Straight in front of you was a wall. That wall was really a door, although it didn't look like one. You had to dial a secret number on the telephone for that wall to open. And then you went in there, man, and you disappeared into the back part.

Up in the back studio, in the apartment there, I had all the furniture custom-designed. I had two couches with scorpion tails which met like an arch. Underneath the arch, I made a round dome. I put a TV monitor painted gold under there. The couches were maroon, the floor was purple and the coffee table was shaped like a huge boomerang.

If you sat down on the couch, there were a lot of buttons under there that you could push. If you wanted cocaine, you punched a button and out of that dome a drawer would come out with cocaine in it. Or you could press the 'weed' button and weed would come out.

On the TV screen in the middle, mash one button and you would see the front door, mash another and you could see down the hallway. Other buttons monitored other parts of the building.

To see into the secret parts of the building you had to have a key to open the part to the other buttons, which would let you see what was going on in the control room of each studio. They would let you see what was going on in my office, or upstairs. You could see and hear what was going on anywhere.

Sometimes I would go up there in that apartment and just sit there and listen around the building, listen around the rooms. Some chick might be in there giving some guy head. I'd be lying up there, just pushing buttons and looking at this chick going down on the guy, and then I'd switch to another room and some guy would be telling another girl that Ike is a dirty bastard. 'What you want with that motherfucker? Ike has all these women,' he'd be putting me down to this broad.

When I told a girl that I had these cameras all over the

building, she would say, 'I bet you got cameras in the bathroom.' I didn't have any cameras in the bathroom, but they thought I did. It was a heck of a place.

I had a bar in there, made like a horseshoe. Over the top of it hung a gong. And then there was a kitchen. The doors in the studio were shaped like eggs set straight up. But there was no knob on the door to the bedroom in the apartment. You could go in and close the door, but you couldn't get out unless I let you out.

In the bedroom there were three steps up to the bed. I had a bunch of buttons on both sides of the bed. You could turn on a blue light and make it bright, soft or dim; a white light, and make it bright, soft or dim; or a gold light. You could make your own mood under there. And there was a button you could press that would make the side panels of the bed close. I could see you outside, but you couldn't see me in there. And I had big, thick blackout drapes. I could punch a button and they would close.

At the foot of the bed I had a record-player. It could play records, cassettes and reel-to-reel tapes. You could open up the top of this unit and there was a big 30in TV.

Above the bed here the ceiling was all mirrored. It was square. I had two bedposts from the floor to the ceiling on both sides. Hidden behind the mirror was an infrared camera which could see in the dark. If I wanted to film with it, I just had to mash 'record' and turn out the lights. Some chick would be giving me head or something and I could be filming it, and she would never know.

The band boys didn't know about this camera. They would all say, 'My old lady is just like Tina, she don't care what I do.'

So they going to prove that shit to me. I say, 'Hey, you want go up to my bedroom? You can go up there and lay that broad.'

This guy would go up there and be giving the broad head, doing all kinda shit with the chick. From whatever office I was in, I had the key to the bottom part of the control panel. I would mash 'record,' I would film him doing it.

So I had all the band boys fucking around with other girls and giving them head and getting head, doing all kinds of freakish shit. I got them straight. So for a Christmas present I was going to tell them, 'Hey, I want all of the band to be at the studio at six o'clock. I got something to show you.' Then I was going to show them that I got film on all their sex activities, then say, 'Now, you said your wife won't get mad about you doing it, so when you bring her down Christmas, we going to show the film.'

Anyway, the studio burned down, so I never got a chance to do it.

When you walk in the bathroom, to the left, there is a closet, maybe 10ft long. It had a mirror where you could powder your face. That left wall was all my clothes and shit. In the corner was a floor safe where I kept my money. There were two or three face bowls and I had an eight-jet Jacuzzi with a door on it. We used to have a lot of fun up there.

Some girl, I don't know who she was ... man, I am downstairs recording, and this girl gets in the Jacuzzi with my cashmere coat and puts it on the floor to step on while she dries off. Would you believe that? She took a damn $3,000, $4,000 coat and put it on the floor so she could dry off.

The bathroom had the only window in the whole building. Inside the rest of the building you would never know whether it was day or night. Sometimes I would be recording up there for four or five days and the only way I knew that this length of time had passed was that the people who were hanging with me would keep disappearing and coming back in fresh clothes. Otherwise, you could stay up there for three or four days and not know you'd been up there that long.

I never went home. When I first built the place, I'd go home once or twice a week. Tina would bring me food down there, or send the maid with it. We led separate lives, except when I was going to record. If I came up with a good song or something, I would call her down there. Sometimes I would call her at night and say, 'Hey, baby, I got this song, it goes like this. This is the highest note you gotta sing. Is it too high?'

I just woke her up. She's in her bedroom, four o'clock in the morning, and I'm telling her to sing out real loud. And she would do it. She said, 'No, it's high enough.'

It was a lot of fun, thinking about this shit. I was five or six minutes from the studio. We would record and I would create

song after song after song. I was creating so many music tracks
I had to hire some writers to write words for them. I was
creating too fast. I hired Leon Ware, who is a big songwriter.
I used a lot of songwriters.

I had a deal with the record company whereby they would
give me $1,600 a week for writers. They was to pay half. I told
them I had eight writers and was spending $3,200 a week in
total. So United Artists were paying half and I was paying half,
but I didn't really have but a couple of writers.

I wrote a lot of songs, and started Tina writing songs too. I
would put my stepdaddy's name on some of them, Philip Reese
– he was dead by then – or I'd put 'written by Ernest Lane'.
Ernest never wrote no songs. I would put anybody's name on
as producer or writer. I did a lot of screwy stuff.

Hiring out the main studio made money. The Rolling Stones
came there to record, and Frank Zappa, Bobby Womack. Leon
Haywood recorded his hits there, and the Gap Band, Three
Dog Night, Billy Preston, Natalie Cole and Chaka Khan. Every
artist who was about anything came through there.

Around the corner, Ike also had two rehearsal studios
which he hired out. But he didn't rent out his own studio,
reserving it for his exclusive use. In spite of the through
traffic, he judges the studio to have been a failure – and
cocaine was at the root of the problem. His own output,
too, began to falter as the drug took its toll.

I put up the studio for one reason and was using it for another.
There were so many people in that studio, man, because there
was so much cocaine in there. People just wanted to come
there to get high. I defeated my own purpose. I never did open
the other offices I had planned down the street to help
musicians and acts and things.

Snorting cocaine can make you forget you are tired. It gives
you a false energy. And when you come down, if you don't
have some more, then you in trouble, 'cos you going to be
feeling like shit. But you have as much of it as I had, and when
you get real tired your body shuts down. You draw some and
it does you no good, so you fall asleep.

Ike would fall asleep across the mixing desk. Or, if he managed to get home, doped up, Tina would lay him across her lap and feed him while he was asleep. Mel Johnson, Nancy's husband, says Ike is the only person he has ever seen who could eat while he was asleep.

Ike also had other troubles.

The first time I got in trouble with the police was about a blue box. It had to be 1970–71. The studio was just built.

A blue box is a thing that allows you to charge your phone calls to someone else. You dial a number and when it rings you push the button on the box and the number you're calling becomes your phone number. I can sit there all day making calls and they going to be charging that phone. So you dial an office number, and as soon as you punch the button they charge all your calls to that company – and they don't ever notice. I bought a couple of those.

In my studio, I had a booking agency named Sputnik. This guy was running my booking agency 'cos he didn't have no money, that mother. He was doing a good job, and he was using this blue box.

But they made a gadget that could trace the blue box. While we were out of town one week, Dave, this boy, was making a phone call on the blue box and this voice came in and told him, 'Hey, we know you are using a blue box.'

What he should have done was stop using it, and if he had told me, I would have made him stop using it. But nobody told me shit. So he kept using it and they traced it to my studio.

So one day, I am sitting there in the studio and in come all these damn Feds. They found the blue boxes and arrested me. I got this lawyer, Paul Caruso, who in some kind of way got me off the hook. I paid $3,000 or whatever it was and I got out of it.

At that time, there were a lot of women around in the studio. I was doing everything you could fucking name. Sometimes I would be sitting mixing at the board and two girls would be under the console sucking my dick. If you looked in, it would look like I was in there by myself. Sometimes I would go out into the studio and dim the lights and take three or four girls and freak off. There wasn't no AIDS or nothing in them days. You could do anything. It was just fun, fun, man.

One time, I was at the studio and it was one of my friends' birthdays. This guy always wanted to have sex with my women, probably just because they were my women or someone I'd had before. This really made him want to be with them even more.

I had one of my secretaries get eight girls I was going with or had gone with. Real pretty girls they were, stacked like brick shithouses, man. Two of the chicks were black and the rest were white. It was my birthday surprise.

I called this guy on the phone and told him to come down to my studio. The girls were already there waiting. They were all wearing nothing but men's shirts, no bottoms. I hid them upstairs in the apartment section of the studio. When he arrived, I sent him upstairs to get me some orange juice, knowing that he wasn't going to come back down. He went up and was gone for about twenty minutes. I finished the recording I was working on and went upstairs to check on him and see what was happening.

He had never been in this type of situation before and he was too excited to get a hard-on. I tried encouraging him. I sat on the couch between two of the girls. I had another girl sitting on each of my knees. On the floor, held between my feet so that it was pointing upwards, was a magic wand vibrator. As I fingered a girl with each of my hands, another girl squatted down between my legs on top of the vibrator.

After about fifteen minutes of this, my friend had made his way over to the bedroom doorway, where he was standing, surrounded by three women. He had one girl kissing on each of his nipples while the third girl got down and was pulling and sucking on his dick. The girl who was giving him head was the kind who refused to be outdone. She was determined to get him hard.

Then I had to go to the bathroom. When I squeezed past them, he looked at me with a real perplexed expression on his face. His dick still wasn't getting hard, despite her best efforts.

When I came back from the restroom, I noticed that she was beginning to get him a little hard.

Now this guy was a car salesman. So, just to be fucking with him, I asked him, 'Hey, how much do you have to put down on a new car?'

He looked up at me, losing his concentration, and said, 'Oh, fuck.'

As he spoke, his dick went limp again. So I got those three girls in the bed and we had a nice foursome together. And I wound up fucking all eight of those women myself.

This guy is an old friend, and whenever I talk about that birthday present I gave him, he says, 'Ike, tell the whole story; you gave them to me but you fucked them all yourself!'

Ike concedes that he is oversexed and that there was no way Tina alone could have kept him-satisfied. Despite his excesses, he still managed to maintain the loyalty of the women closest to him. Yet because of drugs, he would lose them all.

I love sex, I love pretty girls and I love honesty and sex without games. I respect a woman to be just herself. If she's a whore and she is asked that, just be honest about it. If she is a groupie and admits it without me even asking her, well, I respect that too. Her being whatever she is wouldn't change my intentions one way or the other. I can admire and respect this kind of people.

My special women at the time were Ann Thomas, Tina, Rhonda and Ann Cain. Those were like my women. And Tina was *the* woman.

By about 1974, my nose got fucked up really bad. I'd burned this hole through my nose. Somebody told me you could smoke cocaine so your nose wouldn't get sore. You get the same effect.

I thought they meant put it in a cigarette and smoke it. So I went and bought a kilo of coke and sifting it filled up cigarettes with it.

Don't get the wrong idea, Tina never did no cocaine – even though she was sometimes high without knowing it. We were sifting a whole kilo and she was sitting in the dust – she had to get high. She was sitting there laughing, but she wasn't even aware that she was high.

But smoking cocaine in a cigarette don't do nothing but make you horny. That's when I found out that's not what they were talking about. They were talking about freebasing.

I paid a guy $2,000 to come down from San Francisco to show me how to make freebase. He taught me how to make it out of ether and drops. Man, I liked freebase 'cos you took a hit off that and it would last you a couple of hours or something.

When I first started taking it, I thought, man, this is the lick. Snorting it, you had to be doing it every few minutes, but with this shit you didn't have to do it that often. That was beginning of the freebase shit. Then it stopped lasting two or three hours. Just as often as you would sniff on cocaine, that's how often you would be putting that fucking pipe in your mouth. Same difference.

On top of that, the high didn't last no time with this freebase. But, man, it's addictive. If you got people around you, you could smoke up to $2,000, $3,000-worth a night, and that ain't shit. And that's what I did. I had a lot of folks around me, more people in my studio than in any club in LA. I had the stuff there free and they were stealing it anyway. If you looking for girls, it's at Bolic. If you looking for dope, it's at Bolic – and it's free. So why wouldn't they be there?

Right now I wish I knew where there was a Bolic, so I could go get the girls. They can have the dope – just give me the girls.

I had a big glass-topped table, 8ft or 10ft long with eight chairs. The chairs' backs were 5ft tall. And I had a picture painted of me on the wall, like nude, just lying down, and I used to sit at that table and take a big turkey-dropper. I was making freebase out of ether and drops.

I would take this big old turkey-dropper and make it in a big old fruit jar. I would measure it out and suck it up. And I would skeet it down the table, watching the little beads grow up. It looked like a forest, man. There was so much cocaine on the table. You would take a razor blade and just draw it up and put it in the pipe.

A lot of people use a torch and things to burn stuff. I bought an electric soldering-iron and cut the end off it so it fitted right down in the neck of the pipe. And I put this thing in there and the soldering-iron in there, so then you don't need no more matches.

Sometimes I would be so tired, I would sit at this table fighting sleep. One time I got a hole in my leg. I went to sleep with the soldering-iron in my hand.

Another time I was incoherent and asleep in the bed. I had a little rack the soldering-iron hung in. It was on, and I had cocaine right there by the bed.

Man, I was dreaming I was smoking a cigarette and I reached over and got this red-hot soldering-iron with my first two fingers and brought it to my mouth. Then I woke up and saw it was the soldering-iron. That fucking thing didn't start burning me until I became aware that I had it to my mouth.

Sometimes the cocaine would make me talk too much and I would leave the soldering-iron in the pipe too long. I have been high-running my mouth talking and the neck of the pipe's been hot, and I've put the wrong end of the pipe in my fucking mouth, too.

Tina says that she hated me doing cocaine. The only thing I think she could have hated is that I would stay up for seven, eight days in the studio without any sleep, and when I was doing cocaine I would never go home. My house was only three miles from the studio but I never went home. I think she hated what I was doing with cocaine and the people I was hanging with, the people who were doing cocaine with me and the girls and the whole thing. It kept me away from her and the kids. I think, if she thinks about it, that's more what she disliked than me doing the cocaine.

Some people, when they do cocaine, they got a total different personality. They do all kinds of shit. They're tripping. They start seeing things; they start thinking things. They doing all kinds of stuff: peeping out of windows, searching on the floor to see if they can find a rock, all kinds of stuff.

Tina said my personality changed, but my personality didn't change. What it was, man, was that when I'd been up for six nights with no sleep, I was more irritable. I was more edgy. You could piss me off quicker.

I feel that I was just like I am now. The difference in me now is that I don't talk about what I am going to do, I do it. When

I was doing cocaine, I would sit up and philosophise and procrastinate. I would talk about what I was going to do, but I wouldn't do shit. I'd work on one record for two months. At first, the song would sound like a smash hit, then the next day I'd change all of it. It didn't matter, because there was always a bunch of people with me, tagging along for free cocaine. I had a lot of freeloaders who were always around me, saying, 'Ike, I love you. Ike, I love you.'

I was giving away mink coats. Somebody came by with chinchillas and minks and I would give them three or four ounces of cocaine for five or six or seven of them, and all kinds of dresses for women and things. They would come round and I would just give them four ounces of coke and I'd take whatever they had – diamonds, I didn't care what it was. I would just give them what they wanted, and then I would take the mink or whatever and just give it away. Just stupid, man. I gave away three fortunes. It was an experience. I don't regret it, but I wouldn't do it again. A lot of people never had the chance to experience how it feels to give on that level, but I did. It is kinda selfish, but I don't regret it.

Tina ain't got no mind for no business. She ain't never been about business. As long as Tina can go shopping, she don't care nothing about no money. I know that for a fact. She bought 125 pairs of shoes in one store. I would go to Hong Kong and I would buy $10,000-worth of hair. It was like buying $100,000-worth of hair in the States. It was her hair, she paid for it. She's not the type who checks her finances. She never knew if she had $100,000 in the bank or whether she got $100 million. She doesn't care about that as long as she can go shopping. She's always been like that.

She's lying about not having her own money. She would come down to the studio and I would give her $20,000 and Ann Thomas $10,000 to go shopping. We went to Paris, France, I gave her $80,000 and she went shopping. She was gone an hour and a half and still owed $15,000 at the store. What does she mean, I didn't give her no money? I think that is the way she feels because when she started writing songs she said, 'Ike, put me on salary as a songwriter so I can have my own money every week.'

Tina is justly proud of writing 'Nutbush City Limits'. But she just wrote the words: Ike provided the music.

After she learned how to write songs, I put her on salary. I gave her the $400 a month we give the songwriters. That's $100 a week. $100 ain't going to buy shit. The dresses she wears cost $100 to $10,000 so what good is $100? To her, that $100 felt like she earned it. If I give her $200,000 to go shopping it meant nothing, 'cos she didn't feel she'd earned it.

It was greatly to Ike's advantage that Tina spent so much money on clothes during the androgynous period of the early 1970s. Back then, he didn't bother to buy clothes. He was small enough to fit into hers.

16 I've Been Loving You Too Long

In a case of life imitating art, the climax of Ike and Tina's show was Otis Redding's 'I've Been Loving You Too Long'. Their version, however, suggested anything but that. In fact, it was so hot that it was banned in Austria.

WE WENT TO VIENNA, where we were supposed to do TV. They had seen us doing 'I've Been Loving You' in London, and when we landed, man, they would not let us go on TV. They thought we were going to do that damn song. So I called a press conference, and I told them they were prejudiced because we'd been out to this club and they charged me $1,600 for five bottles of champagne and just a whole bunch of crap, man. Anyway, that blew the controversy up real big.

'I've Been Loving You Too Long' got to be the song that the people want to hear because of Tina stroking the microphone like it's a penis and me talking in the background, saying, 'Hey, baby, I ain't never tried nothing like this before.' And I would, like, slurp, and do the stuff on the microphone with the lights real low. And she'd say, 'Do it some more.' It was real sexy shit.

Today, man, they're doing everything, but then . . . well, it was just the timing of it.

Maybe we would never have recorded it if I'd ever known where we were when I was on cocaine. I was asleep on the airplane on the way to New York, where we were playing Madison Square Gardens. I had no idea where we were, and I couldn't have cared less. All I knew was I would get there, I would go in the dressing room, the curtains would open, I'd come out, I'd do my show, I'd go back, I'd go to the party room and then I'd go to sleep before the next town. I wasn't interested in where we were. Had I known that we were at Madison Square Gardens, I never would have done 'I've Been Loving You Too Long'. Madison Square Gardens is one of the places where you got the stiff shirts, which is the thing that made the record go into the Top Ten. But I didn't know where we were, so I did it. And – bam! – a hit.

> This sexy stage image concealed the root of their problem. While Ike just wanted to live his life, Tina seems to have been expecting that one day he would change and become a regular husband.

She was expecting a lie. Today, I could live that type of life. But then . . . I wasn't living that kind of life when I met her. When I met Tina I had the keys to thirty-two women's apartments. And I was fucking all thirty-two a couple of times a week in the early days in St Louis. Tina knew that.

As I said before, she would go get girls for me when she was going with Raymond. I'd say, 'Tina, go get that girl there, tell her to get a cab and go to my house. That one over there, tell her to wait in the car. And that one out there, act like she is your friend, she ain't with me, and she ride in the car too.' And I'd have all of them. And Tina got these girls for me.

Tina knew that I loved women with big asses, and real curvy legs, or women who would spoil me by giving me exactly what I wanted, when I wanted it. I told Tina all about these girls I was going with 'cos she was my buddy. Tina knows everything I like and don't like about women. So she tried to be all that I wanted, rather than be herself.

It's like, when you meet somebody and you are really straight and honest with them, being what you are, and they accept you that way. But when they get you, or think they've got you, they expect you to change. Well, I don't think that's no good. That's no good at all.

Tina, she started to cry a lot man, but not letting me see it, hiding it from me. Around then, this was 1965, I was really tight with a girl named Gloria. Gloria was a gorgeous woman,

Spanish. I started spending all of my leisure time with her. I was crazy about this girl. I bought her a brand new '65 Pontiac Convertible and Tina found that out and so ... Well, she wasn't mad about me buying the car, she was mad because this girl looked like Sophia Loren. She was very pretty. Tina hated going onstage without me, so when she pissed me off I'd punish her by threatening not to go to work with her and suggesting she went alone.

A couple of times, I told her I had to finish mixing in the studio, but this was something I couldn't help – I had a deadline to get it to the record company. But then sometimes I would get pissed off with her because she was mad because I brought some lipstick home or something. Anyway, Tina never did like to go onstage without me, and so I would use this as a tool. I was just evil, man. I say, 'I'm not going to work, I'm gonna stay home.'

One night, man, we were playing in LA at a popular nightclub on Crenshaw Boulevard and Exposition. Tina was pissed off because I had bought Gloria that car. When she said, 'Ike, come on, it's time for us to get ready to go,' I said, 'I ain't going.'

She kept begging me to go, as the time to leave got near, she came into the bedroom for the last time and asked me to please go. Again I told her I wouldn't. Then she kissed me and said that she was leaving to go to work.

When Tina drove away in her Jaguar XKE, I got this funny feeling that something was wrong with her. After about ten minutes, my feeling of dread intensified. It was only maybe fifteen blocks from where we lived to the club we were playing at. So I jumped into my clothes and flew down to the club.

When I got there, it was time for the show to start, so I didn't go into the dressing room, I just knocked on the door as I was passing and said, 'Hey, time for the show.' Then I went up onstage and started the theme song on the guitar, ready for Tina to join me.

While I was playing, Ester, one of the long-serving Ikettes, came over to me onstage and whispered that I had better come to the back and see about Tina. By the expression on her face, I knew something was terribly wrong. I shouted for the band to keep playing and then I headed for the dressing room.

On the way Rhonda told me it appeared that Tina had taken
some sort of pills. I walked into the dressing room and she was
lying down, her eyes rolled back in her head. She was foaming
at the mouth. Either they had taken her wig off her head or she
hadn't put it on.

I told Rhonda to get the car and pull up in front of the club.
I picked Tina up and put her in the car and rushed to the
nearest hospital. I went to maybe five hospitals in LA and none
of them took suicide patients. Finally I carried her in my arms
into a hospital on the corner of La Brea and Coliseum, and
they told me to take her to the Daniel Freedman Memorial
Hospital. They said that they had the facilities there and gave
me directions.

When we got there, the hospital staff asked me, 'What did
she take?'

I didn't know for sure, but I guessed that they were some
type of sleeping-pills. They had me looking through this pill
book. I called the housekeeper to check any prescriptions there
might have been in the bathroom cabinet.

The housekeeper found something. It seems Tina had taken
all of the medicine out of the capsules and swallowed that
instead of the capsules themselves. The capsules were still
floating in the can, where she had tried to flush them. So the
housekeeper brought them out to the hospital. We found out
later that Tina had taken about forty of the powerful sedative
Tuinal.

She was on the table and they had put her on this respirator
machine with this bag that was breathing in and out when she
breathed. Her tongue was all swollen up in her mouth. As I
watched, this air bag slowed down, then stopped altogether.
The doctor snapped his mask off his face and he shook his
head, like he couldn't save her, 'cos I had been running around
with her for hours, trying to get someone to take her into a
hospital.

I flashed back on some conversation that Tina and I had had
in the past. She used to tell me how there was a little man in
her head. When Tina and I sat down and we had no argument,
no nothing and everything was going great, and she was
apologising for something she did, 'cos I don't like to play

onstage when I'm upset, she'd say, 'Ike, it's a little man who sit at a long table and he got a bald head.' I guess, in reality, she was talking about her subconscious mind. She'd say, 'And this little man started telling me that Ike's doing this, and Ike's doing that . . .'

You understand. This little man would tell her everything about me and all the different women I was fooling around with.

'. . . and he keep me upset and I don't want to bring it to you.'

That's the way we talked when we were OK.

During the times when we had these talks, I brought up the subject of what happens to a person when they die. I would tell her to imagine being at the circus and watching the act where a man is riding a motorcycle around the walls on a circular room. I told her to imagine she was in a room like that and was trying to get out by climbing to the top. The closer she got to the top, the more tired she would become. If she ever became too weak and gave up the struggle, she would drop back down to the bottom and die there. But as long as she kept trying she would be all right.

I walked over to the table to where she was in the hospital. She was lying there all still and unmoving. All I could see were the whites of her eyes and her tongue all swollen and hanging out of her mouth.

I say, 'Ann, if you can hear me, move your tongue.'

And her tongue move a little bit, but the air bag was still stopped completely.

I say, 'Hey, you know what, that bag down there stop moving.'

I say, 'You chicken-shit motherfucker. You always said that you wanted to be as much of a woman as I am a man. You're being a fucking coward. We got these four kids so you're gonna leave them all with me so I gotta take care of them? What am I supposed to do, raise the kids by myself?

'You know,' I say, 'that's chicken shit, this ain't the first time you tried to do this. If you're gonna do it, why do you keep leaving me with these damn hospital bills, man? If you really want to die, why don't you just stop putting me through all these damn charges and go to an overpass and wait until a big truck, an eighteen-wheeler, is coming and when he get almost there, then you jump off. Then I got no hospital bills, I don't have no shit.

'Here I am with all these goddamn bills and all four of these kids that we are raising and so you try to take the fucking short-cut out. Anyone can do that.'

It may sound cruel to you, but this is the way we talked to each other, the way we communicated.

I say, 'That little man keep giving you shit, woman, and you keep bringing me the bills. We don't have time for this. I thought you and me had a bond together. Me and you were going to do it. But no, you want to take the short-cut out, you want to leave it all to me. Our livelihood ain't based on me by myself, it's us as a team. If this is what you call being a real friend, go on and die.'

And when I said that, the bag started breathing.

Tina's life was saved, but she had to remain in intensive care for a couple of days. During her recovery she completely lost her sense of taste, but it returned after she regained her health. It was not Tina's only suicide attempt, however.

Three or four times, she tried it. I don't really know why – I'm not a mind-reader. I'd tell her, you keep pulling the same bullshit. She pulled it somewhere in Germany one time; she took those pills and had to have her stomach pumped out by medical personnel. I'm saying, 'Why you keep doing that?' That's a form of looking for attention right there.

Then this other girl that I was living with back then, Ike Junior's mother, Lorraine, she went and drank some poison. She never expressed to me why, but in my opinion when people try to attempt suicide like that they are looking for attention. Anybody that really want to commit suicide, man, I think they succeed.

And me being the way I was, I didn't stop to think why she was doing it. I let her do what she wanted to do. If she want to die, she could die. It wasn't that I was insensitive, I was just living too fast even to think about her feelings.

But Ike was not unaffected by Tina's suffering. He felt that the problem was that Tina was not frank with him about her feelings.

After the suicide attempt in LA, Tina was OK for a year or so. And then, man, one night, I will never forget it. I had a real expensive Italian car. I got dressed up and I was on my way to see Gloria. I was coming down the hill from the house, and when I got almost to the bottom I suddenly thought about Tina.

A bad feeling came over me, and I made a U-turn on that hill and went back up to the house. When I walked in Tina was down in a corner between the dresser and the wall, cuddled up there, and she was crying so bad, man. That was the worst feeling I ever had. That's when I said to myself, 'Man, what did she do to deserve this?'

I felt like I was really mistreating her. But I was in love with this other girl too. I wanted to do something, but there was nothing I could do. I was torn between the pillar and the post. I didn't like hurting Tina, I really didn't. That time she was showing hurt. I wish today ... If I had known then what I know now, I would never have looked at the other chick again. I would have kept my family together, period. But I didn't know.

Right now, I am trying to make the best out of life. You can't undo what's done. I am not apologising for nothing I did, but I regret a lot of the things I have done.

Tina always acted like she accepted what I did, which is what I wanted to hear. We both lived a lie. She said it didn't bother her. She told me it didn't matter to her about me going to bed with a different girl every night, but it would worry her if I started seeing any of them on a regular basis. It was a lie, but it was what I wanted to hear at the time. It served my purpose, and I played on it. I lived my life as though she didn't mind. And I believed it until the time when I felt funny when I was coming down the hill and went back and she was sitting in the corner crying.

Other times, she was hurt by my behaviour but she hid it. I used to tell her, 'Hey, man, if I am doing something to hurt you, I wish you would tell me.' Because, right or wrong, if I knew how she felt about something, even if I didn't stop doing it, I'd have found another way to do it. I was not going to continue to do something to hurt her and know it. That's the way I felt in my heart.

I don't know if I told her that or not, but that's how I felt. If I am doing something to hurt you and you tell me, I wouldn't say that I'm gonna stop, but you would think I stopped. I would find another way to do it that wouldn't hurt you. I would be more discreet about it.

After that feeling that time, I said to myself she didn't deserve this type of hurt behind the way she was with me. She was giving me all of her. She wasn't no problem to me. I had it all, but I didn't know it. You can't cry over spilt milk, though.

Of course Ike had never promised to be faithful. And it was the sixties, after all. But now, he looks back on all his wildness with a tinge of regret.

You think about it, man. Do you have to get to sixty-three years old to realise that you had the world in your hand and you let it go? You abused it, but you were just young and didn't know. A lot of youngsters today are still making the same fucking mistakes. They got it all, but they can't see for looking. They got everything they looking for right there in their hand, but they out there looking for something else. I guess that's the way life is.

After that, I started showing Tina attention, but I was still fucking around. I wasn't bold with it like I had been. I was more discreet.

I started to be a little closer with Tina – I'd go to a movie with her and the kids. In those days, I thought buying her material things would give her what I wasn't able to give her. But it didn't. Whatever I did thinking I was making up for things led her to believe that I had got jealous and possessive, and she started giving me problems about wanting to break up and shit. Because, I guess, that's when she saw some weakness in me. I was trying to hold it together.

A year before that, if she had been talking about a break-up, I would have said, 'Well, fuck you.' Now I was trying to talk her into staying.

So now she knew I cared about something and my face got watched. She watched my face as much as she could, but you can't watch my face too much because I am going to respond to it. You push it too much and I am going to react. But she did it as much as she could.

That's when I started to hear about her and Johnny Williams, the baritone-player with my band. He was an older guy and Tina was supposed to have really liked him, because he was yellow. That's the way my oldest son's natural father, Raymond, is – one of those yellow niggers with curly hair.

So then I was possessive. I didn't want anybody else to have her. Before she started giving me trouble I don't think I was. It was then I realised that I could lose her and my family.

But I can't take the whole of the blame. My feeling about any relationship is this. Whatever happens, the fault is fifty-fifty. I'll explain what I mean. If you got an old lady and she fuck around all the time, she do that to you every day and you take it, you are just as responsible as she is, for staying there and taking it. Same thing if you're her old man and you come home and beat her ass every day, and she still there, taking it – it is just as much her fault as it is yours. So it is fifty-fifty. She can't say it is your fault just 'cos you beat her.

Say you and your wife break up because you are whorish and you've been messing around and she stayed home and cried. OK, she could say it's your fault because you been messing around. Or say she work all the time and you go gamble off the money. In the final analysis, man, in my opinion, whatever reason you broke up, it's not your fault, it's not her fault. You both got 50 per cent here, because one of you stayed there and took it.

In other words, if I beat Tina every day, if I did what they say I did, if I fought her every day and she stayed there for eighteen years and she took it, it's as much her fault as it is mine. Why did she stay there for eighteen years? If she left at the end of eighteen years, she could have left the second day.

Tina did run away once. These pimps out here in LA, if the

chick don't bring in enough money, they take a coat hanger, wind it up and spank her on the butt with it. One time when I was hanging out with them, Tina done something. She ran away and I caught up with the bus she was on and I got her off and spanked her on the butt with a hanger.

> But Ike's argument is that, given that Tina escaped easily enough in the end, she could have done it at any time if she had really wanted to. At the time, he put down her running off to the same attention-seeking behaviour that motivated her suicide attempts.
> And that was their tragedy. She craved the attention he could not give.

You know, I've never had love for Tina like husband for wife. I loved her like a brother loves a sister. I don't know if she loved me or was in love with me: I think it was more that she was in my corner. We were just two peas in the hub. I didn't always enjoy sex with Tina. She didn't appeal to me like that. She is not my kind of woman. You-all look at her and say, 'Oh man, she is sexy, she is attractive.' She is attractive but she's never had no sex appeal for me. She's got these legs, but there is nothing sensuous about her. I taught her the movements for excitement. She's attractive because of what I taught her, the way I taught her to use her body.

> Ike feels that the accounts of their fights have been exaggerated.

I don't go around slapping. I'm not the type to do that. But I don't take no shit, man – don't nobody be hollering at me like I am no fucking kid or nothing, man. Or doing nasty shit, man. If you want to provoke me, all you got to do is holler at me or call me some kind of fucking name, and you got it. I've got a hell of a temper.
Sure, I've slapped Tina. We had fights and there have been times when I punched her without thinking. But I never beat her. Man, my mother was a woman. I loved my mother. I did no more to Tina than I would mind somebody doing to my mother in the same circumstances.

I hit her with a shoe one time. I picked up a shoe and slung it at her. I was just young and stupid. I ain't justifying anything I did, but I ain't lying, neither. What I did, I did.

But the strains within the relationship – both personal and professional – were enormous.

You see, I've always felt like I was the one who should carry all the worries, whatever they may be. Whenever I saw Tina looking down or worried, looking like maybe she was trying to hide something from me, I would always go and ask her, 'Ann, what's wrong?'

And she would lie and say nothing was wrong. I would repeat myself to her over and over again for as long as those vibes kept coming from her.

Shit, that really messed up my whole concentration on business, especially since the woman I lived with both as a wife and a performing partner was the centre of attraction. I had a lot of problems on my mind, such as which songs to record, the choreography for the stage, arranging, booking, publishing, management and our personal bills, not to mention the expense of the whole group, because I carried that burden on my shoulders, too. I worried about the employees' problems as well as my own. Ike and Tina's name was carrying all that. Our bills sometimes ran from $35,000 to $75,000 per month. I had really to hustle to think of ways to stay above water.

So when Tina got these attitudes, which would last for two or three days, I would finally get fed up. I would end up slapping her or something. Then she would tell me that she was wrong. Most of the time it would end up being about some woman that I was going with whom I didn't think she knew about.

She felt that it was disrespectful, that she was being used and mistreated, while I felt that if she had told me how she felt in the beginning, the fight could have been avoided. Tina had her pride and her attempts to please me caused 99 per cent of our fights.

Our fights were never over me being jealous of another man, they were always about her being secretive and unwilling to share her feelings and thoughts with me. She was afraid she would reveal herself to be jealous, an emotion she knew I despised in other women in the past.

I'm no sadist. I don't really know what a sadist is, but I've never liked hurting people. I've always considered myself as a loving and giving person. But I have hurt people mentally and physically in the past, through being angry or dissatisfied, or because things haven't gone my way. I've hurt people's feelings by speaking out harshly before thinking about what it was I was saying, or by being too blunt. And I have got a terrible temper, worse than you think it is, worse than you will ever know.

Tina is not a masochist, either. If having a fight with your spouse or your loved one makes you a wife-beater, then I am guilty.

Ike admits having a very dominating character, but thinks
Tina managed to confuse the line between business, in
which he was forceful, and their personal lives.

She is the one who put me in control of her life, not me. I was in control of the stage. Now, if she brought that back into the house, that's her fault.

Onstage, I told her everything to do – every single move, which way to wear her hair, what clothes to wear and how to wear them, what words to say, the expression to use when she was saying them. And because I was doing all of that, it rubbed off on to my personal life, to the point where, if I told her to go buy furniture for the bedroom, she would say, 'No, Ike, I don't want to go do that because you may not like it.' She was the one who put it there, not me.

OK, so I was very inconsiderate in many ways, not just to Tina, but to many people. But you've got to understand that I was trying to pull together a black group during those days and it was a hard struggle. To try to get ahead, I found myself having to be aggressive, forceful and even dominating.

From the Kings of Rhythm on, I would tell the drummer every beat to play. I would tell the saxophone-player every note to play. Every step, every time anyone turned this way or that way. That attitude got things accomplished; it was a tool that got results. My shows were enjoyable, and Ike and Tina's bills were always paid.

As far as the band was concerned, this was what I was totally in control of. In the final analysis, it had to be what I wanted. But otherwise, professionally, I was not controlling her. I was encouraging her to go in the studio with Phil Spector and Bob Crewe.

When someone is around you twenty-four hours a day, they just get so they're programmed subconsciously. You're not aware that that's what you are doing, but it is. When you tell them to do it on their own, they've got no mind of their own. You know, it is like someone's taken their mind. But it is not something you do intentionally.

It's not about doing what I say, it's about attitude. If I told Tina to go home because the housekeeper wasn't going to be there with the kids, and she decided she was going to a movie instead while I was thinking she was at home with those kids, that would piss me off. And if I said something to her – 'Where the fuck you been?' or whatever – and she said, 'I went to the movies,' and I said, 'That's not what you supposed to do, you supposed to go home to the kids,' and she said, 'Well, I can do what I want to do,' that would start a fight, right there.

So it wasn't as if Ike expected Tina to do as she was told, though admittedly he has a rather old-fashioned view of sexual roles.

I don't feel that a woman is inferior. I don't feel that she's superior to me, either. I believe we both have a role to play. We are equal partners, but both of us have duties to perform.

I feel that a man was made to do tough shit, not that it is any easier than the woman's shit. A woman's shit – home all day cleaning the house, scrubbing floors, washing clothes and shit – that is a hard job, man. The man's role, doing all this labour or brainstorming or whatever it is, that's hard too. You dig what I'm talking about? I think that this stuff has been stretched too far.

On the other hand, Ike surrounded himself with women –
not just as lovers, but as employees, confidantes and
friends.

I guess that's the reason why people say I am a pimp. Because,
man, I like women friends. I don't care that much about men
friends. They get jealous of me and they start doing devious
things towards me. It always happens.

Rhonda Graam went out of her way to get attention, but in
a different way. She was extremely, extremely good, man. But
she was a woman, and women . . . When I first started with
her, I was up at my house, so I was with her almost daily.
When I built Bolic, I'd be in the studio recording all the time
and she'd be in the office by herself. And man, she started
doing everything to get noticed. She would let shit pack up on
her desk to the ceiling and be there until nine or ten at night
in the office, like she was so busy. There wasn't that much
work to do. She just wanted some attention.

Earlier on, when we were playing Las Vegas a lot, Rhonda
found this house up there in Mount Olympus. I didn't know
how much the house cost, but I said, 'Rhonda, I'm going to get
you that house.'

She so happy, right? So when we go to Las Vegas to play, I
put the money on the table and say, 'If I win it's the money for
your house; if I lose you don't get it.'

And I rolled the dice – I threw 11 and I won it. I won the
money to pay for the house. I gave her that house.

Then we went out on the road and she moved. She took her
clothes out of the house and she left all her furniture,
everything, in the house, left the door wide open and went out
on the road. People could have gone in and taken everything.
It just so happened that Mel Johnson was going up to check
on the kids and things and he passed by and saw Rhonda's
door open. She did that just to get attention, too.

Finally, she pulled a thing that broke the camel's back. She
got so insecure, she became kind of destructive. People'd be
calling in – that movie *Car Wash*, that was supposed to be our
movie. They called me about it first. But when they went to
Rhonda's office, Rhonda never called them back. She would do

shit like that. When I found out that she wasn't returning phone calls and wasn't confirming with me to get answers to different things, I told Tina about it. I said Rhonda was pissing me off so bad that sometimes I felt like just knocking her ass off. Tina said, 'Ike, if you feel that way about it, it is best you let her go.'

I said, 'Maybe I should let her go. But I want to keep her salary going.'

Every time we worked, I wanted to give her the same amount she would have gotten if she had been working too. I wanted to keep that up until she got a job.

Tina was cold. She said, 'If that's what you want to do, but I wouldn't give her nothing.' So Rhonda came strolling into the studio and we sat down to talk to her. Tina said, 'Ike wants to give you your salary, the same money you always get every time we play, until you get a job.'

She said, 'Oh no, Tina, I wouldn't want you to do that.'

Tina said, 'I'm glad you understand.'

I would have said, 'You gotta take it, I don't mind,' but Tina said, 'I'm glad you understand.'

Well, I thought Rhonda was gone, but she wasn't. She went up to my house and started living at my house with the kids. So that was what Rhonda was doing until me and Tina broke up.

But Ike did not see this as a sign that perhaps the end was coming.

I never thought it would happen in life. I thought Tina and me were too close for something like that to happen. But man, I've learned in this lifetime that anything you wasn't born with, you can do without.

Regardless of what you think is going on, it is nowhere close to what is really happening. Like they say, when your left eye jump and your flesh begin to crawl, you can bet your bottom dollar another mule is kicking your stall. You can never tell what is on a woman's mind. She can be hugging and kissing you and quitting you all at the same time.

Tina wanted, I believe, to leave before I signed another

record contract and got her tied up for another five years. Our contract with United Artists was ending. I had been searching for a record deal for six months. I had shopped a lot of different deals trying to get another contract and finally I landed one with Al Bennett at Cream Records. He was going to get me $150,000, then I was going to get $150,000 guaranteed per year for four years, whether record sales reached that figure or not. It was a five-year contract with two one-year options.

I finally landed the contract on a Monday. We were leaving to play Dallas on Thursday, Saturday and Sunday, and by the time I got back home the following Monday, the lawyer would have drawn up the papers and I was going to sign the contract. Now, I have power of attorney over Tina Turner – Tina, you'd better check if it's still good.

So Tina has got to break up with me before I get back to town, 'cos if she don't and if I sign that contract she is hooked to this record deal for another five years. She has to do it right there – on one of those four days we're in Dallas.

What happened was – and this is goddammed women for you, man – I had been up for five days in the studio recording. That Thursday morning, when the time came for us to go to Dallas to play, the car pulled up in the alley at the back of the studio. Claude, my trumpet-player, Ann Thomas, Tina and Rhonda came in to get me. I had been up for five days, I hadn't had nothing to eat and I was really tired. I didn't even change my clothes. I just ran upstairs to the apartment, pulled on my coat and reached in a bowl for a handful of those little chocolate kisses, those chocolate things inside silver, because I knew I was gonna get hungry when I came down.

So I got outside to the car and my hands were full. I reached to Tina and said, 'Hey Tina, hold these.'

She just looked at me and snobbed her nose and looked away.

I said, 'Hey Claude, hold these,' and I held them out to Claude, who was riding with us to the airport. Claude took the kisses from me and I got in the car. Now, she knows damn well this is the way to get me to knock her ass off man, to start ignoring me and shit. I don't get no shit like this, man. I wasn't the type, still ain't the type. You ask me something, I am going to answer you. Don't turn up your nose at me with no reason. So I said, 'Hey, Tina, what's your problem?'

She just hunched her shoulders.

So we get to the airport and now I'm getting irritable. This is really plucking on my nerves. It is almost like she's messing with me.

On the airplane, when Tina and I were together, I would never fly first class. I went coach, so that Ann Thomas could sit on the outside and Tina by the window, and I would get in the middle and lay across both of them and sleep until we got where we going.

Meantime, I have been doing so much cocaine, staying awake, that I have got this hole through my nose and it is raw all up behind my eyes. I was really fucked up. When I got to sleep and come down off the cocaine, I was trying to put my finger up behind my eye, up my nostril, man. I was trying to put my hand up behind my eyeball. It was hurting me just like when you have a sore and you put some kind of liniment on it, like putting alcohol on an open wound. It was painful, man. I put some more cocaine in there to deaden it. That's how bad it was.

Tina didn't want me to do coke. She was right. Every time I told her my nose was in pain, she'd say, 'You ought to leave it alone. Why you keep messing with it?' Like anyone would do if they loved you.

Now this is the part that brought on the last fight. It started when she was digging at me on the airplane. I asked her something and she turned up her nose at me again. I guess I was too tired to respond. I fell asleep.

When we got to Dallas, I'd been up a long time and I was incoherent. I got in the limousine. I had just woken up and it felt like someone had put iodine, or something else that burns, up my nostril. Then blood started running down my lip. I say, 'Ann, give me a Kleenex.'

Tina turned her head and looked out of the window.

I said, 'Hey, d'you hear me talking to you? Give me a Kleenex.'

She snobbed up her nose and looked back out the window. I said: 'You motherfucker, you.'

I said to Ann Thomas, 'Ann, give me a Kleenex.' She gave me a Kleenex to wipe the blood and stuff off my nose.

Then Tina laughed. I guess she was trying to use psychology on me. I told her, 'You don't laugh when I'm in fucking pain. I been with you when you had TB. I been with you when you had yellow jaundice. I been with you when you tried to commit suicide. I been with you through every fucking thing. Now you going to laugh at me when I'm in pain?'

Man, my nose is killing me and I don't have any cocaine with me. It's with the instruments and stuff.

I said, 'What the fuck's wrong with you?'

Whatever she said to me, man, I was really out there. I slapped the shit out of her. She did it again. Bam. I slapped her again.

And when I slapped her that time, she jumped up in the limo and put her knee in my chest. I said, 'You motherfucker.' I grabbed her by the windpipe to pull her off of me. And I punched her and punched her.

When I hit her, there was blood coming from my eye or something. There'd only been a couple of slaps in the car. I don't know if it was her nose bleeding or if her lips was busted, but there was blood where I hit her. All she was doing was kicking her legs. She wasn't trying to hit me or nothing. And she said, 'You won't ever find nobody to stick with you like I did. You'll see.'

And I said: 'Fuck you! Fuck you! Fuck you! Fuck you!'

Anyway, we go on to the hotel and sit down in these love-seats, or whatever they is, at the foot of the bed. And I sit on this thing, and Rhonda say, 'You want something to eat?'

And I say, yeah. So Rhonda order some food and I lie down on that thing and I go to sleep, and that's the end of it. When I woke up she was gone.

The effect was devastating.

We had to cancel everything I had booked. My life ain't been right since then. Because that was all of my life, man, building the Ike and Tina Revue. Not trying to feature Ike Turner, but building Tina – I wasn't thinking about building Ike. So I wasted my whole life building something and then it got taken away from me.

Ironically, Ike had already recorded an album that, he believes, would have put Tina where her new manager, Roger Davies, put her in the mid-1980s. Only Ike would have done it ten years earlier.

Tina never believed that you could be a superstar unless white folks put you there. She never believed that a black could put you there. This album would have put her there.

But the world had changed. Ike remained rooted in the sexual liberation of the 1960s, while Tina was swept up in the women's liberation of the 1970s.

17 Poor Fool

Ike does not think that Tina's flight was as final as has been made out.

AFTER WE BROKE UP, I got a letter from Tina's lawyer. She had him write it out. She wanted to keep everything like it was: she didn't want to handle no money, she wanted me to get a house for her and the kids, and offstage she didn't want to be Tina Turner no more. But everything else would remain the same.

She was just tired of the embarrassment of being Mrs Turner when I was travelling with four women and fucking all four of them. And the public knew I was going with all four of them.

She never saw me kiss another woman or nothing like that. I don't give none of them no affection in front of each other. But they all know. She would know that I was probably up in this other woman's room. She'd know that I probably bought this mink coat this girl is wearing – she'd assume it, she didn't know it. This is shameful to Tina, embarrassing to her.

But I wasn't thinking like that then. I turned down the deal she offered. My lawyer advised me to take it. It made sense, rather than breaking up. But I told her to go fuck herself. If it ain't going to be like it was, then I didn't want no part of it. I wasn't going to compromise my manhood.

She called me at the studio one day. I said, 'Hey, I don't know why you calling me on this damn phone. If I wanted to find you, I could find you. You don't think I can?'

She said, 'I know you can.'

I said, 'You bullshitting me, yessing me, now. I'll show you.'

I picked up the phone after I talked to her and called a

detective agency and told them I wanted them to find her. They told me to send $250. I sent that down by Robbie, one of the Ikettes.

While Robbie was right there with the $250, one of this company's agents was at a market and saw Tina. She had her wig off, but the guy recognised her. He called in and said, 'Hey, I got the suspect right now.' He followed her to where she was staying. The agents came by and took me up there to show me where she was. So next time Tina called, I said, 'I know where you are. You're at Shorter's house.'

Three weeks after we split up, Tina and I met for a meal at Ship's Restaurant in LA. We sat and we talked and we had fun and whatever and then I took her home. I don't know what I said to her that night. I know it was the first serious conversation we had after we broke up. But I remember that Tina said that after eight or nine years we might get back together again.

But then Ike Junior cut his finger and I could not find my Blue Cross card. I called Tina to get her card, but she was going to a baby shower and did not call back. She said later that she wanted to have some fun before she called. This got me mad. She don't care about the kids. I took my .38 and went looking for her up at Laurel Canyon. I spent all night looking for her, 'til I got real hungry, sick to my stomach. God was with me that night, boy. Anywhere I'd see that bitch – bang! bang! bang!

Another night I was in the studio at the console. The console is up high and down below it, in front, are some theatre seats where people can watch the band playing through a glass wall. I can't see who is down there when I am up at the board.

I was talking to Dennis Rubinstein, telling him how dirty Rhonda was being. She'd been giving Mike Stewart from United Artists records of how much money I had been making and how much I had saved.

Meantime, I don't see this guy sitting down there at the front. This is the truth, on my mother's grave. This guy on the theatre seats was a friend of Dennis Rubinstein's. He got Dennis to look in the office for Rhonda's and Tina's addresses. I knew where Tina was living, but I didn't know where

Rhonda was. I ain't never been to Rhonda's house in my whole life. This sonofabitch went to Rhonda's house and shot inside it with a shotgun. He got up on her roof and sets her house on fire. Then he drove by Tina's house and fired the shotgun. To this day, they think I did that. I had nothing to do with it – I didn't even know about it until the next day. I guess the guy just felt sorry for me and was trying to put the fear in them. I don't know what he thought. He told me later that he did it. He said he thought Rhonda was a dirty bitch, so was Tina, to do that to me. Tina thinks I did it, but I didn't.

I told Rhonda that I was sorry, but I didn't set her house on fire and I didn't shoot in her house. It was not me. I told her I didn't know nothing about it until after it was done, which was the truth. But I don't think she believed me.

Tina was going to take Ike Junior on the road with her. I went out to the airport. A bodyguard got out of her car. He was just a big kid, he didn't know nothing about fighting – he didn't know nothing about nothing. I guess he thought 'cos he was big, that would scare people. It had no bearing on me at all.

I took the keys to Tina's car from him and went down into the airport and onto the airplane, just walked on, past the guards and everything, to see if Ike Junior was on there. But he wasn't on there. So I left and went home. There wasn't no conflict, no nothing.

I had six black-belt karate guys with me. I went back and gave the keys to her bodyguard and said, 'Why don't you go back to school? I don't want to see you no more, not even in hell.'

But the movie confrontation, at her comeback concert, where I'm supposed to have threatened her with a gun, that never happened. I never went there.

There were guns at Bolic, though. Ike's friend and fellow musician Rickey says that after negotiations between Ike and Tina's lawyers had broken down, a threat was made to burn down the studio. The Mafia was mentioned and Bolic became an armed camp, stacked with cases of hand-grenades and machine-guns. Ike says that the only guns at Bolic were those left as security in drug transactions. However, the police got wind of the arms cache and raided the studio. The machine-guns were hidden on the top of the drum baffle. Officers failed to find them when all the time they were directly above their heads.

It was then that Ike fell into a deep depression as he slowly realised that everything he had created was slipping away from him.

When Tina left, I didn't have but $80,000 in the bank – enough to pay one month's bills. That was all the money I had in the world. I got scared. I panicked. I thought, how we going to pay all these bills when we're not working?

I didn't think, if we're not working I won't have all them bills, 'cos I wouldn't have twenty-six people flying every weekend. There won't be that for me to pay. A lot of things weren't going to be there for me to pay for if Tina and me weren't together.

I had some tax-shelters I had done the year before, some oil-wells up in Calgary, Canada. I had never earned more than $300 out of that investment, but when Tina and I broke up, all at once, these oil-wells gave me $6,000. The next month it went up to $14,000, the next month $22,000. Then it went up to $56,000 a month. This helped me for a while.

Once we reached $1 million, the company was audited. They found that these people were paying me in Canadian dollars, which are worth less than American money. So this company owed us $180,000 and the auditors filed a suit against it. The company stopped the distribution without notice because of the suit. Everything got hung up, man, and it has been that way since 1982. I don't know what is going to be done about it – I got to call somebody and find out.

I had also invested in 310 apartment units in Anaheim, 1515 North Street, I think it was $125,000. I was one of the major shareholders. Something happened and the building got in trouble and started losing money. There were Jewish people over there and the other people did not like them staying there. Anyway, they needed money and kept on losing it. I gave them

$100,000 and became a general partner. I owned 51 per cent of it. All of a sudden, the damn thing started making money. The note was $26,000 a month. I was getting about $4,800 a month off that investment, which was pretty good. They traded in some property on the deal, some houses down Huntingdon Beach, on Santa Barbara Lane – houses which had a miniature golf course and a dock at the back where you could tie your boat. It was a nice place. But we ended up with a whole pile of shit and we got fucked out of it somehow – I forget how.

> Although Ike and Tina were never legally married, Ike says they got divorced to divide the community assets.

Lawyers is scumbags, man. When they hear 'Tina Turner', they go wow. They get all kinds of big ideas. When we went down to court to talk to the lawyer, Tina said she didn't want anything but the divorce. She didn't want none of the property, she didn't want nothing. She wanted to keep the name. She didn't want no royalties. She didn't want no nothing. I could have everything. And this is what the court did.

Meantime, Tina and me met in the hallway of the courthouse. We were just sitting down side by side, talking; Tina's lawyer comes up and takes her by the hand and sits her across from me, on the other side of the hall. He didn't want me talking to her. I guess he was scared she'd change her mind about the split.

> The split between Ike and Tina Turner – both personally and professionally – was now irrevocable. Suddenly, Ike was alone.

Here I am with a car with no motor. How am I going to get where I am going – push it?

Before Tina and I broke up, I had twenty-five people around me every day, telling me they loved me. 'Oh Ike, I love you, I love you, I love you.' All that bullshit. To them bastards it ain't nothing but a word, man. They don't mean shit.

Then I found myself alone for the first time in, what, thirty years? None of the 'I love you' assholes were there then; none of them. When they thought I had no money, they was all gone. There I was in this big, $2.5 million studio by myself, 'cos they thought I didn't have no money. There was nobody there but me. I had a microphone way out over the console. When I turned it on, it automatically shut off the speakers, so I could sing into it and listen through the headphones.

I started crying, man, and I mashed 'record'. And I started singing.

> Lord, I don't know how to pray,
> So I'm going to sing you what I have to say.
> You took away my Momma B.,
> She was the onlyest true friend to me.
> Right now, God, I need Momma B.,
> Because I need someone that's really close to me.
> So God, I'm sure you understand and see,
> Why I need to talk to my Momma B.
> 'Cos Lord, this world is hard.
> I feel so all alone.
> Every time I think I have a friend,
> Before the relationship starts, it ends.
> So God, I am sure you understand and see,
> Why I need to talk to my Momma B.

Anyway, I sing that and I am so alone I started crying. I stopped the tape. When my secretary and everybody heard that, and the people at the record company, they said man, you need to put that out. But I wouldn't put it out because I was crying on it. So I got somebody to write the words off. She wrote the words off. But there were too many words to say. I could never put all them words on no record. The way I was singing, they were just coming to me off my head.

> Ike sorely missed Momma B., his mother, because Tina was the only other woman in his life who had given him a sense of security.

Out of all the women I have gone with, Tina was more of a

mother to me. I ain't never felt like she was no woman of mine. She don't appeal to me as no woman of mine. Never. But I felt protected. If I got sick, couldn't work no more to support my family, I felt as comfortable with Tina as if I was with my mother. I never expressed this to Tina, but that's the way I felt. I felt secure. And it's not the singing, either. The singing don't have nothing to do with it. She do it, even scrubbing floors. It was her loyalty.

From the beginning, if I told Tina to shoot a man, she wouldn't think twice. She would pull the trigger. We had that kind of relationship. We was one person. I didn't give a shit about shit. If I wanted to get out there on the street with two guns and start shooting, I didn't give a fuck about the police. If I'm set up with cocaine, I don't care if the police come here and take me to jail. You don't give a shit about nothing when your mother's got her arms around you.

Now, I wasn't thinking Tina was my momma. It is today I am thinking about that. At that time I was not even aware of what made me what I was. But I never felt that security with any of my other women.

I told my sister about the recording I had made, and two years later, when she got real, real sick, knowing she was going to die, she called me. She said: 'Sonny, I would like to hear that record you sang about Momma.'

She wanted me to come to St Louis. She wanted to see me real bad. And the way she sounded, man, I had to go, because she sounded like she wasn't going to see me no more. So I said OK.

I couldn't find the damn tape nowhere, man, absolutely nowhere. I couldn't find that fucking tape to take with me. The day I was fixing to go to St Louis to see my sister, somebody working in the studio blew the goddamn speakers. On the way out the door, they say, 'Ike, where are the speakers?'

So I pulled down the ladder and went up in the attic to show him where the speakers were so he could replace them. When we got back to the ladder, where you hold on to something to make your first step there was the Momma B. tape sitting there. So I took it to St Louis.

My sister was all the way gone with the cobalt treatment and all of her hair was gone. The cancer had settled in her lungs and in her spine. She didn't have no strength in her back so she was bent all the way down in the bed. But she put on the headphones and listened to the tape.

And she said: 'Sonny, you say you don't know how to pray. You praying here.' Like when I was singing I was praying, you know?

She really loved it. I don't know what happened to the song after that. I don't know whether I left it there with her, 'cos she died that night.

But I regret going to see my sister. This is why today, man, I don't go to nobody's funeral and I ain't going to the hospital to visit anyone, either. I don't want to remember people like that. I can't picture my sister no kind of way but how I saw her in the hospital. I don't want to remember nobody like that. I want to remember them healthy. I don't want to remember them up in some hospital dead or dying or something. That's a screwed-up memory, man.

Ike had not been totally deserted. Ann Thomas stuck by him. He had the money to buy cocaine, which attracted girls, and there were other women in his life, too. Yet at his lowest ebb this was scant consolation.

I am in my bedroom. Ain't no TV on. I bought this house for over a quarter of a million dollars, and here I was sitting in it alone. I was totally spiritually drained. It was like I was in the dark, like what the fuck am I living for? What am I going through all this for? All these depressions and shit?

I was just sitting there in that room, man, on the side of the bed. I was just so down, just tired. And I kept on telling people I was tired, but I didn't know what I was tired of. I wasn't tired like I couldn't get up and play the piano or go chop wood. It's like everybody was draining off me. It's everybody but yourself. It's Ike Turner loves everybody, but who loves Ike Turner?

I don't know where Ann Thomas was. I was going with two other girls, Nanya and Mary Lee. Mary Lee was a big singer around St Louis in those days, and Nanya was just a very pretty girl from Ethiopia. Those girls weren't with me that night. Nanya was in the house, but over the other side where she was living, and Mary Lee was at home.

It was around 1.30 in the morning. I had a .57 magnum pistol. All at once, man, as I sat on the side of the bed, I reached down and got this gun and put it in my mouth. And then I blinked and pulled the trigger. The gun clicked and the hammer hit the bullet and put a dent in it, but it didn't shoot. At that moment, the phone rang.

It was one of the Ikettes, Marcie Thomas, asking if I was all right. Then Nanya opened the door without knocking. She called me Dracula. She said, 'Dracula, you all right? You all right!'

While I was talking to her, I got a beep on the phone and it was Mary Lee – 'Ike, are you all right?' I guess they all felt it.

Mary Lee and her husband got up and came over to my house in the middle of the night. And Mary Lee said, 'Ike, God didn't want it to happen.'

He put you here for a special reason, she says. This is why you didn't do it. It's like you were put here to do a certain thing and you haven't completed what God put you here for. 'Ike,' she said, 'it ain't like you physically tired, you spiritually tired. It's almost like you carrying the world on your shoulders. Now you sitting up and you feeling depressed, like you are concerned about everybody's problems, but nobody is concerned about yours.'

When you get in those kinds of moods, it is very easy to get into that who-loves-you type of thing. I was forty-seven years old or something. I done given all my youth to my family and to the whole shit. How was I going to start over at this late stage in my life?

With my investments, it wasn't as if I was worried about money. I had all the money I wanted. I had two new Mercedes, I had this house – I had everything I wanted, man. I had a trillion women, if I wanted to call a woman.

What most people kill themselves over or get worried about – I got all of that. But what I don't have, man, is what my mother used to give me. When somebody wanted to beat me up I would make it to my mother and she'd put her arms around me and protect me. I don't have that. People get security mixed up with wealth. I got wealth, but I'm not secure at all. I don't feel protected. When you get that way, man, it's a bad state of mind to be in.

Ike acknowledges that what he should have done – as he had planned sixteen years earlier in St Louis – was to find another Tina and go on. He had two good candidates to hand.

In the 1970s, after Tina and I broke up, I could have asked Chaka Khan or Natalie Cole. They would have helped me – they would have done anything for me on the friendship side. Chaka can sing her ass off. She can beat Tina ten to one as far as singing is concerned, but she is not a performer.

Instead of doing that, man, I got really insecure. I got afraid of rejection, thinking that the public wouldn't accept me. And I just started procrastinating and philosophising and staying in the studio.

Nor could Ike return to the blues, though he had released a solo album of blues numbers called *Blues Roots*. The problem had been there from the beginning, when he could barely bring himself to play a boogie-woogie in front of a hall full of kids at Myrtle Hall.

A lot of people like to hear me sing blues, a lot of people. But what I think I'm real good at is organising. I'm a good arranger, I'm a good producer; I was good at teaching somebody else how to do it instead of doing it myself.

I overcame the problem to the point where I could walk onstage and do the thing I did with a guitar. But I don't have enough nerve to get up and sit in on another group. A lot of musicians, they go up on stage and jam. I never did that in my life. I ain't got that kind of nerve.

You see, I built that career standing in the background. I built something I knew the public wanted to see. I was totally confident that they were going to like my show. I made Tina and them perfect. I knew it was something the public wanted.

If I called a promoter and asked him about playing a date, he wasn't going to tell me, 'No Ike, not right now, later.' They wanted the Ike Turner Revue, they wanted Ike and Tina. We had that demand. It was OK. I knew I was wanted.

Without the Revue, I lost all confidence. Maybe I don't look shy, but I am. Just in the last year, I got so I would talk to girls. Before, if you introduced me to someone, then I'd get to know her. But as for going up to a girl and asking her to dance, I would never do that in my life. Because if she told me no, I would go through the hole. I am totally afraid of rejection.

I hadn't thought about doing nothing, definitely not playing no music – scared me to death. I just went into a fifteen-year party.

18 The Fifteen-Year Party

Ike married his great and enduring love Ann Thomas in
Las Vegas on 11 April 1981. For a while life was peaceful.
The trouble started when Ike was involved in a shooting
incident.

'IKE TURNER SHOT THE PAPERBOY FOR HITTING A DOG WITH A NEWSPAPER.'
That is the biggest bunch of shit. This is what happened. I
owned half a block with my studio, Bolic, and also an
apartment building across the alley behind it. I had six
units, big apartments.

A lady moved out and left her dog with us, a real friendly
dog. Ann would let the dog outdoors to play sometimes.
Meantime, I had a place in Bel-Air where I went a lot to do
dope. That day I was out in Bel-Air and Ann was at the
apartment in Inglewood. She heard the dog yelping. This
'paperboy' had the dog down in the garage where the cars were
holding him by the leash and hitting him across the nose with
a newspaper. This paperboy – well, he ain't no paperboy. This
sonofabitch is forty-nine years old. He is 6ft 4. And he is an
arrogant motherfucker, man. He did things to other people in
the neighbourhood on his paper round. But because I was Ike
Turner, they put it in the newspapers that I shot the
'paperboy'.

Anyway, Ann ran down the steps and grabbed the leash
from him and asked him why he was hitting the dog. He said,
'This motherfucker been fucking with me for eleven days.'

Ann told him, 'Well, then you know he's not going to bite.'

And that's when he took his hand, the palm of his hand, and
hit upwards in a blow to her chin. 'Shut up bitch,' he said. She

195

came upstairs, crying, and called me in Bel-Air. So I got some bodyguards of mine and came over to Inglewood. When I got there he was gone. I stayed there. About two or three days later, I was upstairs, lying on the bed, and my daughter came running upstairs calling, 'Daddy, Daddy.'

She said, 'The man who beat Mommy up is out there.'

I came running down the stairs with my bodyguard, but when I got out on the street, the paperman was fixing to get in his car. And he had a little girl in the car with him, I think it was his daughter. I went out to the kerb and said, 'Say, I would like to talk to you for just a minute.'

So he got his ass out. Like I said, he's already over 6ft tall, compared to 5ft 10 or whatever I am, but even so he stands up on the kerb to look down on me from even higher up, his arms folded like Mr Clean. He said, 'Yeah?'

I said, 'A few days ago there was a problem between you and my wife. I would like to talk to you and straighten it out, so we won't have any further problems. I don't even really know what happened.'

He said, 'Well, why the fuck don't you go ask her?'

I made a sign with my fingers and said, 'OK, peace, man, peace.'

I went back to the apartment to ask her what had gone down, 'cos I really didn't know how it actually started. The bodyguard said, 'That cat got a piece, man. He wouldn't be talking to you like he is unless he got a piece.' That's the first time I ever heard anybody call a gun 'a piece'. He said, 'For a guy to talk like that – there are two of us – he got to have a piece.'

I went on upstairs and talked to Ann. Then I just reached up and got one of my guns. I had a bunch of guns. I had a .38 Smith and Wesson, one of them long ones with a long barrel on it.

I went down them steps and out the door. This guy was about 20ft or 30ft from my apartment. He saw the gun in my hand and he said, 'What you going to do, shoot me?'

I said, 'Good idea.'

First I fired in the air. Then I saw that he was serious. Then he turned his shoulders to me and I couldn't see his right hand. I saw him look down at his hand like he had a gun.

He got down and I'm thinking he's fixing to come up and shoot me. So I shot him, right through the calf of his leg. He went hopping down the sidewalk, then he jumped the fence and went on somewhere.

The police came and wanted to take me to jail, but when I went to court with the guy's lawyer, I was found not guilty. There were other people in the neighbourhood, women, he had abused in a similar situation. It was a joke, man.

In 1992, I did the John Brandimier radio show in Chicago. It was real popular. John Brandimier was a musician also, so we were playing, having a ball on the radio. I was playing the guitar and he was beating this little drum. Someone else was playing the harmonica. Then he said, 'Ike, I got a surprise for you.'

He starts playing this thing some kids wrote: 'Ike Shot the Paperboy'. It went:

> The paperboy,
> He wasn't a fan.
> He wasn't no paperboy,
> He was a full-grown man.

Despite Ike's abiding love for Ann Thomas, the marriage failed.

When I got out of jail in 1991, Ann Thomas called and wished me good luck. I told her I would like for us to get back together. She say, 'Well, Ike, too much done went on between me and you.' I guess she thought I might get mad and jump on her. I don't know what she meant. I haven't heard from her since then.

The daughter I had by her, Mia, is now twenty-three, twenty-four years old. We're pretty close, but I don't never see Ann. But, man, she had everything I liked. And her mother hated my guts. If she had known that Ann was going with me when she was seventeen years old, her mother says, she would have 'eliminated' her. Women say a lot of things when they mad.

I started partying with a lot of girls, just having orgies and all kinds of stupid shit. You know, drugs make people do all kinds of crazy shit. I went to this place called Carolina Pines out on Century Boulevard. The restroom had two swing doors. Just as you came in the door, there was a latrine there for you to stand there and pee. About 20ft down to the left were some bathrooms. The janitor was in there mopping the floor. Right inside the door by the latrine he had a bucket the shape of a watermelon with two rollers in it. You put your feet on them and they closed up to wring out the mop. The janitor was down the other end mopping when I walked in and was standing there peeing. As I turned round to zip up my pants, this guy walks in the door. He looked at the bucket, then he put his hands together like he was going to dive into a swimming pool. He dived straight into that bucket. There was blood everywhere. I ain't never seen nothing like that before in my life. This guy was high on angel dust. I guess that shit told him that it was a swimming pool.

You get some people, man, who get paranoid when they do coke. Some girls who did cocaine at my studio would run to the window and start peeping out. I don't know what they were looking for. They just got paranoid.

One time when I was doing dope, I met this fine girl and rented a room out at the Pacific Hotel, right off Route 405. I had my guitar-player Jackie, with me. I got two rooms, each with two beds in it. Between the two beds they had a telephone. I went into my room and got my clothes loose, 'cos I was going to party for a few days. I had my stuff with me – six pairs of shoes, maybe two or three suits, a bathrobe, pyjamas and shit. Jackie had the same. I got maybe half a pound of cocaine, already cooked-up rocks.

After I was through taking a shower, I sat there smoking. I ain't got nothing on but a black velvet robe – if you look, you see my dick. So this girl knocks on the door comes in. She sits down on the side of the bed, acting so dainty with her short mink on.

I say, 'Do you want a hit?'

She says, 'Oh yes, I'd appreciate that.'

So I put a rock on the pipe and I hold it to her mouth and burn it for her. She took this big old draw. And when she let it out she started looking around the room like she was scared of something. She put her hand on the bed like she was ready to raise herself up. I said, 'Oh, no. You're not one of those, are you?'

'What you talkin' about?'

'You not one of those people who hit the pipe and start looking out the curtains, thinking the police are coming and all this bullshit, are you?'

'No, no, no, no, no.'

But she started looking. She tried to be cool but she all cooled out.

After fifteen, twenty minutes, she began to come down. Before I put another hit on the pipe I said, 'I better give you about half what I gave you before.'

She say, 'No, I can take it, that's your imagination.'

I say, 'Why don't you pull off your clothes so that you lay down and stuff.'

'That's OK, I'm fine right now. I'm just trying to relax.'

'OK.'

Meantime, I put some more on the pipe.

I had the telephone in bed so that when it rang I could answer it. I noticed that there was a space under the foot of the door.

So I put another big rock on, put the torch to it and she takes this long draw and starts tripping again. Meantime, I pick up the phone, dial Jackie's room and whisper, 'Jackie, put a pair of shoes outside my door.'

So Jackie goes out of his room next door into the hallway and puts some shoes outside my door so it looks like somebody's standing there. That girl saw them shoes and jumped up on the bed, screaming.

I said, 'Girl, what's wrong with you?'

She said, 'Look, look, look!'

'Look at what?' I said. 'I told you you were one of them kind of people. I would rather smoke by myself than have somebody paranoid around me.'

She said, 'Please look. I'll give you anything you want, just look.'

I bent down and said, 'I don't see shit. Ain't a damn thing there.'

She said, 'Look! You ain't looking.'

'I ain't? I don't see nothing.'

She's sitting there so nervous, man, looking at the door, looking at me, looking at the door, looking at me.

Meantime, Jackie moves the shoes. So I say, 'Let me see what you talking about.' I raise up out of the bed and get up and look.

'There ain't a fucking thing under that door, you see?' I say. I open up the door. 'There ain't nobody out here, see?'

'But there was somebody standing out there.'

I say, 'That's your fucking mind, man, I told you you were one of those people.'

I flicked the TV on.

She said, 'Ike, give me another hit.'

I said, 'I don't like to fuck off my dope like this with people who get paranoid and shit.'

So she went into the bathroom for a minute to pull off her clothes. I guess she was going to play on me to get another hit. While she was in there, I called Jackie and said, 'Put three pairs of shoes outside the door.'

She came back in with just a towel wrapped around her and sat on the bed with her back to the door. So I started feeling her titty and shit. I got my finger up, playing with her and shit.

She say, 'Give me another hit.'

I put the rock on the pipe and she takes this big, big, big hit. She turns around and looks at that door.

She jumps right up from the floor on to the bed and starts making like she is running. And I say, 'Girl, what the fuck's wrong with you?'

She says, 'Look! Look! Look! There's three of them at the door.'

'There ain't nobody at that fucking door. You are out of your fucking mind.'

She ran into the bathroom and slammed the door. When she done that, I called Jackie and told him to remove the shoes.

Then I get another idea. I got a pair of plain coveralls and hung them behind the net curtains and put a cap on top so it looked like there was a man standing there. She came out of the toilet and screamed. I said, 'Girl, what's wrong with you?'

She said, 'Now tell me you don't see that.'
I said, 'There ain't no fucking thing there.'
She said, 'Oh God, God . . .'
I called Jackie to come on through and said, 'Jackie, can you see anything?'
Jackie say, 'No.'
That girl ran off out of that door with that towel wrapped around her, and I ain't seen her no more from that day to this. She left her clothes, everything.

Cocaine attracted other pretty girls who would do anything for a rock of crack, but no matter how many girls he had in how many hotel bedrooms, nothing could disguise the fact that the loss of Ann Thomas marked the beginning of the end.

When Ann and I broke up I really started going downhill. All at once, without notice, those $56,000 cheques every month – the oil money – got cut off. The $5,000 I was getting from those units in Anaheim stopped too.

I let the house in Mount Olympus go and moved out of it. I can't remember whether I sold it or not. Maybe I still own it, I don't know. To start with, at least, I had it managed by a management company, and rented it out. That earned me $3,000 a month and my outgoings were $2,600 a month, so it would pay for itself. That's why I say I don't know if I still own it. Maybe I do. I'll have to check it out.

I'd just sit up nights and procrastinate and philosophise and philosophise and procrastinate. I'd say, 'Tomorrow, I'm gonna put my band together. Tomorrow, we'll go and cut a record.' But tomorrow never came. You just don't follow through and you just go down, down, down, down.

I don't give a damn who you are, or how strong you are, cocaine is stronger than you. I've heard a lot of people say, 'Man, nothing is gonna control me.' Those same guys I see coming back saying, 'Hey, man, where can I get some blow?'

What I'm saying is, cocaine would make a hooker out of a queen.

Events exacerbated this downward spiral. In 1981, the studio burned down. Worse, the insurance had lapsed.

I was pretty sure that Stevie Wonder was buying the studio, so I didn't renew the insurance, and the damned thing burned down. I was the number-one suspect. The fire inspector had been going around asking questions and all this shit. It looked suspicious to him, the whole half a block burning down.

But what I don't understand is that when the firemen got there it was forty-five minutes before they turned on the water. They said the reason they couldn't put out the fire, the reason they couldn't go into the building, was because it was so well insulated. If it was well insulated, it should have made it easier for them to isolate the fire. But I think they just let my fucking building burn. They'd seen all these white girls going in there twenty-four hours a day, partying and things, and they just let it burn, man.

Right now, when I think of that studio, boy, I think of the things I did while I was there and the studio itself, the way I built it – it was like something out of a James Bond movie. It feels like a dream, man. It don't seem real. It's like a fantasy, like it never really happened. That's the way I think of my whole life during that period. I would just love to relive it.

But nothing would bring back the dream, and, without a studio, Ike found himself totally frustrated. Still, there was always the pipe.

With the studio burned down and investments frozen, Ike had no income. That's when he made the transition from cocaine to crack.

One minute I was handling my own publishing company, my own booking agency, my own management, my own recording studio, my own production company – there were about six things I was doing by myself. I would hire people, but I would be the one telling them what to do daily.

I was the bandleader, too: I was telling Tina everything to do and say onstage; telling the Ikettes every step to make, the musicians what notes to play. Then, all of a sudden, I had nothing to do. It's like I was lost. If a guy is doing ten or eleven things every day, for twenty, thirty years, then all at once finds himself doing nothing, he's hurting pretty deep.

I found contentment in drugs. I didn't care. As long as my bills were paid, it was OK. Then, when it got so my bills weren't paid, I sold everything – lost everything – and I still didn't give a shit, man.

I don't really know the difference between crack and cocaine. Freebase is the same as crack. So let me straighten this out.

During the time I was snorting cocaine and freebasing, I was getting it straight from Peru, so I would say it had to be at least 80 per cent pure. I started buying cocaine in kilos, pounds and shit, so I was getting the better grade – the best you could get here in America.

But later on, as my money went down and down, I started buying eight-track, half an ounce or one ounce. That's when I started getting this shit with 10 per cent cocaine in it. And when you start buying a sixteenth, shit like that, you getting rubbish. You ain't getting no good shit.

You see, you start buying it from this guy. Now he puts a 50 per cent cut on it. This guy buys from that guy, who has already put a 50 per cent cut on it. And he bought it from yet another guy, who has also put a 50 per cent cut on it. By the time it gets down to you, you got 10 per cent cocaine and 90 per cent of procaine, lanocaine, benzocaine and all other kinds of 'caines to make it up. You buy $50 to $100-worth – well, you just getting shit watered down. This is what they're talking about when they talk about crack. Now you cook that shit up with baking soda, which makes a little round, hard rock. When you take that, it's the same thing as freebase. But you got only 10 per cent cocaine. The purity is not there. That's what makes it crack.

And when you start buying in smaller amounts you're more likely to get in trouble with the police. When you buy a kilo you don't have to go nowhere. The man brings it to you, you don't have to go nowhere to get it. But when you're buying $100-worth, $150 – a gramme – it is going to be gone in five minutes and you got to drive way across town to buy some more. And you keep making these trips backward and forward, backward and forward. You draw the police to you.

It certainly drew them to Ike. He was arrested twelve, maybe fifteen, times – he can't remember. Not that he wasn't trying to give up.

I tried two different rehabilitation centres – $9,000 for thirty days first time, $14,000 for eleven days the second. Everybody who is in there is in there for the same reason. They all want to leave drugs, or to get a certificate to show the judge that they have been to a rehab. But I was not going to rehab just to stay out of jail. I wanted to stop. There were about fourteen or fifteen people at the meetings every day. You are all sharing the same thing – you want to get sober, you want to clean up your life. After the medical tests, they sat us round a huge vat of cocaine, cooking up rocks, while we had electric-shock treatment. Meanwhile, there would be dealers with 3 kilos in the trunks of their cars outside.

Then when your time comes to get out of there, by the twenty-eighth day, you get scared, 'cos now you are fixing to go back into the real world. And who do you know in the real world? All the people you know are cocaine people. They all do the same thing you do. So you're going to go back around the same people, man, and seeing them do it every day, it's got to make you want to do it again too.

The real key to quitting that shit is, when you quit it, after ten days, or however long you've stopped for, you need to go someplace else and be involved in something new. That's the key. For me, it was all too easy to fall back.

I'd just got out of rehab and I picked up this girl. And the girl say, 'Hey, Ike, buy me a rock so I can blow some smoke on your thang.'

I went and bought her a rock and she started giving me head. Next thing I know, she is blowing that shit in my mouth. There it goes. Yeah, one puff is too many; a thousand ain't enough.

You'd be trying to smoke for free. I ain't never been no dope-dealer, no shit like that. I didn't do it like that. But say an ounce cost $600. If somebody comes and says, 'Hey, Ike, sell me a half-ounce of yours,' because he doesn't want to drive someplace to get it, I say, 'OK, $600.' That way I got my half-ounce free.

I wasn't in the market to deal in cocaine, I don't ever want to think I did that. But I have sold cocaine to a friend of mine or whatever.

But all that opens you to the possibility of being set up. I was living over another lady's house, Lady Catherine's, in Baldwin Hills. My close friend Rickey came to me and said, 'Hey, man, I got a friend who wants a pound of cocaine. Good cocaine. Can you handle this?'

I say, 'Yeah.'

So Rickey brought the guy. I called the guy I buy my cocaine from and he brought the stuff. Rickey and I gave it to the guy and we made a couple of thousand dollars apiece off the transaction.

Meantime, seven months go by, and then Rickey comes to me again, and says, 'Hey, man, Eddie' – a guy who used to be a producer for Motown – 'Eddie got this guy who wants a pound of cocaine, man. But he want the kind of cocaine you got. Can we handle it?'

I say, 'Yeah.'

'Okay,' he says. 'Shall I call my guy?'

It was $12,000 or something like that. So the guy comes round and says, 'Hey, Ike, I got this broad out in the car, would you give me a hit to take to her?'

I say, 'Yeah.'

So I gave this bastard a whole gramme of coke. I just put it in a piece of paper, wrapped it up and gave it to him. He was going to some hotel with this girl.

Then he said, 'Can I have some, so I can show the people what we going to get?'

So I gave him some more in another paper and he split. I didn't know that this asshole had the police around the corner, that the people he is buying it for are the police, 'cos Eddie is Rickey's friend, not mine. Rickey didn't know either.

Anyway, the man is satisfied, but I explained he'd have to wait: 'Man, we can't get it until tomorrow morning.'

Next morning, Rickey came and woke me up out in North

Hollywood. 'Hey, man,' he said. 'They ready to do the deal. Eddie's waiting to hear from his man.'

I said, 'Where's Eddie?'

'He downstairs,' Rickey said.

A few minutes later, Rickey came back and said, 'Eddie wants to come up and talk to you.'

I said, 'Oh man, he want to come up here and get a hit.' I just had a funny feeling. I said, 'I don't feel right about this shit, man. Something feels funny. That motherfucker ain't wired, is he, man? Make him pull off his clothes. Make sure he ain't wired.' It was just a feeling I had. I said, 'Take this robe down there. Make him put it on before he come up here. Then you'll know he ain't wired.'

So Eddie came upstairs and he wasn't wired. Then I tried to call my guy, my connection, but couldn't get no answer. Eddie made a call on the phone. Then he said, 'Ike, everything will be all right, right?'

'Yes, soon as I get in touch with my man.'

'Will it be that long?'

I said, 'No, as soon as he answer the phone, we should be able to get it.'

Meantime, the police think I am talking bullshit and that I've already got the cocaine there. But I can't get through to my man, so I say, 'Man, let's just go on out there. He could be out in the garage or something.'

When we came downstairs, there were two cars parked on the street. There was a white guy in one car and a Japanese-looking guy in the other. Eddie was in his little red sports car. Eddie introduced us to these two guys.

Now, meantime, Rickey has a briefcase. Ain't nothing in there but tapes, but the police think the dope is in there.

I said, 'The three of us can't ride in this little red thing. Rickey, you ride with the guy behind.' Meantime, this guy goes around to the trunk of the car and pulls out a flight bag, the kind you carry on airplanes. He puts his foot up on the bumper and unzips the bag and pulls out the money in there. And he says, 'Here's the $12,000, plus $2,000 apiece for y'all. Is that right, Ike?'

The second guy is wired so he can get my name on the tape.

The first guy says, 'Man, my wife is a fan of yours. Hey, Ike, give me your autograph, man.'

So I gave it to him. He said, 'Boy, Jodie is really going to like this.'

That was the police signal for them to come on in. Police came out of trees and out of every fucking where – sixteen of them. Boy, they swamped us and slung us down on the ground. They arrested us, but we had no dope. We were on our way to get it. They busted us too soon.

They took us to jail and booked us on conspiracy. They got my voice, but we hadn't done anything. Even so, they were going to hit me with six months, but I went into rehab before I went to court. So when I did go to court, the judge read that I had been to rehab and that I was getting my life back together. So he said, 'Ike, I am going to give you six months' suspended sentence. Up with hope and down with dope.'

I was glad, man. He let me go. I had been to court about seven times by then, and it kept getting put off, put off, put off. I was glad to get out of that thing.

But Ike did not stop smoking dope, and not all his arrests were so serious. Nor did he acknowledge that sooner or later he was going to go down.

There are a million people doing dope right now, as much as I was doing, almost, and they've never been down.

I stayed at the Beverly Hills Hotel for a week and stole all the towels. Every time I ordered food, I stole all the plates, the silverware. I just wouldn't send it back. I had four or five big boxes of stuff and no car.

I called Rickey and said, 'Hey, partner, come get me.' I had all this cocaine and shit, too. He came and picked me up from the Beverly Hills Hotel in a phutt-phutt car – a raggedy-ass backfiring car that ain't got no business in Beverly Hills. He picks me up and we don't get five blocks from the hotel before the police pull us over.

Here we are with all these pipes, all this cocaine and the police pull us over.

He says, 'Driver's licence?'

I gave it to him.

'Ike Turner,' the cop says.

The man opens the trunk and sees all this stuff with Beverly Hills Hotel written on it. I don't think the guy would have said nothing if I hadn't had so much stuff: coffeepots, everything – boxes of it. He called the hotel.

Man, that was the most embarrassing thing that happened in my whole life. When the man from the hotel came we were lying on the street with our hands behind our heads. And he said, 'Ike, I'd have given you this shit, man.'

I felt real small.

Ike was pretty lucky. Most of his arrests resulted in a 'DA reject', which meant there was not enough evidence to prosecute. In fact, he is proud of the fact that he never actually got caught with cocaine on him. He took the sensible precaution of hiding his stash under the gas flap. Nevertheless he did go to jail.

They caught me at a crack house, man. I don't really remember it, I got busted so many times. Anyway, the judge gave me thirty days in jail and I was going to have to serve sixteen out of the thirty.

I was living with a broad named Nina then, and right before I had to go to jail, I saw this movie called *Scared Straight*. In that they were raping people in jail.

Man, it scared the shit out of me. When I saw that movie, I definitely didn't want to go to jail.

Around that time I had a boil between my balls and my butthole, near my ass, and I had to have it operated on. Somebody told me, man, if you go in the hospital part of the jail, you ain't going to be in the mainstream. So when I heard I was going to go to jail, I pulled out those stitches in my butt and I strained to pop it open a little bit. Then I went to the doctor and he wrote out a note for me that said I needed to have sit-baths two or three times a day. I would have to be in the hospital part to have those.

But when I went to jail, they gave me a red wristband and put me in protective custody – where they put O.J. Simpson, or where they'd put the President, if he was in jail. I didn't know they would automatically put me in protective custody. So I'd bust my butt open for nothing.

This self-inflicted wound would flare up painfully four or five times a year until, finally, in 1995, Ike got it fixed.

I was really going crazy, man. You see, after Tina, after Ann Thomas, I didn't want no more regular woman. I just wanted to stay by myself and have all of them, have whoever I wanted to have. That's the way I made my mind up, I would fuck around. Then I met Jeanette, who's white.

Jeanette Bazzell and I were living all over the place, staying at this house, staying at that house, sleeping on floors. We would just stay anywhere, man. Boy, me and Jeanette, we lived all over Los Angeles, man, anywhere they would let us stay for free. If there was somebody who was doing dope we would give them dope to stay with them.

I got to the point where I had absolutely nothing at all. I was going to sleep with no money. I was looking in drawers and things to find enough pennies to come up with a dollar. I remember a place here called Oke Diner. You go in there man, and you buy one of their Oke sandwiches for $2.50 – that's enough to feed six people, man. I got to be one of their favourite customers. I would wake up in the morning hungry and I would go to Oke's to get enough stuff to feed me and Jeanette.

Mostly we hung out in South Central LA. You could not stop your car there. If you stopped, niggers would swamp your car real fast. They'd all be in your car saying, 'Hey, I got the best dope, I got the best dope.' You couldn't even slow down – they'd all be in front of you like bees. On all these corners there was nothing but dope-dealers, man. All you do is pull up the car and say, 'Hey man, give us an eight-track.'

I wasn't even thinking of no future. I was just living day by day. I thought about putting my band back together and getting back onstage. But I just felt that I was daydreaming to even think about it.

While I was hitting rock-bottom, Tina was becoming a star.

I don't have no feelings about it at all. I don't know whether I dissociated myself from her or what, but I'm not proud because I discovered her, taught her to sing. And I'm not sad about it, either, or jealous or envious.

It's just like, if I look at the charts and I see Elton John has a Top Ten record – well, great. If it's a song I like, I like it. I don't feel good about it or bad about it, it's just a song I like.

I was sitting at home watching TV when I saw Tina come on and do that damn song, 'What's Love Got to Do With It'. As soon as I heard it, I called her sister and I said, 'You tell Ann that if she do that record just like she did on TV, she got a smash hit.'

But there is one thing about Tina's new act that I don't understand. She says she didn't like the image I portrayed on her. But what is she doing now? When you look at it, she's doing the same damn thing today.

Tina's success inspired Ike to try to do something with his own life again.

She was playing at Caesar's Palace, Las Vegas, and I came with an idea. I thought it was a good idea for me and Tina. You see, everybody compares Ike and Tina with Sonny and Cher. So I wrote a play for television called *Ike and Tina, Sony and Cher – The Broken Pieces Put Together by Crazy Glue*.

I wrote all the songs for it. For Sonny to sing, for me to sing – and for me and Tina to sing, and Sonny and Cher to sing. I had put the whole play together and I went to Las Vegas to tell Tina about it.

She said, 'Ike, this is a fantastic idea. But I think I would be putting the buggy before the horse. Right now, I don't have no pull with the manager, with the record company or nothing. If I had two hit records under my belt, then I could demand what I want. Later, when I get a couple of hit records, maybe we could do it.'

And so I said, 'OK.'

That is the last time I saw her.

Nevertheless, Ike was, at last, trying. He was also playing again.

When I first tried to get clean, Marie Times told me about this girl who could really, really sing. She wanted me to help produce the girl. So she introduced me to Barbara Cole, and we all went to Florida to produce the record.

But as soon as I got into the studio to record 'Black Seducer', I had to turn round and fly back to LA to go to court. I had to fly all the way back from Miami to California, and I walked into the courtroom and it was a DA reject.

In 1988 this guy Richard Drury was managing me and I was just putting my band back together. He paid for renting the bus and the instruments and all this stuff. One of the first shows I played was in Vallejo, California. Someone brought me a note on the bus. I don't remember the exact words, but it said something like: 'I am your daughter from Pat in St Louis. I would like to talk to you.' Now, normally, I don't go for that shit. But when this girl got on the bus it was just like looking at my own self.

In the meantime, Ike's comeback faltered.

I was still secretly doing cocaine. This damn chick – used to be my Ikette – she went back and told Richard Drury, and he dropped me right away and started managing her. She a damn throat-cutting cow. I was trying to get things back together, but that knocked it out from under me. I was already in trouble with the law.

Ike was already swimming against the current when allegations that he was a wife-beater surfaced. These culminated in the book *I, Tina.*

Tina got real, real big. The bigger she got, the more she talked about me. Every time she said something, she would go a little bit further – to see if I would take it.

For example, she made a statement that we raised four kids but she only felt like mothering one of them. The one she felt like mothering was not mine. That's when I started disliking her, 'cos I treated all four of those kids like they were mine. I felt like all four of them were mine. Well, I thought she said

things like that to try to get a response from me, to see if I
would say anything, or do anything. If I didn't, she would go
a little further next time. So she jump on it, jump on it, jump
on it. But until now I never responded. It was a continuation
of the way our relationship had always been. She'd push and
push to try to get some reaction.

Today she won't have nothing to do with nobody who knew
Ike and Tina, except for Rhonda and Ann Cain. But those two
work for her now. Anybody else, she don't have nothing to do
with them.

At first, she was using this black boy to do all the arranging.
He copied what I'd been doing. But when she got big enough,
she didn't need him no more, so she dropped him. Now there
are no blacks around her at all. She ain't got nothing for black
people. She don't like them. She's just forgotten where she's
comes from, man. I don't know this Tina. I don't know her, I
don't like her, and I don't want her.

The Tina I knew was a lady, a good woman and a sweet,
kind mother – she was everything a man would want in a
woman, I think. I abused it, but it was what I loved.

Man, I wouldn't give a fuck if today's Tina had a trillion
dollars, she couldn't do nothing for me, man. Absolutely
nothing.

Sure, I might need money – I might need it desperately – but
I am man enough to get it without stooping or compromising
my standards.

Anyway, I got busted and I didn't have shit. Some boy had
it and the police put it on me.

I went by a place I used to go to do dope and where a lot of
girls hung around, down at Second Street, off Melrose and
Normandy. I had been going there daily, doing coke. This guy
who owned the place borrowed some money from me and gave
me a throw rug to hold. So I went by there to get my money.

He said, 'Ike, do me a favour, drop these two people off.'

I said, 'Where they going?'

When I heard they were going to Century City, I said, 'Man,
that is the opposite direction from where I'm going.'

He said, 'Please, man, do me this favour.'

It was a black guy with a white chick. I didn't know neither one of them. I took off flying. I had a spare tyre in my car, a flat. I didn't have the key to the trunk so the tyre was in the back seat, and the three of us had to sit in the front. The white girl was sitting in the middle and the black guy on the other side.

Anyway, I was driving how I drive – fast – and I see this police car come in behind. The guy said, 'Aw, shit, I'm dirty, man.'

I said, 'Motherfucker.' Dirty? I need this like a hole in the head.

So when I got to the corner, I turned left, let his window down and told him to drop the stuff out. He told me he had.

If he had dropped it where I said, when I was making the turn, the police would have rolled right over it and never seen a thing. But he didn't drop it.

I went on half a block and pulled over. The policeman came over and said, 'Let me see your driver's licence.'

I gave it to him.

He said, 'Ike Turner? Let's see your bag.'

My bag was sitting right here. I gave it to him. He looked inside and there was a pipe in there. I had forgotten it was there.

He said. 'Where's the other stuff that goes with it?'

Meantime, there is a woman cop standing on the passenger's side of the car. She aims her gun at this black guy sitting there.

'Keep your hands on the fucking dashboard.' That's what this woman kept telling him. But he kept dropping his hands down.

This black guy, he was one of those anti-police guys. He hated policemen. He kept being smart-mouthed with the cop.

So the policeman said, 'Oh, you one of them smart mothers. You come out the car.'

But that woman cop who's standing there, she saw him put the shit under the seat. They got us out and the police say, 'Ike, is this yours?'

I said, 'No. The pipe is mine, but the dope is not mine.'

Anyway, they put the dope on both of us, though not on the girl. When we went to the judge, the judge let us out on OR – own recognisance.

But when this other dude got out, he took off. I don't know where he went to. So the only person they got left is Ike Turner. I am in deep shit. This got me all of the time.

When Phil Spector heard about all this, he sent for me. I went to meet with him and he promised me that I wouldn't go down. He offered help, I didn't ask for it. He was the one who said he'd see that I didn't go to jail. While I was out on bail, I called Phil desperately for a month or two or three months. I wanted to see if he could help me get a lawyer, 'cos I didn't have the money for an attorney. But I couldn't get him on the telephone. Then I went to jail. And after I got out, two years later, then he called.

> Without Spector's money to buy him a top-flight attorney, Ike had to turn to a less high-powered lawyer. Ike was found guilty of possession with intent to distribute. He appealed, and was still out on an appeal bond when he was arrested again.

The other time I got arrested, I'd been over at a dope house. Jeanette called and told me she had cooked, so I was on my way home in a hurry.

The night before, I had left my photo album in a friend's car. He was a white dude from Africa called Norman. On my way home, I was passing pretty close to his house so I cut across to drop by and pick up the photo album. I parked right in front of the apartment building, where it was no parking, so I left my lights blinking and the motor running. I rang the thing on the door and told him, 'It's Ike. I come to pick up the photo album.'

Norman lived on the third floor. I ran up the steps – I didn't even use the elevator. When I got to his apartment, he said, 'Ike, lend me your car just for a minute. I want to go down the street to the Seven-Eleven.'

I said, 'Man, I'm on my way home right now.'

He said, 'I'll be straight back. The Seven-Eleven is only two blocks.'

I said, 'Well, OK.'

So he took off in my car.

There were two girls in Norman's apartment so I sat down to have a smoke with them. After about half an hour, I called Jeanette. I said, 'I lent Norman my car and he didn't get back yet. As soon as he gets here, I'll be home.'

Another thirty minutes, and he still didn't come. So then I called Jeanette and said, 'Hey, I'm coming to pick you up.'

I asked Norman's girl where the keys to his car were. She gave me the keys, and showed me which were the keys to his car and which was the key to the elevator to go down and get it. I asked one of the girls to ride with me. So we went downstairs and got Norman's car.

I am speeding on my way to pick Jeanette up and this cop was stopped at a doughnut shop, right by a red light. There were several cars there and there wasn't no left lane for a car to make a left. Everything was straight on.

The car in front of me was making a left turn from the middle lane, so when the light changed to red I couldn't back up. In comes this cop behind me. I said, why is this asshole following me? I drove on for two or three blocks.

And finally, man, I say, let me see if he is following me. I turned right, he turned right. I go left, he go left. He followed me straight to the address on Fuller where I was staying. When I arrived, I didn't have the remote to open the electric gate, so I had to park on the street. But just as I pulled up by a car to back in, the cop, he turn on his lights.

I backed into the parking space and he came round to my side of the car. He said. 'Put your hands on the fucking steering-wheel. If you make any funny moves I am going to blow your fucking brains out.' He pulled his gun on me.

Then he said to the girl, 'I saw you when you threw that out of the car.'

So he got me out of the car. 'Cos he's by himself, he's scared. He got me out of the car, walked me over to the kerb, handcuffed me and sat me down on the ground. Then he went round to the girl's side of the car and got her out.

When he got round to her side, he said again, 'I saw you when you threw that out.' And he pointed with his flashlight over at the grass.

She said, 'I didn't do nothing. I didn't do nothing.'

This is about 10.30 at night, man. The neighbours heard it.

Then, he walked her in front of the next car, where I could not hear what they were saying 'cos I was sitting down on the kerb on my own. When he came back, he shone the light in my face and said, 'Ike Turner, you didn't think I saw you when you threw that out.'

I said, 'Man, you ain't seen me throw nothing out.'

'Cos he done found out who I was, he is going to put it on me. Then he gets on that radio and calls his buddies and tells them, 'You be surprised what I got.'

So these other police, they arrive. When they get there, then he start to rambling in the trunk. He finds a gun in there, and he say, 'Hey, look here what we got. Ike, this is not your gun either, is it?'

I said, 'I guess it belongs to Norman. He is chief of the Fire Department. So it's his gun and I am sure he would have it registered. I didn't know it was in there. It don't belong to me.'

Then he puts me in the police car and takes me to the police station. Now, I was already out on bond from the other thing before. While we in the car he got on the radio and said, 'Last night I couldn't bust a grape. Guess what? I got Ike Turner tonight.' He was just bragging to every cop he can find, man. Even when he see one down the hallway, he bragging. He got me.

They fingerprinted me and booked me. They only put the cocaine on me, they didn't bother with the gun. They put my bond at $2,500. You need 10 per cent of that to call a bondsman to get out, so that means I need $250.

I didn't have but about $100 in my pocket. I didn't have enough money to get out. So the next morning, about eight o'clock, they came and took me out of my cell and brought me upstairs to the narcos. And the guy tell me, 'Hey, Ike, look, you don't need no more trouble, man. One hand can wash the other one. You help me, I help you. We know you know big-time dope-dealers, people who deal in pounds and kilos.'

I said, 'Mister, I don't get involved in politics.'

He said, 'OK, you want to be fucking smart? We'll show you how to be smart.'

He took me back to my cell, then he came back about five minutes later and said, 'Now you got the gun.'

Up till then I had only got the dope.

And he said, 'Your bond is $10,000.' So now I need $1,000 to get out.

I called Jeanette to tell her to come and get me out, but she didn't have the money to post bond. She tried to call Phil Spector, and couldn't get the sonofabitch on the phone. Then she called his secretary and said, 'Ike is in jail, I have a painting I can sell.' So Jeanette pawned two $12,000 paintings to Phil Spector for a lousy $1,000 to get me out.

But the police were not finished with me yet. I thought that's all the bastard was going to do, put the gun on me.

Two days later my lawyer calls and says, 'Hey, they want to revoke your appeal bond.'

I said, 'Can they do that?'

He said, 'Well, I'm going to argue it.'

When I went down there for him to fight it, the district attorney said I was a threat to the public. I had no business being on the streets. The judge agreed with him and slung my ass in jail. I was expecting to go home, but I was taken into custody right then. Man, I thought I was coming back home that day.

Ike's appeal bond was revoked and he went to jail on 13 July 1989. He had to stay there seven months before his appeal came up. Meanwhile, the other charges against him were dropped.

19 Tough Enough

GOING TO JAIL IS THE GREATEST THING that ever happened to me, because I got my life back together, man.

First of all, it got me off drugs. I wanted to stop before I went into jail, but I just couldn't. My whole environment was crack. Everybody I knew was into it. I used to say to myself daily, if I could go five days without this shit, I would never go back to it. So when I went to jail, I was locked up in a cell and I went a week or something without even thinking about it, just 'cos I was scared. Later on, I saw people doing it constantly in jail. They were smoking it, snorting it, doing all kinds. You got heroin, everything in there: there was more drugs in jail than on the streets.

One guy played guitar with me. The guy up in the tower that looks over the yard, saw him doing some heroin and shipped him out to another pen.

Anyway after I was in there about a month and was off coke, this warden named Perez told me he wanted me to be a trusty. A trusty can go to the store all the time; he can walk around in the jail. So I would go to the store and buy stuff. I paid 50c for a bar of candy and I could sell it for a dollar. Whatever amount of money you spent at the store, you made a dollar on every dollar you spent. I was making $500 a day in jail. I ran thirty-two stores. I had these guys running the stores for me, and I gave them all $50.

Once a hustler always a hustler. Ike had to get close to the guards to check out when people were being released before giving them money to trade.

I didn't know coffee was so addictive. After eleven o'clock the inmates are not supposed to be out, but these guys would crawl down under the one dorm to the next dorm to get one bag of coffee, man. If the man in the tower saw him crawling he would shoot him, but that's how addictive coffee is.

In six months, I saved $13,000 – and you are not allowed to have but $40 in jail. The prison officers liked me, and they used to put the money on the books so I wouldn't get caught with it.

One guard, a Spanish dude, had a hard-on for Ike Turner. I could feel by the way this guy acted with me that when he got off work, he go back home, and he say, 'Guess what, I had Ike Turner mopping floors today.'

This sonofabitch came into my cell substituting for my regular officer. It was Christmas night and he say, 'Ike, come with me.'

It was about 11.30 at night, and this bastard took me up to the central stairway. He had me get buckets and some sheets. He had me tear up these sheets and tape some mop handles together so I could reach way up and scrub. He had me taping this shit together. He was going to work my ass off, boy. He was the type who would probably try to beat on me, then put me in the hole where nobody could see I'd been beaten.

Anyway, he moves off. When he turned the corner, I dropped that mop and I hauled ass. I ran through into the next cell block and beat on the door. The officer in that block let me in and said, 'Turner, what you doing out here?'

I told him, 'Man, that guy done took me out of my cell and made me wash up by the steps, man. He knows that ain't right.' He took me back to my cell and I got on my bunk and fell asleep. Next day, I told one of the higher authorities that every time this Spanish guy came on he did some funny shit to me. This high-up say, 'I am going to give you a hallway badge, a PM badge and AM badge'. With a hallway badge you could run the hallway, and the AM and PM badges showed which shift you were working, morning or afternoon. And I had a trusty's badge as well, so I had four fucking badges.

He says, 'Whenever this guy comes on, show him the opposite badge and tell him you're not working that shift.'

That guy just had to pick on Ike Turner. He was the only one to give me shit. And there were other guys working in the jail who were supposed to be assholes, but they didn't give me no shit.

There was a woman officer who also had it in for me, though. She was called Sergeant Ford.

Every night I got fucking hungry around three o'clock in the morning. This warden Marlinatto used to go up to the kitchen and get me some food. One night I was starving and I told Marlinatto, 'I'm hungry, man.'

He said OK. He walked me up to the kitchen and got the cook to fix me some eggs, meat and shit – nice shit. I want to take some back to the fellows who are up with me right? So I got this big old arm of shit coming back down the hall and Marlinatto is walking right alongside me, 'cos you can't go nowhere without a guard that time of night. So Marlinatto walking right along. Up walks this damn woman – she is a women's libber.

She said, 'Turner, you hungry, huh?'

I said, 'Yes ma'am, Miss Ford.'

She said, 'I see.'

Shit, that cow mad, man. The next day, she had me moved out of where I was, in the 2200s, where they put drunk drivers and soft criminals. She moved me up the 3000 floor with the big-time dope-dealers, gang-bangers and real criminals. Man, I hated it up there. She was getting me away from the warden I knew, who made it easy for me, and putting me around some new ones. But it don't take me no time to learn them, and they like me.

One day up on 3000, I was lying on the top bunk. I was still running my store. I took some Babe Ruth candy bars. Right down by the door, there's a hole. And this big fucking rat comes in and tears the paper off a candy bar, just like a man, and eat that whole candy bar out of there.

Another time some new guys came in there. They'd been up all night being booked, and they were so tired. I saw one so tired, he put his money in his shorts, in that little part where your dick comes out. He put his money in there and lay there and went to sleep.

The inmates look at this and say, 'You kidding?'

One of them took a razor-blade and cut the guy's shorts and got the fucking money out. That poor guy woke up and he ain't got no money and he ain't got no shoes. He ain't got shit.

That was an experience, man.

The hardest part was doing without pussy. That's the only thing I missed in jail. You ain't got no woman, you ain't got no car – you just fucked up like that, man. At night, the lights would go off in the jail and you would get to sleep for a minute, doze off, and then you would see the sheets going up and down – ding, ding, ding, ding. The sons of bitches were getting it on with themselves.

> After seven months in the county jail, Ike's appeal came up. It was denied.

The judge said, 'Mr Turner, you got a history of arrests. Where there's smoke, there's fire. I am going to give you four years in the state penitentiary.'

My head hit the table. So that was it. They took me back to the county jail to wait for the thing to pick us up and take us to the CMC, the California Men's Colony. But it was good that it happened to me because it made me. I used it positive.

> So Ike became prisoner number E48678 at the California Men's Colony in San Luis Obispo. And that was the end of his lucrative career in the grocery business – in the state penitentiary, prisoners were not allowed to handle money. They were given dockets instead. But life was not too tough.

People might be attracted to me because I'm Ike Turner, but I don't think that is the only reason. I think I have a charisma or something. People just like me as a person. Me being Ike Turner has some bearing on it when they are getting to know me, but the things the guys did for me in the CMC, I think they did because of me, my personality.

I got along with the Mexican mafia, the Crips and the Bloods. The Bloods would go to the store for me on the days the Bloods were allowed to go, and so would the Crips – and there are only certain days when they let each gang go to the store.

Most times, if you get along with the officers, the prisoners think you're a snitch. And if you get along with the inmates, the wardens call you a trouble-stirrer. But they never did that with me. I got along with everybody in there, boy. They were good to me. All of them were really, really good to me. They treated me like I was no damn criminal, man. I just didn't have no privileges.

When I first got to the state penitentiary, there was a lady named Mrs Philmore, who was real, real good. The lady in the library where I worked, Miss Hoffman, she was real nice too. Another lady I called 'Spoon-Booty' – Miss Donnell. I can tell you her real name, 'cos I ain't never going back there, no way. She was a guard, security at the library.

Miss Donnell was one of those women who like to boss men, but she couldn't do shit with me. They would let me go to another yard or something. She would see me over there and say, 'Turner, come here. What are you doing over there? You get back to your yard.'

She a bossy heifer, man. Anyway, I like her and she like me. We had a lot of fun together. I ain't talking about no love nor no sex, just these mischievous things that she would do. Like one time, man, she was pissed at me and she said, 'Turner, go get that bucket up there.'

She had me fill it with water and get the mop. I thought I was getting it for someone else, because my job was library clerk. I was letting out books and stuff like that. But she turned to me and said, 'I want you to mop up.'

I say, 'Miss Donnell, it ain't my job. I ain't mopping no floor.'

She said, 'Are you disobeying a direct order?'

I said, 'Whatever it is, Miss Donnell, I'm not going to mop no floor.'

She said, 'I tell you what, you stay here after the library close.'

So when the library close, she came up to me and said, 'You fronting me off in front of these other inmates.'

I said, 'Miss Donnell, I ain't doing nothing. You doing it all yourself. You going to tell me to mop some floor. I ain't never mopped no floor in my life, and I ain't going to start now.'

So anyway, she smiled. I had a good relationship with her.

There was another officer named Peter Garcia. He was real good. He helped me around the jail, tried to protect me and showed me the things to do and not to do to keep from getting in trouble.

But the state penitentiary was not always as comfortable as Ike makes it sound. Once, when he had a prison visit, the man sitting next to him was stabbed to death.

After I was in jail for a couple of years, and it was almost time to get out, I got scared of leaving. Now you coming back to reality.

I was clean, and I knew I would never mess with drugs again because I tried it in the CMC. I bought a dime rock.

You know, people always saying if you were try it again you are hooked back up to where you left off. They tell that damn lie. I bought a dime rock in jail, man. The guy gave me the pipe and put it on there and I smoked it. That was the nastiest shit I ever tasted in my life. I hated it. I hated the way it smelled; I hated the way it made me feel. There is no way in the world I would ever fuck around with it again.

Ike served two years, two months. Prison, he thinks, made him a better man. But he has every incentive not to go back.

The lieutenant of CMC, Mr Lyons, he was fantastic. Last thing he said to me when I left there was, 'Ike, with the talent you got, if you ever come back to this jail again, I personally am going to whup your ass.'

20 On the Road Again

WHEN I GOT OUT OF JAIL, I was scared. The warden knew that there would be a lot of press there, so he tried to sneak me out before they arrived. But they had helicopters and followed me and got me anyway. I came on to LA and held a press conference with my daughter, Tawanna.

Then Little Richard gave me $1,000 or $2,000 to get me started. He was there for me when I needed it. But all those people I done gave cars to, all those people I done gave diamonds to – I gave away a lot of shit in my lifetime, boy, just gave it – they nowhere to be seen.

I was released up where Tawanna was. She works with the Highway Patrol up there. I moved in with her, then I sent for Jeanette and both of us were living at my daughter's house. I went to a few rehearsals with Tawanna, and her band. She sings and plays guitar, too. She is a real good singer, man.

After I'd been to two or three of their rehearsals I went to where they were playing and sat in on the keyboard and did a couple of numbers.

Then I met this guy Bobby Watson and Geta, a blues singer, a white guy. He's got a good voice and he can play the blues, boy. I started to put together a show.

I moved into Bobby's house, but then it got into some hassle, some sort of jealousy thing between him and Jeanette. I stayed for a few months, then I decided to move out, get my own place.

We got us a two-bedroomed apartment in Fairfield, California. Arnie Melby, Tawanna's husband, moved in – he and my daughter had separated – which made it easier for me.

The rent at that time wasn't but $480 a month. He paid half and I paid half. He had a steady income. I didn't, but I could hustle that little bit a month.

Then I got to play in Jimmy's Lounge up in Oakland. I was trying to record also. I met this guy Eppie and his wife, who were into management. Eppie bought me an overcoat and gave me a suit. He and his wife were really helpful. We started getting little jobs around the place. I only had but one suit, and if I had to do two shows he pulled his suit off and gave it to me so that I could do the second one.

Eppie owned this big centre where he rehearsed kids. He had this sound system in there, so I didn't have to pay for a rehearsal hall. He gave all that to me, and he put up a recording studio in there and everything.

I booked some dates in LA and Eppie was going to handle the money. The first date was the Strand at the Roosevelt Hotel, then we were going to play the Hollywood Hotel and the *Arsenio Hall Show*.

This woman in LA set up the *Arsenio Hall Show*. She pulled us down here. I told her that I was not going to do the show with just me and the Ikettes. So she called back and said, 'They will take you and the Ikettes and a rhythm section.'

I said no.

Then she called again and said that they would take the whole entourage.

Meantime, I flew in to play all three dates. I needed all three to break even. I couldn't get this woman on the phone before we left, so Eppie used his credit cards to rent the vans and cars we needed. The TV station was going to pay us back our hotel bills.

When we arrived in LA, this woman told me the *Arsenio Hall Show* had been cancelled. That put me in trouble – the money I had to pay out for the vans and the hotel bills and the food and shit put me way in the hole – about $2,500 in the hole.

So I called the network and the lady from the *Arsenio Hall Show*, she say, 'Ike, we're so sorry, we would have taken your show any time. If we commit to seventeen people or a hundred people, we do it. But this woman here representing you, she was the worst. We tried her all day long yesterday. And she got real ignorant and hung up the phone on us. We just couldn't communicate with her. Any time you want to do the *Arsenio Hall Show*, you call us or you get someone else to call us, and we will gladly reschedule the show.'

Meantime, I am still in trouble, 'cos I got to play the Roosevelt and Hollywood Hotels two nights.

While we were playing the Roosevelt Hotel, Vernon Minow, a guy who used to record at my studio, came over there. Vernon has real long hair, like a hippy. He said, 'Ike, I'm going to buy a hundred tickets to come and see you. I got money now.' So he reached in his pocket and put $2,500 in my hand. Boy, that was a godsend. I paid my band and everything.

After that, man, Vernon was helping me survive. We did a TV show and they paid for the rooms for us to stay another few days. It was for BET, Black Entertainment Television. The hostess of the show, she was so excited. She wanted to be an Ikette for a day. So we dug her out a Tina wig and taught her the dance steps. We had fun that day. It was supposed to be just a one-hour show, but they did an hour one day and an hour the next.

So Vernon said, 'Why don't you come over and stay at my hotel and I will pay for your room and give you a limo to travel in every day.'

I told him no, but some kind of way I ended up at his hotel. When my bill reached $1,700, Vernon came up with the money to pay it.

I went with him to meet a limo out at the airport. I was sitting in the back and Vernon said to this guy, 'Give me some money.' I don't think this deal had nothing to do with no dope. The guy reached in his bag and pulled out a big bundle of twenties. Vernon said, 'I don't want this shit.' And he threw it on the floor. Then the guy gave him some $100 bills. I don't know how much Vernon gave me then.

But Vernon had a falling out with the people he got all this money from. He was going to do a concert for them. They got cold feet, and Vernon got mad at them, and they decided not to give him no more money.

So that stops Vernon's money. Now he's in trouble and I

can't help him. So he went to sell some jewellery and he made contact with Tom Gilbert with Lenny Marmor. Lenny was a fan of mine. He is crazy about my music like you wouldn't believe. He just believe in Ike Turner, man, he is a hope-to-die believer in me.

So Lenny says he will pay for my recording so we could cut four or five sides, which would be $25,000 or $30,000. Then, when I got a record deal, I would pay him back his money off the top. That was my deal with him.

I told him that I was going to need money to live on while I did that. So Lenny said, 'No sweat. After the 15th, when my daughter gets married, I will be 100 per cent behind you,' and he gave me $500. I was staying at the Trade Winds Hotel, and every week, man, he would give money for the bill and money to live on. He was 1,000 per cent behind doing this thing.

One weekend, Jeanette and I went to stay down at his house in La Costa, near San Diego. Boy, I loved it down there. Lenny said, 'If you want to move down here, move down.' So with his wife, Karen, and his daughter Robin, we went around looking for apartments. We found this place in Carlsbad and moved all the furniture from Fairfield. Over there, my bills got to be, what $1,500 a month? He paid them all, and gave me $500 a week to spend.

I went and got Vera Hamilton, an ex-Ikette. She sang the shit out of a song I wrote called 'Do All I Can'. We cut that, and we redid 'Sexy Ida'. We did eight or ten tunes. But I never gave it to the record company because, by then, trouble was looming again.

Back in 1988, Disney made contact with me through a lawyer. I was in South Central LA, then, and the lawyer was in Laurel Canyon.

He told me that Disney wanted to give me $45,000 for agreeing to someone playing me in Tina's movie. I didn't have no money then, and $45,000 sounded like a million. So I said, yeah.

He said that they were going to give me $15,000 then and $30,000 if they did the movie. They had five years to decide. He said Walt Disney weren't that sure that they were going to do no movie on Tina – that was the bullshit he was telling me.

And I didn't have to do anything but give them permission for somebody else to play me in the movie.

I don't care who's gonna play me in the movie. Tina and I are not together – whoever she wants, it doesn't matter to me. He said nothing about me signing away my rights to sue them if they portrayed me wrong.

Anyway, I am all eyes for this $15,000 so I can get back over there to that cocaine. I fucked up and signed the contract without reading it properly. So I got that $15,000 and went and bought cocaine. I found me a place to stay and put my band together, bought me a car – whatever $15,000 would do.

I got out of jail on 3 September 1991, and in 1992 the five years they had to make up their minds whether they were going to do the movie or not were up. Now I read the contract and find out that I have signed away my rights to sue them if they show me in the wrong light. So then I was hoping that Disney wouldn't send this $30,000, but the money came. I talked to some more lawyers about it and tried to get out of it, but we didn't talk to the right lawyers, man.

I don't believe you can sign nothing, legally, that can put your life in danger, not for no amount of money. And my life is in danger, man. A lot of people who are real fans of Tina's want to stick something in me for what the movie said I did. I don't believe that is legal. Anyway, they got away with it.

> Ike was not consulted at all by the movie's producers, but he did happen to drive by when filming *What's Love Got to Do With It?* was underway.

When they were doing the movie up at the house, I was riding by there one day with Lenny Marmor. They had big trucks parked alongside the street. I didn't know nothing about who was playing who, but anyway, this guy Larry Fishburne comes over to the car and puts his hand on the window and says, 'Hey.' He had on some flash bellbottom pants. He say, 'Hey, man, I think you're going to be real proud of what I'm doing in the movie. Will you show me how you walk?'

Then it dawned on me that this guy was playing me in the movie. I got out and showed him how I walk.

He said, 'I turned down this movie three or four times until they fixed the script so it showed some parts of you as a musician. If you beat her as much as they had it, when did you have time to make her a star? I think you will be real proud of what I've done.'

I am very proud of what he did. I think he did a fantastic job, though the job he did isn't really me. But he did great overall, from what he had to work with, because they never wanted him to meet me.

If he'd met me he couldn't play the kind of dude they wanted me to be in the movie, 'cos I ain't that kinda dude. I got temper, and I'm dominating and all that shit about what I want as far as music is concerned, but I ain't what they had me be.

When *What's Love Got to Do With It?* came out, Ike suddenly found himself public enemy number one. He is particularly outraged by the rape scene in the film. No rape allegation appeared in Tina's autobiography, *I, Tina*. And, according to *Ebony* magazine, Tina was 'not at all happy with some aspects of the film'. It was noticeable that she did not stand behind the movie when it was released.

Some people said, 'Ike, you going to be finished. Man, people going to hate your guts.'

A lot of women saw the movie, and if they are not open-minded and see it as a one-sided movie, they actually believe I am that type of dude. Tina and me, we had our fights, but we ain't had no more fights than anybody else.

I think the rape in that movie was the lowest thing they could ever have done. I am sure that Tina would agree that is something I would never do. I think that anyone who rapes a person, man or woman, or sells drugs to a minor, should have their eyes plucked out. 'Cos that is the lowest thing anybody could ever do to anyone. I don't think anything can justify a person raping or selling a kid drugs.

The movie gave me high notoriety. It did me no good, it don't put no money in your pocket. They say that all publicity is good publicity. Well, that maybe true in a sense, but it don't help you financially.

I wasn't angry with Tina about it, not at first. Before the book came out, I think I could probably have stopped it. People had told me a little bit about what she had said, but I figured that she had just done it to get sympathy from the public.

See, when Tina and I broke up this was the time of the beginning of feminist stuff. I think things like this helped boost her career, so I never would defend myself against shit like that, or rebut anything she said.

I'm sitting there doing nothing with my career, having fun with the cocaine and the girls and stuff, so if that's going to get her where she got to go, so what?

But then when I got out of jail I got my life back on track and now I'm clean – I don't need this in my life, man. If she started bashing me again today, I would take a real nasty attitude, because she has reached her goal. She's up there, man. Now I got to get there. I don't need any more bashing. I don't think I deserved it in the first place, regardless of what happened in our personal life.

Whatever I did, it's done. I can't undo the past. I'm sure we all have done things that we regret. I'm sorry for the embarrassment that I put her through with girls and things, but I was just young and didn't know no better, and I was just having fun. I hope she can forgive and forget.

In the meantime, I got a problem. I got the best show in the world, but it is hard for me to get work. That movie hurt me so bad, man, in so many different ways. My fucking career, man. I got a good show and everything, people are crazy about my show. But there are people who won't even come and see it because of the way I am portrayed in that movie. All the negative publicity makes it hard for me to get started.

See, some people are sons of bitches. I called a booking agency. The man there is this guy I've known all my life, since I been into music. Little Richard gave me his number and said, 'Call him, he'll get you some work, man.'

So I had Andy Ania call him. He said he'd call back in ten minutes. So he calls back in ten minutes and says, 'Hey, man, nobody in the office interested in booking Ike Turner.'

That's a cold thing. Man, that hurt me. That was a rejection.

Then, up at B.B. King's Club in Century City, B.B. announces that I am in the audience and tells a story about how good a producer I am and how I put a band together, all of this stuff. He builds me up for my talent. So I asked B.B. if he could get his booking agency to get me on some tours with him, because it would really help me.

Maybe he is too busy with his career, but man, I need to keep my group together. I can't hold them if they don't work. I asked him to ask his agency, but that's all I can do. I can't be getting on my knees.

And when the Rolling Stones toured America in 1994, they wouldn't help, either.

I know I got a bitching show right now, and I tried to call Keith Richards a million times. And I called Ron Wood a million times. I can't even reach them, man, never mind get on a show with them. But I know my show is better now than it was with Ike and Tina. That's how phoney people can be. Maybe this was the reason why Mick didn't call me this time. Maybe they figured that my show would be too hot for them, like we was in 1969.

I read some of this shit Keith Richards is supposed to have said about me. I can't believe it. I thought we were tighter than that. He may not have said it, you can't believe everything you read.

But there ain't no reason for anybody to favour me or Tina – just be real about what it is. I never got a call from any of the Stones. That tour would have meant the world to me. It would have exposed me to a lot of kids who don't know me and it would have opened a lot of doors.

Although his career was taking another hammering, Ike was beginning to put his family back together.

That's another thing I got pissed off at Tina about. Our son Ronnie played with Tina after we broke up. They played somewhere out of the country.

The band always get to work before the star. Ronnie and

them got to work, set up all the equipment and stuff, did all the sound checks. Then Ronnie went outdoors. And when the limousine pulls up and Tina steps out of the limo, Ronnie walks up there and kisses her, 'cos that's the way he's raised. All my kids have been raised to be affectionate.

But from what Ronnie told me, Tina said to him, 'Don't ever do that again.' And she fired him.

I don't believe that she fired him just for that – I think it's more likely that she fired him for his drinking – but I believe she did tell him not to kiss her in public like that. You know, he'd just walk up and grab you and hug you and kiss you like that. He'd kiss me like that. That's how he was raised.

When I got out of jail, Ronnie played with me. I used Ronnie on bass when I first put my band together. She's got to know about that.

The split had a devastating effect on the children. One Ike found living in a shelter for the homeless in South Central LA. And there has been involvement with drugs – though, with Ike's help, one son has been weaned off.

Michael hasn't seen Tina for years. Ike Junior don't see her, but he gets money from her every once in a while. But Ike Junior would ask her for money; Michael wouldn't until lately. That's a damn shame. Ain't no way in the world that one of those kids needed something and I wouldn't give it to them, man.

Craig, I haven't seen since 1976. I wouldn't know him if I walked up on him.

Ronnie sees Tina all the time. He is the only one who belongs to me and her. And Craig, he don't belong to me, and he sees her all the time. The two not of her blood she don't see at all. Which is a damn shame, 'cos I felt all four of those kids were mine. I really felt that Craig was my son and I still do.

There is no communication with any of the rest of Tina's family.

All of them are so scared. Her mother, her sister and her niece won't associate with anybody who has anything to do with me.

But some people have stood by Ike: Mel Johnson and his wife, Nancy, who have known both Ike and Tina since they were all together in St Louis, and mutual friend Norris Williams.

When I played at the Roosevelt Hotel, Bobby Womack gave me two stage suits and two pairs of shoes. Years ago I gave him money to pay off his bills and his note on his car, so I consider him a friend of mine.

He had a Rolls-Royce and a Mercedes. I said, 'Man, look if you see a time you're not going to be able to keep your Rolls-Royce, let me know. I know a lot of strings you can pull before you lose something.'

Man, his pride and shit – he lost it and he didn't even let me know. I really hated that, but I understood it. It's that pride. But the way I look at it, damn, he gave it back to the white man before he'd let me have it.

Gradually, public perception of Ike Turner has begun to turn around.

Slowly, through the television and the radio, people are beginning to see me and hear me and know what I really have in my heart, and accept me for what I am. Not taking me for the way I am portrayed in that movie, but judging me for my music – which is the way it should be – not for the way I live, or the way they think I lived, my life.

Believe it or not, man, people can feel whether something on TV is real – when you are real and when you are phoney. I did some interviews and I think they did a lot for me. People got to realise that that movie is a one-sided thing. Anyone with common sense can see that it is one person's view.

Now, some people see Tina as a woman scorned. Women, when they get mad, they turn on you. They might say anything or do anything. Some people think it's that, so there's mixed feelings out there.

One TV appearance in particular made the headlines. Ike went on *The Geraldo Show* with Jeanette Bazzell. Geraldo asked her if she would marry Ike after seeing the movie *What's Love Got to Do With It?*

She said, sure. Ike was nothing like the way he was portrayed in the movie. Then she said she wanted to be a June bride. Ike was then asked to name the day. He said the 31 June.

The newswires picked this up and grandly announced that Ike was engaged. But of course, there is no 31 June. Nevertheless, Ike says he is as good as his word. He is prepared to marry Jeanette on any 31 June.

Ike has also been picked up on by a new generation of gangsta rappers. In one Ice-T number, the lyrics go: 'I don't want to be like Mike, I want to be like Ike.'

The movie does not seem to have harmed Ike much on the Continent, either.

A lot of Spanish and Italian kids who see Larry Fishburne in that movie, they think that's the way a man's supposed to be anyhow.

And Ike has a 1–900 number in America 1–900–990–IKE1 – which people can call to hear his side of the story.

21 Battle of the Bands

Ike is all too painfully aware of where things went wrong in his life.

CAME TO A SPLIT IN THE ROAD and I took the wrong road, man. The split was when I started doing drugs. I took a left when I should have taken a right. It brought my life down to zero, man.

Other rock stars have taken drugs and got away with it.

We was Ike and Tina. Tina didn't do drugs; I did.

Joe Cocker, he drank like a fish. Finally he got his head back on and he's pulling back up again. But he destroyed his life like I destroyed mine.

You see, my career never really got started. When I met Tina, I forgot my own career. Then I was afraid to go back to it after I started with her. So now I am scared to go back to the guitar, I am scared to go back to the piano.

But if you think back, I put out an album called *The Edge*, and there's only Ike on that album. But, well, that's where my head was when Tina and me broke up.

The drugs are all behind him now. He won't take more than half a cup of coffee, does not drink alcohol and is appalled if anyone smokes a joint within range of his nostrils.

I got six years going on seven clean. As a matter of fact, I intend to be a role model for all present drug-users, demonstrating that you can get back to your original self, look good again, and feel good about yourself again. But it is going to take complete change: new surroundings, new friends, new places to go; and you're gonna have to keep busy. There are ways to get off the drugs and stay off them, but an idle mind is the devil's workshop.

And I got a new Revue, the Ike Turner Revue. I will say this point blank, I have the best show in the whole world. It's a hot show, man – I'm talking way hotter than it was when it was Ike and Tina. I have four girls, and let me tell you something for a fact, we just got the award for the best performance of the year in Japan.

I did a show like Ike and Tina's because I figured that kids who are twenty-five years old today, when Tina and I broke up nineteen years ago, they were about six years old. They've never seen a show like we did then. That would be something for kids to see.

But now they are trying to bring me out front. I don't know whether I am going to make it. Man, I am an organiser – I ain't no goddamn artist. I put together a show, I am not the one who is supposed to be out there doing all that shit.

I hope that somewhere along the line Tina and I can work together in some form. I feel that this is something the public would want to see, even if it is just one trip around the world, one time. I think of that as a fun tour. A musical battle between Ike and Tina onstage would be something the public would go for, and so would I. 'Ike and Tina back together' would make the front page of every newspaper in the world.

It would be no sweat off her back if we went on tour together. It is nothing out of her pocket; it is not a degrading thing to her. We don't even have to talk. If she don't want to see me, she don't have to see me. She can just go and do her show, stay at whatever hotel her people stay at, and I can stay wherever.

But I just think, financially, in the condition that I am in these days – I just think it would be advantageous to both of us. And a lot of people would like to see Ike and Tina together.

So what is keeping them apart?

At first, I thought it was the managers and shit. But I haven't made any effort at all to say nothing to her. I tried hard before we parted not to let it break up, now I got no more ammunition. I ain't going to go licking ass with her to do something. But the damn market has turned around. It is hard to get record deals. It is a bit easier for her, it's rougher for me on account of I been away from it for eighteen years. But I never want to feel within myself that she reached out and picked me up because I fell to zero. If I was doing a tour with her, I'm doing it myself.

I could make the first approach – it would be the way to do it, but it takes you right back to the possibility of rejection again. Tina is so big, she ain't like the Tina I know. She done got to be like she is a star and shit, like everybody else is smaller than her.

I don't think she would act that way with me – in fact, I am sure she wouldn't.

The possibilities of an emotional reconciliation are even more remote.

I have always loved Tina – I love her right now. But I don't like her. I don't like her at all. She ain't the one I know. I think she forgot where she came from.

She don't like blacks. She forgets that she is black. She don't associate with blacks. I've never been in love with Tina in my life. I love her, I really love her, just like you love your sister, as I've said. We were for each other, man. Everything else was on the outside of us.

Tina may live in a different world, but Ike certainly hasn't forgotten where he has come from.

About eight months ago, I went down to Mississippi, where I was born. I walked over the neighbourhood. All over where I used to live, man, where I'm from. And I looked at that neighbourhood and I said, 'God brought me from here!' Boy, that's unbelievable.

I went there with Jeanette. On the way back, I was pulled over for speeding. It was a black dude. He said, 'Brother, look, if one of these honkies stop you, you're going to be in real trouble, driving at 130mph with a white woman in the car in Mississippi. Between here and Memphis, there are fifty or sixty highway patrols. There have been a lot of accidents on this road and they are trying to slow things down.' So this dude, he escorted me. He stayed on my bumper all the way to the state line.

> Ike feels that he can still make a comeback, possibly by basing himself in Europe – he would like to live in Germany. He thinks that black music in America is in trouble.

Tina said that when she went to record companies in America they said she was too old – and this was before she made it. It was six or ten years before she could get a record deal. So she went to London. That's where she got herself started again, because America has more followers than doers, man.

Black radio stations and black disc-jockeys, they've sold out, man. They sold out the black race. Creative talent? Our kids don't know a fucking thing about it. Today, you don't have any Otis Reddings, you don't have any Jackie Wilsons. There are no more Roy Browns, no more Louis Jordans, no more Joe Texes or B.B. Kings. Blacks are ashamed of the blues.

You listen to white music, man, and you got country, you got bluegrass, you got rock 'n' roll, you got rock, you got acid rock – you got a trillion kinds. Among blacks what have you got? You got black women that sing like Anita Baker and Whitney Houston, but you ain't got no Elton Johns or Rod Stewarts.

Man, we got all kinds of talent around, but you know what we settle for? We settle for a loop. All you hear from black men today is rap shit, man. We're settling for a damn loop. And you got to be putting the women down, you got to be talking about dope. There ain't no decent black shit out today, man.

Believe me, I love all kinds of music, I really do. So I can't say I hate rap. There is a little rap that I like. I like Salt 'n' Pepa . . .

He should. Their 'Shoop Song' is one of his, and the royalty cheques are rolling in.

... but man, I don't like Snoop Doggy Dog. I don't like nothing he do. I don't like that talking about, the bitch this, the bitch that. I don't like people putting people down. If you can't say something good about people, don't say nothing at all. The black kids today don't know nothing about being creative; they don't know anything about what comes straight from the gut. When Elmore James really hollers out you can feel his soul within his voice. They don't know nothing about this. All they know is the guy on the corner is driving a damn Mercedes or a Rolls-Royce and he got chicks all over him and he got pockets full of money, 'cos he sell dope.

Blacks want to stand on their fucking own and tell whitey to go kiss his ass, but it's the blacks who sold out the blacks, man. For what? A dollar. They don't know what they can do, or what they can't do. I think that blacks have just got to get up off of their asses and put their foot down and say, we are not going to disgrace our women and call them bitches. And we are not going to tell our kids that the way to get a Mercedes and a pocketful of money, man, is by selling dope.

We got to take a little starving if that's what it takes to get our dignity back. We got guys like Rod Stewart, Elton John and all this shit amongst the blacks. But these rappers, man, they end up in jail. They get caught with a fucking gun in their pocket and a gramme of cocaine.

Los Angeles County Jail is supposed to have only 5,800 people inside. They got over 10,000 people in there – 98 per cent black, man – blacks and Hispanics. It's a damn shame.

I used to do dope, so I understand the dope side of it, but there has got to be something done about black music today. I think entertainers owe that to the younger generation. We owe it to them to express things that make the world better, not to tear the world down.

If I had my life over again, I would live it much the same way. But I would give my kids more of me. I gave them all the material things. I had housekeepers, but I didn't spend a lot of time taking the kids to Disneyland and doing fun things with them because we were on the road for eleven months of the year. So I think that part would be different.

And Tina and I didn't have a fun life of our own – you know, like going out to the movies and enjoying ourselves, or going skating, or going on vacation. It was all work. I regret that. But as for the other part, I have no regrets.

All of this shit that it took to make me what I am today, I don't regret any of it. I love me today. Maybe if I hadn't done what I did in my past, I wouldn't feel this way about myself now.

And when I say Little Richard copied my style of playing from 'Rocket 88', when I tell them that shit about Elvis Presley, nobody believes it. I don't care whether they believe it or not. I ain't on no ego trip. I don't care about the glory or nothing.

Man, I don't give a fuck about any of it. They can say what they want to say. I am going to say it like it is.

Epilogue
by Nigel Cawthorne

I started down the long road that culminated in this book in 1993, shortly before Tina's movie *What's Love Got to Do With It?* came out in England. There was a documentary on Channel 4 about Tina. In it were Mick Jagger, Elton John and David Bowie. They all praised her to the skies, as well they might. But they said nothing about Ike.

As even the most cursory reading of the history of popular music shows that Ike Turner began rock 'n' roll – the music that made Jagger, John and Bowie very wealthy men indeed – they could at least have made a nod in his direction. The only person who had anything good to say about Ike was Tina herself. And Ike's only appearance in the documentary was in the blue uniform of the California State Penitentiary.

So when *What's Love Got to Do With It?* came out, I went to see it. As a Hollywood biopic in the tradition of *The Eddie Cantor Story*, it was good as far as it went. However, it depicted Ike as a hulking brute dominating a petite Tina. I knew from 1960s album covers that Ike was slight and that Tina is a strong and – not to put too fine a point on it – beefy woman, muscular and powerful. Would you dare hit Tina Turner? She would tear your head off.

Nevertheless, most people took the film at face value. You could walk into any pub in London, mention the name Ike Turner and be greeted with a one-word response: wife-beater. It seemed to me that Ike Turner had been tried in the court of world public opinion, found guilty and sentenced without anybody hearing the case for the defence. This offended my sense of justice – as I am sure it would that of any decent person. But more than that, Ike Turner was a significant

241

human being. He had made a great contribution to the world, and yet he had been written off by mere accusation.

Tina's book, *I, Tina*, made it clear that she could be pretty violent too. In cases of domestic violence, once it comes to blows, people begin to live in their own separate realities, and there are, after all, two sides to every story. Most people get little more than a wrecked house, a broken heart and a few stitches in the casualty ward. But Ike Turner, this son of Mississippi, seemed to have suffered little short of lynching. So I determined to do something about it. So what if he was a wife-beater? Even a murderer gets a counsel for the defence.

It took me about three weeks to track down his phone number. I called him and asked him if I could write a book about him. He said, 'Sure'. I felt that at the time he was not getting too many phone calls.

Then came the hard part. Publishers go to the movies too, and, although they are liberal by nature, they have to sell into a market that is not. Besides, these days publishers – especially American publishers – have to be seen to be politically correct. And Ike Turner, with his chicks and niggers and mother-fuckers, is anything but that. But, eventually, I found a British publisher to take the book on.

Then came the really hard part. Have you ever tried to make a deal with an old rock 'n' roller? These guys want cash in their pockets before they go onstage. They have been ripped off by the white man once, twice, probably a hundred times too often. My literary agent earned every penny of his 10 per cent.

So then I went to California to hang out with the guy. He was, of course, charming. Women fell at his feet, despite the reputation the movie had given him. He genuinely prefers women to men.

While women fawned over him, in banks and shops and on the street, many men saw him as a hero. One black guy even told me, 'The man had to do what he had to do. The bitch is a ho.'

Ike has a volcanic temper and he can be scary to be with. But he can also be kind and generous. The singer Barbara Cole told me that after she had an operation for polyps on her vocal chords, he took her in and taught her to sing again. And while

I was there, Ike helped one of his new Ikettes and her four children to escape from an abusive husband. I suggested that he set up the Ike Turner Refuge for Battered Wives, though I doubt he would get support from many women's groups.

The man works tirelessly. He hands out pictures and handbills and signs autographs as though he were a politician running for office. But he knows that it all counts. He presses the flesh in the soul-food restaurants in which he eats twice a day and will even pull over a police car to hand the officers a glossy ten by eight, signed with a hand-written message – perhaps 'What's love got to do with it? Not a goddamn thing'. This is the way he reaches his public.

He drives a gold Mercedes and dresses like a rock star. He has a studded leather jacket, painted silver, purple suits, collarless shirts, leather riding boots. His hands are heavy with chunky gold rings and bracelets. And round his neck hangs a gold scorpion encrusted with diamonds. Scorpio is his star sign, but it would suit him anyway.

He is certainly a dominating character. Travelling anywhere with him, you become an acolyte, you get to stand behind him like a minder. You get to run out to the car to get more pictures, to dial phone numbers or hold things for him. I have stood just a couple of months of this. How did Tina manage eighteen years? But then, when you are alone with him and he plays the piano or the guitar and sings an old blues song, or you hear him composing, you know you are in the presence of a genius.

He and I made an odd couple hanging out in the clubs and after-hours joints of Los Angeles: a streetwise black from the Deep South and a suburban white from the Home Counties. Could this have been why, in a bizarre incident involving one of Ike's players and his girlfriend's stolen car, my computer was sold in a crack house in San Diego for one rock of $10? That is where the first draft of this book now resides.

We made an even odder couple when we travelled back to Clarksdale together. 'You and me couldn't have done this back then,' Ike pointed out as we sped down Route 61.

Clarksdale is about the size of Reigate, only in terminal decay. It was a bit like going to the Isle of Wight or Staten

Island – leaping back forty years. People were friendly, but suspicious. Guns bristled in pockets.

We visited the house where Ike was born, the places he had his first sexual experiences, his father's chapel, the funeral home where the corpse fell on him, the stores where he worked, the Riverside Hotel where he hung out with Robert Nighthawk, and John Lane's house, where he first heard the music of Pinetop Perkins. It was all so much smaller than I had imagined – except for the cotton compress where he saw that brutal murder. That was huge. We also visited the gas station where Denzil Turner, the epileptic, was shot.

The Alcazar Hotel was closed, though Ike obligingly sat on the pavement outside in the same spot where he watched the white girls with their little mink stoles getting out of their boyfriends' daddies' cars and wished for something he thought he could never have. But the radio station, WROX, was still broadcasting from the second floor and Early Wright was still doing his Sunday morning spiritual show.

We could not make out whether the town was now integrated. Ike was convinced it was not. As we drove out through Oakhurst, he barked repeatedly: 'Ain't no niggers living out here.'

We also discovered that just two years ago, the municipal swimming pool was filled in after a series of racial incidents. It seems that in Clarksdale, blacks and white still cannot get used to using the same water.

Despite his background, Ike is untainted by racial prejudice. He is simply brutally frank about it. The only colour he is the least bit concerned about is the colour of money – greenbacks or pink cashiers' cheques only, thank you.

We travelled back up the long, flat road which Ike took on his bike, clinging to the back of a truck, more than fifty years ago, past the serrated cotton fields, past the derelict sharecroppers' shacks, past the anonymous place where his mother and father are buried, past the outlying school where he once played and past the turn-off where the highway patrol had picked up Ike and the Kings of Rhythm in 1951, when they were on their way to their first, historic, recording session.

Ike was able to identify the cutting where he was forced to

let go of the truck. When we reached Memphis, we went to the Peabody Hotel. On the piano in the lobby – which bore a conspicuous sign reading: 'Do Not Touch' – Ike thundered out a boogie-woogie. When reprimanded, he apologised, explaining charmingly that when he had first come to Memphis, niggers were not allowed in the Peabody. Now he was staying in the celebrity suite.

Then we went to Sun Studios, which he had not visited since the early 1950s. He thought they had closed down. When he walked in the door he went straight to a piano and played, incongruously, the theme from *Chariots of Fire*.

Ike Turner is a maddening individual. His little goatee beard and his square-cut hair, raised slightly at the sides like horns, make him look like the devil. He has a diabolical laugh. But he is undoubtedly a human being – a tough, talented, irrepressible, complex human being.

When Ike went down for drugs, he did not complain that he was from a broken home. There was no special pleading. He took his punishment like a man. Now he asks for only one thing. He is sixty-seven, and he just wants to perform his music.

Ike Turner has contributed to the world. He has certainly given more than he will take away. He has suffered more than his accusers. Who could deny him that?

Notes on the Ike Turner Discography

Compiled by Ray Topping, June 1995

During the years 1951 to 1955 Ike Turner was employed as a talent scout and a sideline musician for the Modern Record Company of Los Angeles, owned by the Bihari Brothers, Jules, Saul, and Joe. Through these years Ike accompanied Joe Bihari on many field recording trips in the southern states and Ike's piano skills were featured on most of these sessions, backing artists such as B.B. King, Howlin' Wolf, Elmore James, Jimmie Lee and Artis, Ben Burton, Houston Boines, Brother Bell, Charlie Booker, Baby Face Turner, Driftin Slim, Sunny Blair, Junior Brooks, and Boyd Gilmore. Between 1958 and 1959 Ike Turner also backed up Otis Rush and Buddy Guy on various Cobra sessions.

Ike switched to playing guitar in 1953, and by early 1954 Joe Bihari and Ike built a makeshift recording studio, in a disused Greyhound bus station in Clarksdale, Miss., using his Kings Of Rhythm as studio musicians. They cut many sides for the Modern, RPM and Flair labels. Some of these artists were one-time members of the Kings of Rhythm who worked as vocalists and musicians and include Clayton Love (pianist), Dennis Binder (pianist), Billy Gales (drummer), Lonnie 'The Cat' (L. C. Cation) (drummer), Billy 'The Kid' Emerson (pianist), Eugene Fox (The Fox, Sly Fox) (saxophonist), Jesse Knight Sr (Fender bassist), Johnny Wright (guitarist), J. W. Walker (pianist), Bonnie Turner (pianist).

In 1980 I started a reissue series of these modern recordings for Ace Records that included three albums, ACE CH 22, CHD 146, and CHD 244. These are now out of print. However to coincide with this publication Ace have released a CD, *Rhythm Rockin' Blues*.

The Personnel of The Kings Of Rhythm

The Kings Of Rhythm or Delta Cats 1951
Ike Turner (Pno) Jackie Brenston (Vo-bari sax) Raymond Hill
(Ts) Eugene Fox (Ts) Willie Kizart (Gtr) Willie Sims (Dms)

The Kings Of Rhythm 1953/54
Ike Turner (Gtr/Pno) Raymond Hill, Eugene Fox, Bobby Fields
(Saxes) Bonnie Turner (Pno) Jesse Knight (Bass/Gtr) Bob
Prindell (Dms)

The Kings Of Rhythm 1956
Ike Turner (Gtr) Raymond Hill, Eddie Jones, Jackie Brenston
(Saxes) Annie Mae Wilson (Pno) Jesse Knight (Bass/Gtr)
Eugene Washington (Dms)

The Kings Of Rhythm 1957/58
Ike Turner (Gtr) Carlson Oliver, Eddie Jones (Ts) Erskine
Oglesby (Bari) Fred Sample (Pno) Jesse Knight (Bass Gtr)
Eugene Washington (Dms)

The Kings Of Rhythm 1959/60
Ike Turner (Gtr) Eddie Silvers, Rasheed Ishmael (Norman
Rich) (Ts) Marvin Warwick (Bari) Fred Sample (Pno) Jesse
Knight (Bass Gtr) T.N.T Tribble (Dms)

The Kings Of Rhythm 1962/63
Ike Turner (Gtr) Jess Herring (Tbn) Mac Johnson (Tp) Rasheed
Ishmael (Ts) Eddie Silvers (Ts) Marvin Warwick (Bari) Ernest
Lane (Pno) Sam Rhodes (Bass Gtr) Thomas Norwood (Dms)

The Kings Of Rhythm 1964/65
Ike Turner (Gtr) Russell Jacquet (Tp) Clifford Solomon (Ts)
Ray Phil Davers (Bari) Ernest Lane (Pno) Sam Rhodes (Bass
Gtr) Thomas Norwood (Dms)

The Family Vibes '70s
Ike Turner (Gtr/Keyboards) Claude Williams (Tp) McKinley Johnson (Tp) Edmund Burks (Tbn) Jimmy Smith (Ts) J. D. Reed (Ts) Jackie Clark (Gtr) Larry Reed (Pno/Ts) Warren Dawson (Bass Gtr) Soko Richardson (Dms)

Discography

Jackie Brenston and his Delta-Cats: *Vocal* 1951
Rocket 88   Chess 1458
Come Back Where You Belong   Chess 1458
Independent Woman   Chess 1472

Ike Turner and his King's of Rythm (sic): *Vocal* 1951
Heart Broken And Worried   Chess 1459
I'm Lonesome Baby   Chess 1459

Jackie Brenston and his Delta Cats: *Vocal* 1951
In My Real Gone Rocket   Chess 1469

Ike Turner singing with Ben Burton Orch: *Vocal* 1952
You're Driving Me Insane   RPM 356
Trouble And Heartaches   RPM 356

Mary Sue: *Vocal* 1952
Everybody's Talking   Modern 880
Love Is A Gamble   Modern 880

Bonnie and Ike Turner: *Vocal Duet* 1952
My Heart Belongs To You   RPM 362
Looking For My Baby   RPM 362

Ike and Bonnie Turner: *Vocals* 1953
Camping In Canaan's Land   Sun (Unissued)
Way Down In The Congo   Sun (Unissued), Charly (UK)
                                                   CR LP 30103
Old Brother Jack   Sun (Unissued), Charly (UK)
                                                   CR LP 30103
Love Is A Gamble   Sun (Unissued), Charly (UK)
                                                   CR LP 30103

Johnny O'Neal with Ike Turners band: *Vocal* 1953
Trouble   Sun (Unissued)
Devil's Dream (Johnny's Dream)   Sun (Unissued), Charly
                                                   Sunbox 105

Ugly Woman	Sun (Unissued), Charly CR LP 30103
Dead Letter Blues	Sun (Unissued), Charly CR LP 30103
Peg Leg Baby	Sun (Unissued), Krazy Kat LP 7427

Billy 'The Kid' Emerson: *Vocal* 1954
No Teasin' Around	Sun 195
If Lovin's Is Believin'	Sun 195
Hey Little Girl	Charley (UK) LP CR 30187

Billy 'The Kid' Emerson: *Vocal* 1954
I'm Not Going Home	Sun 203, Charly (UK) LP CR 30187
The Wood Chuck	Sun 203, Charly (UK) LP CR 30187
When My Baby Quit Me	Charly (UK) LP CR 30187

Eugene Fox: *Vocal* 1954
Stay At Home	Checker 792
Sinners Dream	Checker 792

Lover Boy: *Vocal Ike Turner* 1954
Why Did You Leave Me	Ace (UK) LP CHD 244
Love Is Scarce	RPM 409
The Way You Used To Treat Me	RPM 409
Nobody Wants Me	Crown LP 5367
Nobody Seems To Want Me	Ace (UK) LP CHD 244

Lonnie 'The Cat': With Bobby Hines Band & members of The Kings Of Rhythm: *Vocal* 1954
I Ain't Drunk	RPM 410
The Road I Travel	RPM 410

Clayton Love: *Vocal* 1954
Wicked Little Baby	Modern 929
Why Don't You Believe Me	Modern 929

Dennis Binder: *Vocal* 1954
I Miss You So	Modern 930
Early Times	Modern 930
You Got Me Way Down Here	Ace (UK) LP CH 22

Mat Cockrell: *Vocal* 1954
Baby Please	Flair 1037
Gypsy Blues	Flair 1037

Raymond Hill: *Ts* 1954
The Snuggle (Inst)	Sun 204
Burbon Street Jump (Inst)	Sun 204

Ike Turner & Orch: 1954

Cubano Jump (Inst)	Flair 1040
Loosely (Inst)	Flair 1040
Cuban Get Away (Inst)	Flair 1059
Go To It (Inst)	Flair 1059

(Note: Above titles reissued on Crown LP 5367 and retitled respectively 'Hey Miss Tina', 'The Wild One', 'Bayou Rock', 'Stringin' Along')

All The Blues All The Time	Crown LP 5367

Billy Gale and his Orch: *Vocal* 1954

Night Howler	Flair 1038
My Heart In Your Hands	Flair 1038
A Woman Just Won't Do	Flair (Unissued), Ace (UK) LP CHD 244
I'm Tired Of Being Dogged Around	Flair (Unissued), Ace (UK) LP CHD 244

The Flairs: *Vocal Group* 1954

Baby Wants	Flair 1041
You Were Untrue	Flair 1041

Young Jessie and The Flairs:

Why Do I Love You	Flair (Unissued), Ace LP CHD 225

Richard Berry: *Vocal*

Real Good Lovin Man	Ace (UK) CD CH 355

Ike Turners Kings Of Rhythm: *Unknown Vocalist*

Goodbye Baby	Modern (Unissued), Ace (UK) LP CH 22
Love My Baby	Modern (Unissued), Ace (UK) LP CH 22

The Fox: *Vocal* 1954

The Dream Part 1	RPM 420
The Dream Part 2	RPM 420
The Dream (Alt Take)	Ace (UK) LP CH 22

Little Johnny Burton: *Vocal* 1954

Why Did You Go Away	Modern (Unissued), Ace (UK) LP CHD 146
Talking About Me	Modern (Unissued), Ace (UK) LP CHD 146
Walk My Way Back Home	Modern (Unissued), Ace (UK) LP CHD 146
One Day	Modern (Unissued), Ace (UK) LP CHD 146

Ike Turner: *Gtr* 1954
  Canton Mississippi Breakdown (Inst)   Kent LP 9001

N.B. Wrongly credited to Elmore James on this album. Ike cut this instrumental at the end of Elmore James' recording session.

Jesse Knight & his Combo: 1954
  Nobody Seems To Want Me   Checker 797
  Nothing But Money   Checker 797

The Sly Fox: *Vocal* 1954
  Hoo-Doo Say   Spark 108
  I'm Tired Of Beggin'   Spark 108
  My Four Women   Spark 112
  Alley Music   Spark 112

J. W. Walker: *Vocal* 1954 (Rel 1970)
  J Ws Blues   Kent LP 9012
  Sitting Here Wondering   Kent LP 9012
  Can't See You Baby   Ace LP (UK) CHD 146
  Why Won't You Be True   (Unissued)

Johnny Wright: *Vocal* 1955
  The World Is Yours   RPM 443
  Suffocate   RPM 443

The Trojan's: *Vocal group with Ike Turner's Orch* 1956
  As Long As I Have You   RPM 446
  I Wanna Make Love To You   RPM 446

Billy Gales: *Vocal* 1956
  I Miss You So   Modern (Unissued), Ace
                           (UK) LP CHD 146

Willie King: *Billy Gales Vocal* 1956
  Peg Leg Woman   Vita 123
  Mistreating Me   Vita 123

The Rockers: *Vocal Group* 1956
  What Am I To Do   Federal 12267
  I'll Die In Love With You   Federal 12267
  Why Don't You Believe   Federal 12273
  Down In The Bottom   Federal 12273

Billy Gales with Ike Turner's Rhythm Rockers: *Vocal* 1956
  If I Had Never Known You   Federal 12265
  I'm Tore Up   Federal 12265
  Take Your Fine Frame Home   Federal 12272
  Let's Call It A Day   Federal 12272

Billy Gales with Ike Turner's Kings Of Rhythm: *Vocal* 1956
Do Right Baby	Federal 12282
No Coming Back	Federal 12282
Just One More Time	Federal 12287
Sad As A Man Can Be	Federal 12287

Jackie Brenston with Ike Turner's Kings Of Rhythm: *Vocal* 1956
What Can It Be	Federal 12283
Gonna Wait For My Chance	Federal 12283
Much Later	Federal 12291
The Mistreater	Federal 12291

The Gardenias: *Vocal Group* 1956
My Baby's Tops	Federal 12284
Flaming Love	Federal 12284
Miserable	Charly (UK) CRB 263
You Found The Time	Charly (UK) CRB 263

Ike Turner & His Orch: *Clayton Love Vocal (1)* 1957
Do You Mean It (1)	Federal 12297
She Made My Blood Run Cold (1)	Federal 12297, King 5553
The Big Question (1)	Federal 12304, King 5553
Rock-A-Bucket (Inst)	Federal 12304, King 5553
You've Changed My Love (1)	Federal 12307
Trail Blazer (Inst)	Federal 12307

Kenneth Churchill And The Lyric's with Ike Turner Orch: *Vocal* 1958
Would You Rather	Joyce 304
Fate Of Rock And Roll	Joyce 304

Ike Turner, Carlson Oliver & Little Ann: *(1)*
Ike Turner Orch – Fred Sample *Voc (2)* 1958
Box Top (1)	Tune Town 501
Chalypso Love Cry (2)	Tune Town 501

(The first recording ever by Tina)

Ike Turner Kings Of Rhythm: *Tommy Hodge Vocal*
I Told My Girl About You	Sun (Unissued)
Get It Over Baby	Sun (Unissued), Charly (UK) CR 30103
How Long Will It Last	Sun (Unissued), Charly (UK) CR 30103
I'm Gonna Forget About You	Sun (Unissued), Charly (UK) CR 30103
You Can't Be The One For Me	Sun (Unissued), Charly (UK) CR 30103
Why Should I Keep Trying	Sun (Unissued), Charly (UK) CR 30103

Ike Turner: *Tommy Hodge Vocal*   1959
    I Know You Don't Love Me   Royal American 105
    I'm On Your Trail   Royal American 105 (Rel
                                      '65)

Ike Turner and his Kings Of Rhythm: *Tommy Hodge Vocal*   1958
(Rel 1981)
    Matchbox (Version B)   Flyright (UK) LP 578
    Matchbox (Version A)   Flyright (UK) LP 578
    I Know You Don't Love Me No More   Flyright (UK) LP 578

Ike Turner and his Kings Of Rhythm: *Jackie Brenston Vocal*
    You Keep On Worrying Me   Flyright (UK) LP 578

Ike Turner and his Kings Of Rhythm: *Tommy Hodge Vocal*
    I'm Gonna Forget About You   Flyright (UK) LP 578
    How Long (Will It Last)   Flyright (UK) LP 578

Ike Turner and his Kings Of Rhythm: *Jackie Brenston Vocal*
    You've Got To Lose   Flyright (UK) LP 578

Ike Turner: *Ike, Billy Gales Vocals*
    Walking Down The Aisle   (Unissued Takes) Flyright
                              (UK) LP 578

Betty Everett: *Accompanied by the Kings Of Rhythm*
    Every Day Of My Life   Flyright (UK) LP 589
    Every Day Of My Life   Flyright (UK) LP 589
    I'll Weep No More   Cobra 5031, Flyright (UK)
                              LP 589

Betty Everett:
    Darling Tell Me   Flyright (UK) LP 589
    Darling Tell Me   Flyright (UK) LP 589
    Darling Tell Me   Flyright (UK) LP 589
    Tell Me Darling   Cobra 5031, Flyright (UK)
                              LP 589

(All the above sessions are from unissued Cobra masters)

Ike Turner's Kings Of Rhythm: *Tommy Hodge Vocal*   1959
    (I Know) You Don't Love Me   Artistic 1504
    Down And Out   Artistic 1504

Ike Turner's Kings Of Rhythm featuring Ike & Billy: *(1)*
Ike & Carl: *(2)* 1959
    Walking Down The Aisle (1)   Cobra 5033
    Box Top (2)   Cobra 5033

Icky Renrut: *Jimmy Thomas Vocal*   1959
    Jack Rabbit   Stevens 104
    In Your Eye's Baby   Stevens 104

Hey-Hey	Stevens 107
Ho-Ho (Inst)	Stevens 107
Tell Me Why	Stevens (Unissued), Red Lightnin (UK) LP 0047
Hey-Hey	Stevens (Unissued), Red Lightnin (UK) LP 0047
Prancin' (Inst)	Stevens (Unissued), Red Lightnin (UK) LP 0047

(Icky Renrut is Ike Turner back to front)

Ike Turner and the Kings Of Rhythm: 1959

My Love	Sue 722
That's All I Need	Sue 722

Ike & Tina Turner 1960

A Fool In Love	Sue 730, LP 2001, LP 2004
The Way You Love Me	Sue 730, LP 2001, LP 2004

Jackie Brenston with Ike Turner's Orch: 1960

Trouble Up The Road	Sue 736
You Ain't The One	Sue 736

Ike & Tina Turner: 1960

I Idolize You	Sue 735, LP 2001, LP 2004
Letter From Tina	Sue 735, LP 2001, LP 2004
I'm Jealous	Sue 740, LP 2001, LP 2004
You're My Baby	Sue 740, LP 2001, LP 2004

Eloise Hester:

My Man Rock Head	Sue 742
I Need You	Sue 742

Jimmy & Jean with Ike Turner's Orch: 1960

I Wanta Marry You	Sue 743
I Cant Believe	Sue 743

Ike & Tina Turner: 'The Soul Of . . .' 1961

It's Gonna Work Out Fine	Sue 749, LP 2004
Won't You Forgive Me	Sue 749, LP 2004
I Had A Notion	Sue LP 2001
You Can't Love Two	Sue LP 2001
Chances Are	Sue LP 2001
If	Sue LP 2001
Poor Fool	Sue 753, LP 2004
You Can't Blame Me	Sue 753, LP 2001
You Shoulda Treated Me Right	Sue 765, LP 2004
Sleepless	Sue 765, LP 2001, LP 2004

Ike Turner & his Kings Of Rhythm: 'Dance With Ike and Tina' 1962

It's Gonna Work Out Fine	Sue 760, LP 2003

Prancing	Sue 760, LP 2003
The Gully	LP 2003
Twista Roo	LP 2003
Track Down Twist	LP 2003
Potato Mash	LP 2003
Steel Guitar Rag	LP 2003
Double Mint	LP 2003
The Rooster	LP 2003
Katanga	LP 2003
The Groove	LP 2003
Going Home	LP 2003

All tracks on this LP are instrumental and feature Ike on guitar.

Ike & Tina Turner: 1962

Tra La La La	Sue 757, LP 2004
Puppy Love	Sue 757
Tina's Dilemma	Sue 768 (1963)
The Argument	Sue 772 (1962)
Mind In A Whirl	Sue 772
Worried And Hurtin Inside	Sue 774
Please Don't Hurt Me	Sue 774

Jimmy Thomas: 1962

You Can Go	Sue 778
Hurry And Come Home	Sue 778

Ike & Tina Turner: 1962

Make Up	Sue 784, LP 2005
Don't Play Me Cheap	Sue 784, LP 2005
I Made A Promise Up Above	LP 2005
Desire	LP 2005
Those Way's	LP 2005
Mama Tell Him	LP 2005
Pretend	LP 2005
The Real Me	LP 2005
Forever Mine	LP 2005
No Amending	LP 2005
Love Letters	LP 2005
My Everything To Me	LP 2005

Ike & Tina Turner: *'It's Gonna Work Out Fine'*

Gonna Find Me A Substitute	Sue LP 2007
This Man's Crazy	Sue LP 2007
Mojo Queen	Sue LP 2007
Kinda Strange	Sue LP 2007
Tinaroo	Sue LP 2007
I'm Gonna Cut You Loose	Sue LP 2007
Why Should I	Sue LP 2007

Foolish	Sue LP 2007
I'm Fallin' In Love	Sue LP 2007
Good Good Lovin'	Sue LP 2007

Dolores Johnson with Ike Turner's band: 1962
Give Me Your Love	Bobbin 132
Gotta Find My Baby	Bobbin 132

Tina Turner with Ikettes: 1962
Prisoner In Love (No Bail In This Jail)	Teena 1702
Those Words	Teena 1702

Robbie Montgomery with Ikettes:
Crazy In Love	Teena 1701
Pee-Wee	Teena 1701

Vernon Guy with Ike Turner's band & Ikettes: 1963
You've Got Me	Teena 1703
They Aint Lovin' Ya	Teena 1703

Flora Williams:
Love Me Or Leave Me	Teena (release number unknown)
I'll Wait For You	Teena (release number unknown)

Ike & Tina Turner: 1963
If I Can't Be First	Sonja 2001
I'm Going Back Home	Sonja 2001

Little Bones (The Worlds Greatest Singing Cricket): *Ike Turner* 1963
What I Say	Prann 5001
Ya-Ya	Prann 5001
Going To The River	Prann 5006
I Know	Prann 5006

The Turnabouts: *Featuring Ike Turner Gtr* 1963
Gettin' Away	Prann 5002
Cotton Pickin'	Prann 5002

The Nasty Minds:
Getting Nasty	Sonja 5001
Nutting Up	Sonja 5001

Bobby John: 1963
Lonely Soldier	Sony 111
The Bad Man	Sony 111

Venetta Fields: with Ike Turner's band 1963
You're Still My Baby	Sony 112
I'm Leaving You	Sony 112

Stacy Johnson:
Don't Believe 'Em	Sony 113
Remove My Doubts	Sony 113

Fontella Bass: *with Oliver Sain Orch: produced by Ike & Tina Turner*
I Love The Man	Prann 5005
My Good Loving	Prann 5005

Fontella Bass (or Fontella Bass and Tina Turner):
Poor Little Fool	**Sonja 2006, Vesuvius 1002**
This Would Make Me Happy	**Sonja 2006, Vesuvius 1002**

Ike & Tina Turner:
You Can't Miss Nothing That You Never Had	Sonja 2005
God Gave Me You	Sonja 2005

Vernon Guy:
Anything To Make It With You	Sonja 2007
Anything To Make It With You (Inst)	Sonja 2007

Jimmy Thomas with the Ike & Tina Revue:
You've Tasted Another's Lips	Sonja 2004
I Love Nobody But You	Sonja 2004

Ike & Tina Turner with the Ikettes:
Here's Your Heart Pt 1	Innis 3000
Here's Your Heart Pt 2 (Inst)	Innis 3000

Gloria Garcia with the Ike & Tina Revue:
No Puedes Extranar	Innis 3001
Koonkie Cookie	Innis 3001

Ike & Dee Dee Johnson:
You Can't Have Your Cake (And Eat it Too)	Innis 3002
The Drag	Innis 3002

Ike Turner's Kings Of Rhythm: *Jimmy Thomas Vocal* 1964 (Rel 1988)
Feelin' Good	Modern (Unissued), Ace (UK) CHD 244
I Smell Trouble	Modern (Unissued), Ace (UK) CHD 244
Mother-In-Law Blues	Modern (Unissued), Ace (UK) CHD 244
Tin Pan Alley	Modern (Unissued), Ace (UK) CHD 244

Tina Turner Vocal
Five Long Years   Modern (Unissued), Ace (UK) CHD 244

Bobby John Vocal
Dust My Blues   Modern (Unissued), Ace (UK) CHD 244

Vernon Guy Vocal
That's Alright   Modern (Unissued), Ace (UK) CHD 244

Ike Turner Guitar
Twistin' The Strings (Inst)   Modern (Unissued), Ace (UK) CHD 244

Ike & Tina Turner: 'Get It' 1964

Get It	Cenco 112, LP 104
You Weren't Ready	Cenco 112, LP 104
I Believe	LP 104
I Can't Believe	LP 104
My Babe	LP 104
Strange	LP 104
That's Alright	LP 104
Rooster	LP 104
Five Long Years	LP 104
Things I Used To Do	LP 104

N.B. Above album reissued on Capitol LP 571 'Her Man, His Woman' remastered with overdubbed brass and strings.

Ike & Tina Turner: 1964

I Can't Believe What You Say	Kent 402, LP 5014
My Baby Now	Kent 402, LP 5014

Ike & Tina Turner: 1964

A Fool For A Fool	Warner Bros 5433
No Tears To Cry	Warner Bros 5433
You're No Good	Loma LP 5904
It's All Over	Loma LP 5904
All I Can Do Is Cry	Loma LP 5904
A Fool For You	Loma LP 5904

Ike & Tina Turner: 1964

It's All Over	Warner Bros 5461
(I'll Do Anything) Just To Be With You	Loma 2015
Finger Poppin'	Warner Bros 5461

Ike & Tina Turner Show 'Live': 1964

Finger Poppin'	Warner Bros LP 1579
Down In The Valley	Warner Bros LP 1579

Good Times	Warner Bros LP 1579
You Are My Sunshine	Warner Bros LP 1579
Good Time Tonight	Warner Bros LP 1579
Twist And Shout	Warner Bros LP 1579
Somethings Got A Hold On Me	Warner Bros LP 1579
I Know	Warner Bros LP 1579
Tight Pants	Warner Bros LP 1579
My Man He's A Lovin Man	Warner Bros LP 1579
I Can't Stop Loving You	Warner Bros LP 1579
Tell The Truth	Warner Bros LP 1579
Shake A Tail Feather	Loma LP 5904
Oop-Poo-Pah-Doo	Warner Bros 5493, Loma LP 5904
Keep On A Pushin'	Loma LP 5904
You Must Believe In Me	Loma LP 5904
Early In The Morning	Loma LP 5904
Somebody Somewhere Needs You	Loma 2015

The Ike & Tina Turner Show: *'Live'* 1964

Please Please Please	Kent 409, LP 5014
Feel So Good	Kent LP 5014
The Love Of My Man	Kent LP 5014
Think	Kent LP 5014
Drown In My Own Tears	Kent LP 5014
I Love The Way You Love	Kent LP 5014
You're Precious Love	Kent LP 5014
All In My Mind	Kent LP 5014

Ike & Tina Turner: 1964

Am I A Fool In Love	Kent 409, LP 519
I'm Thru With Love	Loma 2011
Merry Christmas Baby	Warner Bros 5493

Stacey Johnson with Ike Turner's band: 1964

Don't Believe Him	Modern 1001
Consider Yourself	Modern 1001

Ike & Tina Turner: 1965

Tell Her I'm Not Home	Loma 2011
Please Leave Me Alone	Edsel (UK) LP 243
Too Many Tears	Edsel (UK) LP 243

Ike & Tina Turner: 1965

He's The One	Kent 418
Chicken Shack	Kent 418, LP 519
If I Can't Be First	Kent LP 519

Ike & Tina Turner:

Somebody Needs You	Loma 2015

Ike & Tina Turner:

Goodbye So Long	Modern 1007, Kent LP 519
Hurt Is All You Gave Me	Modern 1007, Kent LP 519
I Don't Need	Modern 1012, Kent LP 519
Gonna Have Fun	Modern 1012, Kent LP 519

Ike & Tina Turner: 1965

Two Is A Couple	Sue 135
Tin Top House	Sue 135

Ike Turner and his Kings Of Rhythm: 1965

The New Breed Pt 1	Sue 138
The New Breed Pt 2	Sue 138

Ike & Tina Turner: 1965

Can't Stand A Break Up	Sue 139
Stagger Lee And Billy	Sue 139
Dear John	Sue 146
I Made A Promise Up Above	Sue 146

Ike & Tina Turner: 1966

Anything You Wasn't Born With	Tangerine 963
Beauty Is Only Skin Deep	Tangerine 963
I'm Hooked	Tangerine 967
Dust My Broom	Tangerine 967

Ike & Tina Turner: *'River Deep – Mountain High'* (LP 4178) 1966

River Deep – Mountain High*	Philles 131, A&M 1118, LP 4178
I'll Keep You Happy	Philles 131, A&M 1118, LP 4178
Two To Tango	Philles 134
A Man Is A Man Is A Man	Philles 134
A Love Like Yours (Don't Come Knocking Every Day)*	Philles 136, A&M 1170, LP 4178
I Idolize You	Philles 136, A&M LP 4178
Hold On Baby*	A&M LP 4178
A Fool In Love	A&M LP 4178
Make 'Em Wait	A&M LP 4178
Save The Last Dance For Me*	A&M 1170, LP 4178
Oh Baby! (Things Ain't What They Used To Be)	A&M LP 4178
Every Day I Have To Cry*	A&M LP 4178
Such A Fool For You	A&M LP 4178
It's Gonna Work Out Fine	A&M LP 4178
You're So Fine	A&M LP 4178

N.B. Tracks* produced by Phil Spector; Ike had no involvement in these. All others produced by Ike Turner, except 'Two To Tango' by Bob Crewe. The above A&M LP 4178, appeared on a small amount of promo copies as Philles LP 4011.

Ike & Tina Turner:
I'll Never Need More Than This	Philles 135

Ike Turner and his Kings Of Rhythm:
The Cash Box Blues (Inst)	Philles 135

Ike & Tina Turner: 1966
I Wish My Dream Would Come True	Kent 457, LP 519
Flee Flee Fla	Kent 457, LP 519
Hard Times	Kent LP 519
It's Crazy Baby	Kent LP 519
Something Came Over Me	Kent LP 519
Don't Blame It On Me	Kent LP 519
Am I A Fool In Love	Kent LP 519
Over You	Kent (UK) LP 065
Makin' Plans Together	Kent (UK) LP 065
Lose My Cool	Kent (UK) LP 065
You Can't Miss Nothing	Kent (UK) LP 065
Give Me Your Love	Kent (UK) LP 065
I Need A Man	Kent (UK) LP 065
Baby Don't Do It	Kent (UK) LP 065

Ike & Tina Turner: *'Festival Of Live Performances'*   1967
A Fool In Love	Kent LP 538
He's Mine	Kent LP 538
Stop The Wedding	Kent LP 538
Please Please Please	Kent LP 538
If I Can't Be First	Kent LP 538
My Man	Kent LP 538
You Don't Love Me No More	Kent LP 538
It's Gonna Work Out Fine	Kent LP 538
If I Only Had You	Kent LP 538
I Can't Stop Loving You	Kent LP 538
Treat Me Right	Kent LP 538

Ike & Tina Turner & Ikettes: 1968
Betcha Can't Kiss Me	Pompeii LP 6000, 7003, 6006
T'ain't Nobody's Business	Pompeii LP 6000, 6006
It Sho' Ain't Me	Pompeii 66675, LP 6000, 6005
Too Hot To Hold	Pompeii 66682, LP 6000, 6006
A Fool In Love	Pompeii LP 6000
I Better Get To Steppin'	Innis 6668, Pompeii LP 6000, 6004

Shake A Tail Feather	Pompeii 66700
Poor Same	Innis 6668
We Need An Understanding	Pompeii 66675, LP 6000, 6005
You're So Fine	Pompeii LP 6000
Cussin'	Pompeii LP 6004
You Got What You Wanted	Pompeii 66682, LP 6004, 6006

Ike & Tina Turner:

Nothing You Can Do Boy (To Change My Way)	Pompeii LP 6004, 6005
Fed Up	
I'm Fed Up	Pompeii LP 6004, 6006
Beauty's Just Skin Deep	Pompeii 66683, LP 6004, 6006
What You Got	
Cussin' Cryin' And Carrying On	Pompeii 66700, LP 6004, 6006
Make 'Em Wait	Pompeii 66683, LP 6004, 6006

Ike Turner with the Kings Of Rhythm: 1969

Thinkin' Black	Pompeii LP 6003, 6004, 6005
Black Beauty	Pompeii LP 6003, 6004
Ghetto Funk	Pompeii LP 6003
Blacks Alley	Pompeii LP 6003
Black Angel	Pompeii LP 6003
Getting Nasty	Pompeii LP 6003
Funky Mule	Pompeii LP 6003, 6006
Philly Dog	Pompeii LP 6003
Scotty Souling	Pompeii LP 6003
Up Hard	Pompeii LP 6003
Nutting Up	Pompeii LP 6003
Freedom Sound	Pompeii LP 6003, 6006

Ike & Tina Turner: *'Outta Season'* 1969

I've Been Loving You Too Long	Blue Thumb 101, 202, LP 5, 49
Mean Old World	Blue Thumb LP 5
3 O'Clock In The Morning Blues	Blue Thumb LP 5
Five Long Years	Blue Thumb LP 5
Dust My Broom	Blue Thumb LP 5, 49
Grumbling (Inst)	Blue Thumb 101, LP 5, 49
I Am A Motherless Child	Blue Thumb LP 5, 49
Crazy 'Bout You Baby	Blue Thumb 102, 202, LP 5, 49

Reconsider Baby	Blue Thumb LP 5
Honest I Do	Blue Thumb LP 5
Please Love Me	Blue Thumb LP 5
My Babe	Blue Thumb LP 5
Rock Me Baby	Blue Thumb LP 5, 49

Ike & Tina Turner: *'The Hunter'* 1969

The Hunter	Blue Thumb 102, LP 11, 49
You Don't Love Me	Blue Thumb LP 11
You Got Me Running	Blue Thumb LP 11, 49
Bold Soul Sister	Blue Thumb LP 11, 49
I Smell Trouble	Blue Thumb LP 11, 49
The Things I Used To Do	Blue Thumb LP 11
Early In The Morning	Blue Thumb LP 11, 49
You're Still My Baby	Blue Thumb LP 11, 49
I Know	Blue Thumb 104, LP 11, 49

Ike & Tina Turner: 1969–70

I'm Gonna Do All I Can (To Do Right By My Man)	Minit 32060
You've Got Too Many Ties That Bind	Minit 32060
I Wish It Would Rain	Minit 32068
With A Little Help From My Friends	Minit 32068
I Wanna Jump	Minit 32077
Treating Us (Women) Funky	Minit 32077

Ike & Tina Turner and the Ikettes:

Honky Tonk Woman	Minit 32087, Liberty LP 7637
Come Together	Minit 32087, Liberty LP 7637
It Ain't Right Lovin To Be Lovin	Liberty LP 7637
Too Much Woman For A Hen Pecked Man	Liberty LP 7637
Unlucky Creature	Liberty LP 7637
Young And Dumb	Liberty LP 7637
Why Can't We Be Happy	Liberty LP 7637
Contact High	Liberty 56177, LP 7637
Keep On Walkin'	Liberty LP 7637
Don't Look Back	Liberty LP 7637
I Want To Take You Higher	Liberty 56177, LP 7637
Evil Man, Doin' It (Inst)	Liberty LP 7637

Ike Turner:

Love Is A Game	Liberty 56194
Takin' Back My Name	Liberty 56194

Ike & Tina Turner: *'Working Together'* (Rel Feb 1971)

Proud Mary	Liberty 56216, LP 7650

Funkier Than A Mosquita's Tweeter	Liberty 56216, LP 7650
Working Together	Liberty 56207, LP 7650
The Way You Love Me	Liberty 56207, LP 7650
Ooh-Poo-Pah-Doo	United Artists 50782, Liberty LP 7650
(As Long As I Can) Get You When I Want You	Liberty LP 7650
Get Back	Liberty LP 7650
You Can Have It	Liberty LP 7650
Game Of Love	Liberty LP 7650
Goodbye So Long	Liberty LP 7650
Let It Be	Liberty LP 7650

Ike & Tina Turner: *'Live In Paris'* 1971

Grumbling (Inst)	Liberty LP 83468/9
You Got Me Hummin – Ikettes Voc	Liberty LP 83468/9
Every Day People – Ikettes Voc	Liberty LP 83468/9
Shake A Tail Feather – Ikettes Voc	Liberty LP 83468/9
Gimme Some Loving	Liberty LP 83468/9
Sweet Soul Music	Liberty LP 83468/9
Son Of A Preacher Man	Liberty LP 83468/9
Come Together	Liberty LP 83468/9
Proud Mary	Liberty LP 83468/9
A Love Like Yours	Liberty LP 83468/9
I Smell Trouble	Liberty LP 83468/9
Respect	Liberty LP 83468/9
Honky Tonk Woman	Liberty LP 83468/9
I've Been Loving You Too Long	Liberty LP 83468/9
I Want To Take You Higher	Liberty LP 83468/9
Land Of 1000 Dances	Liberty LP 83468/9

Ike & Tina Turner: *'What You Hear What You Get'* 1971
(Live At Carnegie Hall NY)

Piece Of My Heart	United Artists UAS 9953
Every Day People	United Artists UAS 9953
Doin The Tina Turner	United Artists UAS 9953
Sweet Soul Music	United Artists UAS 9953
Ooh-Poo-Pah-Doo	United Artists UAS 9953
Honky Tonk Woman	United Artists UAS 9953
A Love Like Yours	United Artists UAS 9953
Proud Mary Pt 1/2	United Artists UAS 9953
I Smell Trouble	United Artists UAS 9953
Ike's Tune	United Artists UAS 9953
I Want To Take You Higher	United Artists UAS 9953
I've Been Loving You Too Long	United Artists UAS 9953
Respect	United Artists UAS 9953

Ike & Tina Turner: *'Nuff Said*   1971
I Love What You Do To Me	United Artists LP 5530
Baby (What You Want Me To Do)	United Artists LP 5530
Sweet Frustrations	United Artists LP 5530
What You Don't See	United Artists LP 5530
Nuff Said	United Artists LP 5530
Tell The Truth	United Artists LP 5530
Pick Me Up (Take Me Where Your Home Is)	United Artists 50939, LP 5530
Moving Into Hip-Style A Trip Child	United Artists LP 5530
I Love Baby	United Artists LP 5530
Can't You Hear Me Calling	United Artists LP 5530
Nuff Said Pt 2	United Artists LP 5530
River Deep Mountain High	United Artists 50865, LP 5530
Na-Na	United Artists 50865
Games People Play	United Artists 50939

Ike Turner Presents 'The Family Vibes':
Happy But Lonely	United Artists LP 5560
Heep-A-Hole-Lot	United Artists LP 5560
Jumpin'	United Artists LP 5560
Neckin'	United Artists LP 5560
Bootie Lip	United Artists 50901, LP 5560
Soppin' Molasses	United Artists 50901, LP 5560
Sweet	United Artists LP 5560
Sixty-Nine	United Artists LP 5560
D M Z	United Artists LP 5560
I-8-1-2 (I Ate One Too)	United Artists LP 5560
Pardon Me	United Artists LP 5560
Outrageous	United Artists 50913

Ike Turner: *'Blues Roots'*   1972
Dust My Broom	United Artists 51102
You Won't Let Me Go	United Artists 51102
The Things I Used To Do	United Artists LP 5576
Goin Home	United Artists LP 5576
Lawdy Miss Clawdy	United Artists 50930, LP 5576
Rockin' Blues	United Artists LP 5576
Broken Hearted	United Artists LP 5576
You're Still My Baby	United Artists LP 5576
Tacks In My Shoes	United Artists 50930, 50900, LP 5576

Right On	United Artists 50900, LP 5576
Think	United Artists LP 5576
That's Alright	United Artists LP 5576
My Babe	United Artists LP 5576
If You Love Me Like You Say	United Artists LP 5576

Ike & Tina Turner:

I'm Yours (Use Me Any Way You Wanna)	United Artists 50837
Doin It	United Artists 50837
Up In Heah	United Artists 50881
Doo Wah Ditty (Got To Get Ya)	United Artists 50881

Ike & Tina Turner: *'Feel Good'* 1972

Feel Good	United Artists 50913, LP 5598
Chopper	United Artists 50955, LP 5598
Kay Got Laid (Joe Got Paid)	United Artists LP 5598
I Like It	United Artists LP 5598
If You Can Hully Gully I Can Hully Gully Too	United Artists LP 5598
Black Coffee	United Artists LP 5598
She Came In Through The Bathroom Window	United Artists LP 5598
If I Knew Then What I Know Now	United Artists LP 5598
You Better Think Of Something	United Artists LP 5598
Bolic	United Artists LP 5598

Ike & Tina Turner: *'Let Me Touch Your Mind'* 1972

Let Me Touch Your Mind	United Artists 50955, LP 5660
Annie Had A Baby	United Artists LP 5660
Don't Believe Her	United Artists LP 5660
I Had A Notion	United Artists LP 5660
Pop Corn	United Artists LP 5660
Early One Morning	United Artists LP 5660
Help Him	United Artists LP 5660
Up On The Roof	United Artists LP 5660
Born Free	United Artists XW 257, LP 5660
Heaven Help Us All	United Artists LP 5660

Ike Turner presents the Family Vibes: *'Confined To Soul'* 1973

Beauty Is In The Eye (Of The Beholder)	United Artists UA-LA LP 051
Two For Three And Three For Me	United Artists UA-LA LP 051

Takin' Back My Name

El-Burrito	UA XW 278, United Artists UA-LA LP 051
Scratch	United Artists UA-LA LP 051
Garbage Man	UA XW 278, United Artists UA-LA LP 051
The Shakes	United Artists UA-LA LP 051
LA Vamp	United Artists UA-LA LP 051
Ballad Of All Time Blues	United Artists UA-LA LP 051
Journey Through Your Feelings	United Artists UA-LA LP 051

Ike & Tina Turner: *'Live The World Of Ike & Tina Turner'* 1973

Theme From Shaft	United Artists UA LA LP 064
I Gotcha	United Artists UA LA LP 064
She Came In Through The Bathroom Window	United Artists UA LA LP 064
You're Still My Baby	United Artists UA LA LP 064
Don't Fight It	United Artists UA LA LP 064
Annie Had A Baby	United Artists UA LA LP 064
With A Little Help From My Friends	United Artists UA LA LP 064
Get Back	United Artists UA LA LP 064
Games People Play	United Artists UA LA LP 064
Honky Tonk Woman	United Artists UA LA LP 064
If You Love Me Like You Say	United Artists UA LA LP 064
I Can't Turn You Loose	United Artists UA LA LP 064
I Wish It Would Rain	United Artists UA LA LP 064
Just One More Day	United Artists UA LA LP 064
Stand By Me	United Artists UA LA LP 064
Dust My Broom	United Artists UA LA LP 064
River Deep Mountain High	United Artists UA LA LP 064
Let Me Touch Your Mind	United Artists UA LA LP 064
Chopper	United Artists UA LA LP 064
1-2-3	United Artists UA LA LP 064

Ike Turner: *'Bad Dreams'* 1973

These Dreams	United Artists UA LA LP 087
That's How Much I Love You	United Artists UA LA LP 087
One Nite Stand	United Artists UA LA LP 087
Don't Hold Your Breath	United Artists UA LA LP 087
(You Can Have) The City	United Artists UA LA LP 087
Flockin' With You	United Artists UA LA LP 087
Take A Walk With Me	United Artists UA LA LP 087

Later For You Baby	United Artists UA LA LP 087
Rats	United Artists UA LA LP 087
I Love The Way You Love	United Artists UA LA LP 087

Ike & Tina Turner:
Work On Me	United Artists 257

Ike & Tina Turner: *'Nutbush City Limits'* 1973
Nutbush City Limits	United Artists 298, LP 180
Make Me Over	United Artists LP 180
Drift Away	United Artists LP 180
That's My Purpose	United Artists LP 180
Fancy Annie	United Artists LP 180
River Deep Mountain High	United Artists LP 180
Git It Out Of Your Mind	United Artists LP 180
Daily Bread	United Artists LP 180
You Are My Sunshine	United Artists LP 180
Club Manhattan	United Artists LP 180

Ike & Tina Turner:
Help Him	United Artists 298

Ike & Tina Turner: *'Gospel According To Ike & Tina Turner'* 1974
Farther Along	UA 460, United Artists LP UA LA 203
Walk With Me (I Need You Lord To Be My Friend)	United Artists LP UA LA 203
Glory Glory	United Artists LP UA LA 203
Closer Walk With Thee	United Artists LP UA LA 203
What A Friend We Have In Jesus	United Artists LP UA LA 203
Amazing Grace	United Artists LP UA LA 203
Take My Hand Precious Lord	UA 460, United Artists LP UA LA 203
Nearer The Cross	United Artists LP UA LA 203
Our Lord Will Make A Way	United Artists LP UA LA 203
When The Saints Go Marching In	United Artists LP UA LA 203

Tina Turner: *'Tina Turner Turns The Country On'* 1974
Bayou Song	United Artists LP UA LA 200
Help Me Make It Through The Night	UA 598, United Artists LP UA LA 200
Tonight I'll Be Staying Here With You	United Artists LP UA LA 200
If You Love Me	United Artists LP UA LA 200
He Belongs To Me	United Artists LP UA LA 200
Don't Talk Now	United Artists LP UA LA 200
Long Long Time	United Artists LP UA LA 200
I'm Moving On	United Artists LP UA LA 200

There'll Always Be Music	United Artists LP UA LA 200
The Love That Lights Our Way	United Artists LP UA LA 200

Ike & Tina Turner: *'Sweet Rhode Island Red'* 1974

Let Me Be There	United Artists LP UA LA 312
Living For The City	United Artists LP UA LA 312
I Know	United Artists LP UA LA 312
Mississippi Rolling Stone	United Artists LP UA LA 312
Sugar Hill	United Artists LP UA LA 312
Sweet Rhode Island Red	UA 409, United Artists LP UA LA 312
Ready For You Baby	United Artists LP UA LA 312
Smooth Out The Wrinkles	United Artists LP UA LA 312
Doozie	United Artists LP UA LA 312
High Ground	United Artists LP UA LA 312
Get It Out Of Your Mind	UA 409

Tina Turner: *'Acid Queen'* 1975

Under My Thumb*	United Artists LP UA LA 495
Lets Spend The Night Together*	United Artists LP UA LA 495
Acid Queen*	United Artists LP UA LA 495
I Can See For Miles*	United Artists LP UA LA 495
Whole Lotta Love*	UA 724, United Artists LP UA LA 495
Baby Get It On	UA 598, United Artists LP UA LA 495
Bootsie Whitelaw	United Artists LP UA LA 495
Pick Me Tonight	United Artists LP UA LA 495
Rockin' & Rollin'	UA 724, United Artists LP UA LA 495

*No Ike involvement on these.

Ike & Tina Turner:

Sexy Ida Part 1	United Artists 528
Sexy Ida Part 2	United Artists 528

Ike & Tina Turner: *'Delilah's Power'* (Rel 1977)

Delilah's Power	UA 730, United Artists UA LA LP 707
Never Been To Spain	United Artists UA LA LP 707
Unhappy Birthday	United Artists UA LA LP 707
Put Something In To It	United Artists UA LA LP 707
Nothing Comes To You When You're Asleep But A Dream	United Artists UA LA LP 707
Stormy Weather	United Artists UA LA LP 707
Sugar Sugar	United Artists UA LA LP 707
Too Much For One Woman	United Artists UA LA LP 707

Trying To Find My Mind	United Artists UA LA LP 707
Pick Me Up	United Artists UA LA LP 707
Too Many Women	United Artists UA LA LP 707
I Want To Take You Higher	Liberty 56177, United Artists UA LA LP 707

N.B.: This is a compilation of sides from earlier sessions.

Ike & Tina Turner:

Mississippi Rolling Stone	Stripped Horse LP, Spartan (UK) LP 2
Living For The City	Spartan (UK) LP 2
Golden Empire	Spartan (UK) LP 2
I'm Looking For My Mind	Spartan (UK) LP 2
Shake A Hand	Spartan (UK) LP 2
Botsie Whitelaw	Spartan (UK) LP 2
Too Much Man For One Woman	Spartan (UK) LP 2
I Know (You Don't Want Me No More)	Spartan (UK) LP 2
Rockin' And Rollin'	Spartan (UK) LP 2
Never Been To Spain	Spartan (UK) LP 2
Sugar Sugar	Spartan (UK) LP 2
Push	Spartan (UK) LP 2
Raise Your Hand	Spartan (UK) LP 2
Tina's Prayer	Spartan (UK) LP 2
Chiken	Spartan (UK) LP 2
If You Want It	Spartan (UK) LP 2
Let's Get It On	Spartan (UK) LP 2
You're Up To Something	Spartan (UK) LP 2
You're Still My Baby	Spartan (UK) LP 2
Jesus	Spartan (UK) LP 2

N.B. Cuts above recorded at Ike's Bolic Sound Studio, 1973–74.

Ike & Tina Turner & Home Grown Funk: *'The Edge'* 1980

Shame Shame Shame	Fantasy F LP 9597
Lean On Me	Fantasy F LP 9597
Philadelphia Freedom	Fantasy F LP 9597
Use Me	Fantasy F LP 9597
Only Women Bleed	Fantasy F LP 9597
Party Vibes	Fantasy F LP 9597
Lum Dum	Fantasy F LP 9597
No Other Woman	Fantasy F LP 9597
I Can't Believe	Fantasy F LP 9597
I Don't Want Nobody	Fantasy F LP 9597

Acknowledgements to friends who have written and made additions to the Turner Disco during the last 20 or so years who include Mike Leadbitter, Dave Sax, Cilla Huggins, Bruce Bastin, Bill Greensmith and Bill Millar.